QUALITY
of
EARNINGS

QUALITY
of
EARNINGS

The Investor's Guide
To How Much Money
A Company Is Really Making

Thornton L. O'glove

with Robert Sobel

THE FREE PRESS
A Division of Macmillan, Inc.
NEW YORK
Collier Macmillan Publishers
LONDON

The Free Press
A Division of Macmillan, Inc.
866 Third Avenue, New York, N.Y. 10022

Collier Macmillan Canada, Inc.

Printed in the United States of America

printing number

1 2 3 4 5 6 7 8 9 10

Library of Congress Cataloging-in-Publication Data

O'glove, Thornton L.
    Quality of earnings.

    Bibliography: p.
    Includes index.
    1. Financial statements.   2. Business enterprises—
Finance.   3. Accounting.   I. Sobel, Robert.
II. Title.
HG4028.B2035   1987   657'.33   86–25631
ISBN 978-0-684-86375-7

To
Professor Abraham J. Briloff
and Leonard Spacek—
The Consciences of
Accountancy

CONTENTS

ACKNOWLEDGMENTS

ONE OF THE PLEASURES of writing this book is to make some special acknowledgments to those who have given support over the years to the concept and implementation of the *Quality of Earnings® Report* service. In the realm of inspiration, I shall always be indebted to Leonard Spacek, former chairman of Arthur Andersen & Co; Abraham J. Briloff, Emmanuel Saxe Distinguished Professor of Accountancy, Bernard M. Baruch College of the City University of New York; and David Norr, former director of research at First Manhattan Company and the first security analyst ever appointed to the Accounting Principles Board. Their vigorous campaigns over the years in an effort to produce more effective financial accounting reforms have inspired me in my own research efforts.

I wish to take this opportunity to pay tribute to Leopold A. Bernstein, Professor of Accounting, Bernard M. Baruch College. His landmark textbooks on financial statement analysis have been of much assistance to me in providing up-to-date treatment of the analysis of financial statements.

I am most appreciative of the encouragement provided to me early on by Fred Lange, former director of research at Blair & Co., and Wilma J. Engel, an investment advisor consultant for Stolper & Company. They always thought highly of the concept of *Quality of Earnings® Report* and encouraged me to pursue it. Along the way, I was fortunate to encounter Donald Geogerian, portfolio manager at Dreyfus Corp., who has provided me with his insight

and constructive criticism in reference to the *Quality of Earnings®
Report* service.

There never would have been a *Quality of Earnings® Report*
service if it had not been for Alfred Kingon, former research director at Scheinman, Hochstin and Trotta, who thought the service
was direly needed and doable and who hired me specifically to write
quality of earnings reports. His successor at SH&T, Raphael Yav-
neh, provided valuable support in shaping and promoting the
Quality of Earnings® Report concept, at a time when SH&T was
in financial difficulty.

I am grateful to Sidney Brown, former editor of the *Commercial and Financial Chronicle* and current editor of the *Market
Chronicle,* for always being willing to grant me a platform when
I wanted to write an article or comment upon pertinent financial
accounting topics of the day.

I thank my former partner for ten years, Robert Olstein, who
helped me take the *Quality of Earnings® Report* service out of the
developmental stage and place it on the institutional research map.

In conclusion, I most earnestly wish to thank Gail Weinrib,
who has been my valued executive assistant from the inception of
the *Quality of Earnings® Report* service to the present; Jo-Ann Masi,
who, over the years, has rendered worthy service as a key administrator; and Jackie Kinney and Ellen Falk, who helped immeas-
urably in the transcribing and editing of the manuscript for this
book.

THORNTON L. O'GLOVE

INTRODUCTION

EVERY INVESTOR WANTS a magic way to select stocks, a clear set of signals indicating when to buy and sell. And seemingly every analyst who has spent some time watching the market has written a book on just that.

So let's begin by saying that this is not that kind of book. Rather, my work is about an intelligent approach to reading and using reports and other documents issued by corporations to comply with the securities laws and to communicate with shareholders. I believe that an informed analysis of these readily available materials can lead a knowledgeable investor to the kind of conclusion that enables the investor *alone* to make buy and sell decisions.

There is nothing very complicated about what I will say. But while most analysts will concede the importance of the drill, few actually perform it. So the mastery of a small number of fundamental techniques may give you a leg up on some of the financial district's more closely watched pros.

But I am getting ahead of myself, so let's go back a bit. This calls for some biographical information.

In the 1950s, I was a finance major at San Francisco State and it appeared I was headed for a career as a stockbroker. Sure enough, I later worked for several years with an over-the-counter (OTC) brokerage firm and then as a stockbroker at the San Francisco offices of Walston & Co., where I remained for three years.

This was a period when a new issue craze was sweeping the

Street, taking most brokers along with it. I found the mania troublesome. Looking through the prospectuses, I realized that many of the companies had nothing more than a romantic name, high-flown ambitions, and a willing group of brokers eager to place issues and reap the rewards. So they did, for a while at least, while I sat back, watched in dismay, and wondered how usually sensible people could invest hard-earned money without realizing what they were buying.

The answer was obvious: they had not read the prospectuses. Few ever did. So one lesson I learned then was that genuine knowledge may matter little in the short run, especially during the course of an emotional market. After a while, however, manias die and more realistic values reassert themselves. So I watched investors multiplying their holdings and must admit I was pretty envious of how rich they were getting. After a while even those who agreed with my analysis convinced themselves of the true merit of their holdings. But in the end, many of them were wiped out.

What they learned from all of this I cannot say. But the lesson I derived was that there is no substitute for information and knowledge, that markets are imperfect beasts and do not reflect all that is known about a security, and finally, that while analysis can provide investors with a clear picture of the company's operations, it cannot tell them what individual stocks will do tomorrow morning. Moreover, most investors (and analysts) have no clear conception of how corporations can report earnings that are partially illusory; to them numbers are numbers, and they are willing to let it go at that. Long before I heard the term "quality of earnings" I was aware that this was one of the keys to meaningful financial analysis.

Unfortunately, there was no one around in those days who did such analytical work. And as far as I can see, no one on the Street today concentrates his labor on it. There is an important reason for this, to which I will return again and again, and that's because such research is usually negative. Most investors would rather kill the messenger than think about the message.

Suppose a company reported $2.00 per share earnings, and you dissect the number. Do you think the chief executive officer had any reason to understate the figure, that it really was $2.50? No reason at all. But he might have inflated the $2.00 from $1.50 to make his regime look better than it should.

As I said, I soon learned that most of my findings meant bad news rather than good. And who wants to hear bad news? The answer should be: fiduciaries entrusted with large amounts of capital, who upon hearing only optimistic reports from analysts would like to learn the other side of the story. In other words, the pros should seek out bad news, while the amateurs may only want to hear the best about stocks they own. "You don't have to tell me how good a stock is," my clients will often tell me. "There are a dozen analysts out there who will do that. We are blitzkrieged with all the positive stuff. What we want from you is another view, an indication that perhaps the others are wrong."

Almost from the first, I didn't trust what any management said, and this has been reinforced by my research in the field. I suppose it is natural for someone who works day in, day out with corporate books, who knows how accountants can present figures to make a good showing of things, and who knows public relations writers paper over problems with their prose, to feel this way. I always suspect management is trying to hide something. What is it they are trying to do cosmetically? I ask. And I start out by assuming the worst.

Too often I am not disappointed. Of course, usually the closet has no skeleton and if all seems up to snuff, I will let matters rest. And should an analysis of the documents indicate that the company is in much better shape than most realize, I serve notice as well.

So much dawned on me in the early 1960s: even though I realized there might be a highly sophisticated market for the kind of information I was generating, it was years before I could do anything about it.

While at Walston, I made a specialty of examining prospectuses, looking for hidden gems or for stocks to sell or avoid. Because the documents were lengthy, very few brokers would take time out to read them. Accordingly, I concluded that one could obtain some edge on the market by diligently reading a prospectus from cover to cover. By the way, this is still true today even though the institutions dominate the market to a far greater degree than in the sixties.

A desire to obtain a deeper understanding of securities analysis led me to leave Walston and register at the University of California Graduate School of Business. It was one of the most important educational experiences of my life, and the greatest lesson was imparted when I submitted my thesis. The subject was investment tax credits, for which there were two diverse ways of permitted reporting. I held that only the more conservative method was the accurate reporting procedure. My thesis advisor, who was an accounting professor, disagreed and gave me a disappointing grade of B. One of those whom I interviewed on the subject was Leonard Spacek, a legendary figure in the accounting field. A former member of the Accounting Principles Board, he was one of the most distinguished in the accounting profession, as well as an important critic of diverse accounting practices. Between 1956 and 1969, Spacek made 168 speeches around the country, fighting the battle for sound accounting.

When I interviewed Spacek, he was chairman of Arthur Andersen & Co. I was very pleased when Spacek supported my thesis conclusions and suggested that it be published. Subsequently, he sent me a check to help defray the cost of having the thesis bound into a printed booklet, and then took 200 copies for his own use.

In 1967, my M.B.A. in hand, I obtained an analyst position at the Bank of America where things didn't work out as well as I had hoped. Assigned to financial stocks, I came up with some sell recommendations that ran contrary to those of a somewhat stodgy trust department. One did not make waves at B of A in those days, and that was what I was doing. Stated simply, the bank had a list of approved stocks from which trust officers made their selections. Additions and deletions to the list had to be approved by a high-powered investment committee that included some of the top ranking officers of the bank. My superior, the head of the trust department, gave me the impression that I should not delve into the quality of earnings of bank holdings because to do so would be to imply error, which would hardly build confidence in the trust department. Somewhat innocently, I assumed that to be critical was my job. Not so. After six months, I was dismissed, on the pavement looking for work after having been told I didn't have the qualifications to be a securities analyst.

This was the greatest break of my life. Why? Because otherwise I might still be at B of A, going through the motions. But after being fired, I was even more intrigued with the concept of contrary opinion. I had been given a clear demonstration of the fact that most people prefer illusion to reality, if it conforms to a view to which they are committed. This is still the case. Changing people's minds about their investments remains a most difficult task. Standing outside the bank, in shock I must confess, it dawned on me that I could utilize my expertise only if I could find human beings willing to listen and act upon bad news.

As it turned out, I had little trouble finding a new job, this time at Hornblower, Weeks in New York. This had nothing to do with my education and experience. A bull market was on and a shortage of analysts had developed, which helped considerably. At Hornblower, Weeks, I covered just about any company and industry that attracted my attention.

In January of 1968, I met Professor Abraham J. Briloff, a professor of accounting at Bernard M. Baruch College of The City University of New York, who was speaking before the New York Society of Security Analysts. His speech was entitled "Distortions Arising From Pooling-Of-Interests Accounting." In essence, Briloff critiqued the type of accounting associated with conglomerates in making their numerous acquisitions. He opened my eyes to the way that pooling-of-interests accounting made earnings comparisons glow unrealistically.

Professor Briloff was also a prolific writer who published many articles berating the accounting profession for permitting various accounting practices that had the effect of overstating corporate earnings. Briloff, from his academic perch, was doing what Leonard Spacek had done as an executive of Arthur Andersen & Co. To this day, Spacek and Briloff, whom I have always admired as the consciences of accountancy, still inspire me.

In 1968, I joined Blair & Co. as a special situation analyst. Blair had underwritten a franchise operation, which initially seemed quite attractive to me. I wrote a positive research report recommending that the franchised stock should be purchased for capital appreciation. But, after my research report, I changed my mind and then wrote a negative report which prompted an angry call from the company's president. "I can't believe what you people are doing," he screamed. "How can you put out a sell report on a company you underwrote? You brought us public just a year ago!" Words followed, and the upshot was that we were dismissed as the firm's investment banker. The company did stumble badly and subsequently vanished from the scene, along with scores of others like it.

To its credit Blair never called me on the carpet about the firm being dropped as the investment banker of the franchising firm that

I had written a "sell" report on. Yet, the incident shook me up and I realized that it could have cost me my job.

By then I had become convinced my future rested in full-time analysis of financial statements. I would have to seek some other base of operations and this time a place where I would have the full freedom necessary. This would be difficult. In effect, I wanted a job telling people what stocks *not* to buy. Can you imagine any firm, even today, prizing such an employee? A few might have some in-house Cassandras, but their day in, day out reports would not be for those customers whose orders are being solicited.

I then began to look for a smaller firm, which didn't have an investment banking department of any consequence. Luckily, I found such a place in Scheinman, Hochstin, and Trotta. The firm, which was bankrolled by financier Sol Kittay, called itself "the businessman's broker." The research director, Al Kingon, really liked my ideas and gave me a free hand. At about the same time, I talked about my ideas to others and one person, whose name now sadly escapes me, suggested calling the advisories "The Quality of Earnings Report," which I did.

By then the bear market of 1969–1970 was in full swing and I thrived. Investors no longer wanted to learn how to double their money overnight, but rather were looking for excuses to dump stocks and preserve whatever capital remained. It was like shooting fish in a barrel. The market was heading down anyway and I was simply helping it along. One of the first companies I wrote up was the Leasco Data Processing Equipment Corp. The company had reported share earnings totaling $2.71 in 1969 and I made several quality of earnings adjustments that resulted in adjusted earnings of only $1.42 a share. Next I turned to the land development companies and did the same with them. Subsequently, thanks largely to the bear market, Leasco Data and the land companies collapsed in price. Years later, Leasco Data, which was renamed Reliance Insurance, came back and did very well before it was taken private by Saul Steinberg.

So I looked impressive, but who wouldn't have in that kind of market? Soon after, I ran into Bob Olstein who had been an accountant with Arthur Andersen & Co. and then an instructor at Hofstra University School of Business. He had recently arrived at Scheinman, Hochstin, and Trotta as a broker and also performed some research. Initially Olstein didn't seem especially interested in my work; like most brokers and analysts, he was a congenital bull. But one day, after coming back to the office after a short vacation, I found a large number of orders from a money manager based upon a recent Quality of Earnings® research report. Olstein heard about this and we started to talk about the market. Many of his recommendations were going down the tube and he seemed prepared to convert to the bear side, if only for a season.

Olstein was about to take a trip to California. He suggested taking some of my reports with him to see if he could drum up some business. To my astonishment, Olstein returned with six accounts. I had been working for about a year and had only a few institutional accounts. Olstein thought I had gone about things the wrong way. It was his idea to charge subscribers a regular fee and put "The Quality of Earnings® Report" on a more businesslike footing. It was Olstein who decided to charge subscribers $12,000 or more a year in commissions for the service. Olstein provided the kind of vision I clearly needed. So we formed a partnership.

This was in 1971 when, like many other brokerages, Scheinman, Hochstin, and Trotta was having back office problems. The firm had trouble handling its current accounts, and now Olstein and I were about to bring in substantial new business. We were on our way to becoming one of the district's top producing teams.

By Labor Day, because Scheinman, Hochstin, and Trotta was in need of additional capital, it found it necessary to be taken over by Weis, Voisin & Company. The new management appreciated our work, but told us it would be impossible for us to stay. Weis, Voisin & Company participated in quite a few underwriting syndications thus creating a potential conflict of interest with two bears like us knocking some of the stocks its salesmen were supporting. So with this, in November, 1971, Olstein and I went to Coenen & Co., where we were for all intents and purposes on our own.

We remained with Coenen for four years. This was a period of fixed commissions, when the purchaser of 1,000 shares of a common stock paid ten times the amount in commissions than the buyer of 100 shares. All firms made the same charges up to a $300,000 ceiling on one order. One way to pay for institutional research was by commissions, commonly known as "soft" dollars. "The Quality of Earnings® Report" fell into this category. Those institutions that transacted business with Coenen could receive our monthly publication if they racked up $12,000 a year in commissions. We went from approximately twenty accounts to 140 by 1975.

All of this came to an end with "May Day" 1975 when commissions became fully negotiable. Overnight, we lost forty accounts, as some clients preferred lower commissions to our research. But our other accounts held firm, and we were easily able to absorb the decline. But given the new dispensation, it did seem to make sense for us to go into business on our own and we did soon after. We continued on until 1980, when Olstein decided to return to brokerage and account management. We parted on amicable terms, and I continued the publication on my own.

Last year, I thought the time had come to organize my methods and present them in such a way that individual investors might profit from the techniques I had developed over the past quarter of a century. Through mutual friends I met Robert Sobel, a professor of business history at Hofstra University and a historian of the financial markets; over the years, we had often discussed ideas of common interest. Together we planned this book, which you are now reading. We agreed that the goal would be to offer individual investors a means whereby they could avoid pitfalls in the market and maximize their chances of making profits. I firmly believe this can be done, though there are no magic formulas—only hard work, which *only you* can perform.

CHAPTER 1

Don't Trust Your Analyst

INVESTORS, whether novices or veterans, know that decisions about what and when to buy and sell are based upon a mix of fear, hopes, hunches, snatches of overheard conversations, and solid information. Especially information, that is, for all of us like to think we act in rational ways, that our decisions about how to place thousands of dollars are based on more than just a whim. So we try to get information from newspapers, television shows, and private conversations at restaurants, and sporting events, etc. Then we go through business and investment magazines, devour market letters, dial "hot lines," and attend seminars.

Note that all of such information comes from others, people who want to convince you that they have the facts and are able to interpret and digest them, the end product being a recommendation which, if acted upon, will be greatly rewarding. Most investors think these experts have answers—if not all of them, at least some— along with insights, intelligence, contacts, experience, and a feel for the market. Alas, too often this simply isn't so.

I would like to suggest that you can consult an expert whose advice can be trusted, someone who will be on hand whenever you need him or her, and who can be counted upon not to try to deceive. And this is one who isn't dumb, for it takes some brains to accumulate enough money for serious investment.

That expert is *you*, or at least can be, if you make some effort. This is the key message of the book you are now reading, which won't tell you which stocks to buy or sell and when to do so, but rather will demonstrate simple techniques that may be applied and methods of interpreting data that are as readily available as your letter box, telephone, or, in some cases, library. This is more important than a tip on a high tech flyer or a hunch on the next move for copper stocks. The message can serve you well, giving you, the trusted expert, the edge over professional money managers.

It's a cliche which is nonetheless true: give a man a fish and you feed him for a day; teach him how to fish and he'll feed himself for life. That is the goal of this book.

Before delving into what should be done, it would be well to show here and now, and in sufficient detail, why most of the information gathered from the conventional sources must be filtered through a mesh so fine that very little be allowed into that part of your brain where money decisions are made. The discussion might also tell you why some of your investments did not work out very well.

For beginners, consider historian and social critic Daniel Boorstin's definition of a celebrity: a person who is famous for being famous. Boorstin was thinking of the likes of the Gabor sisters and half forgotten starlets who pop up on TV talk shows or are pictured in the tabloids getting off airplanes or petting bogus unicorns at the circus.

They have their counterparts in the investment world. You'll see and hear them on some of the same TV shows, business programs dealing with the Street, and newspaper stories concerning the market. The same people reappear regularly, and they even look somewhat alike. The middle-aged men are grey, bespectacled, and avuncular, the middle-aged women well-coiffed and sharp of eye, while the younger ones of both sexes look lean, hungry, and aggressive. All seem well-to-do. The older ones tend to hedge, while the younger seers make flat-out predictions. And you look and listen—and only half remember just what it was they said, because so much information comes your way.

Next week, when you read or see them again, you will have forgotten just what it was they predicted or thought. All you recall is their faces, voices, and in time, names. They are experts, you think, whose advice should be taken. But don't think that. Remember they are celebrities, individuals famous for being famous.

One of the first things you learn as a broadcast journalist is that the public really isn't interested in what you, the journalist, think when they read news stories, but rather the ideas of individuals important in their fields. That reporter may know much more than the expert interviewed, but he needs quotes for the story. So the TV reporter goes to the office of some senior vice president plucked from the ranks for his charm and way with words, asks a few questions, which are answered briefly (the celebrities know that TV answers have to be short and witty) and then leaves for the studio. Both sides got what they wanted. The reporter has his thirty seconds of videotape, the analyst-celebrity kudos for the firm (his raison d'être), and that night the public will also get something they want—expert advice, or at least so they think.

The same is true for print journalism. Next time you read a stock market story, note that the reporter will quote at least three people in a medium sized piece, more if it is longer. These too are expert-celebrities. And many stories are well worth reading, especially when they deal with industry conditions, political analysis, and economic discourse. But not when the stories are about the market and come out of the same investment house mouthpieces. This time around, instead of a thirty-second interview (complete with wry smiles and twinkling eyes), they need snappy prose and highly quotable thoughts, especially when these conform to those of the writer. "Better a highly quotable ignoramus than an astute scholar who can't gather his thoughts" is the way one newsman put it.

Next, observe that many of those interviewed tend toward the extremes—they either think the market will go through the roof or the floor, though often they tend to be fuzzy on specifics. Say wiggle waggle and no one seems interested. Cry fire and everyone runs. It's a terrific way of grabbing attention, and celebrities need this more than food and drink.

Market letter writers, a special breed, aren't all that different, but they have a decided bias to the bullish side, and for good reason: who wants to pay a few hundred dollars a year for bad news? Besides, it's much easier to write day after day about buys than sells.

Leslie Gould, one of the great market watchers of the 1920s, told a reporter years later that he saw the 1929 crash coming the previous summer. The young man protested. "Mr. Gould, you were bullish up to the very end. I read all of your columns, and the messages were always positive." "Of course they were," Gould snorted, as though talking to an innocent. "If I said, 'Sell everything and go fishing' on Monday what could I write on Tuesday?"

Letter writers know that their readers are always looking for inside information on special situations, those undiscovered growth stocks which will double overnight. They don't want to hear about an overblown issue that should be avoided or shorted. If they don't own it, they won't buy, and if they do, they have an emotional commitment and probably won't sell. And few entertain thoughts about shorting stocks, which is almost anti-American. After all, we go to the track and try to pick the winners; the pari-mutuels don't accept bets on the horse you think will come in last.

Professor William Sharpe of the Stanford Business School puts it this way: "Without short-selling, market prices will be above consensus prices." (A near-perfect example of a concise pithy statement which wouldn't usually find its way into print, because it requires explanation.) What Sharp means is that if ten individuals have opinions on a stock, and the first thinks it should be $1, the second $2, the third $3, and so on until the tenth comes up with $10, the consensus price will come out to around $5. The pessimists—those who believe it should be between $1 and $4—won't do anything, while the optimists will buy, and so the price will come out to $7 or so in the end. "In other words, the price will not reflect all available information but only that held by optimists."[1]

This is understandable in letter writers, who after all may or may not have the credentials to go with their claims to prescience and depend upon hype to gather subscribers. But what about those people who labor at investment firms? Most have put in their time at undergraduate and graduate schools of business, have the requisite initials after their names, are members of the Financial Analysts Federation, which has about 16,000 members, and have put in many years in the field. Surely these worthies merit a respectful hearing. The answer is a hedged "maybe." To put it in the vernacular, you have to know where they are coming from before acting on their advice. Since so many investors rely upon recommendations from their brokers, who in turn get them from their analysts, it would be worthwhile to pursue this matter in some detail.

There are several thousand "sell side" securities analysts at work reading financial entrails and interviewing corporate executives. Major houses may carry upward of fifty, each assigned to specialized tasks, while the small, regional firms may have only three or four generalists. High-powered analysts tend to come from two areas: the M.B.A. programs of well-considered graduate schools, or the industry which they are expected to interpret, while the ideal candidate would combine both. A well-considered computer analyst, for example, might possess an engineering undergraduate degree, have worked for a while at one or more computer firms, have gone on for the M.B.A., and only then trekked to Wall Street for a position.

Most analysts start as assistants to veterans, and after an apprenticeship and a period as journeyman, emerge as full-fledged seniors, receiving salaries of from $80,000–$120,000 plus bonuses depending upon performance, with a number of them in the half million range, and some way above that.

Along the way these analysts develop contacts with managements, which together with required reports are their main source of information. They attend trade shows, seminars run by the industry covered, and are expected to live, eat, and breathe it. Quite literally. Restaurant analysts may have a dozen meals a week at fast-food operations, those in computers will run programs on mainframes and minis to evaluate software and hardware, and auto experts are expected to know as much about the vehicles as they do about their makers' balance sheets. Out of all this will come the familiar write-ups your broker may pass on, and more specialized information for his eyes only.

So far, so good. It's nice to have a real expert on hand when you are investing your funds. The trouble is the analyst is working for the firm that gives him that fat paycheck, and not for you, and that creates complications and conflicts.

For example, he is expected to be on good terms with the managements of companies covered, so he can scout for other business for the firm. Some of this is quite legitimate. As *Fortune* writer Anne B. Fisher has observed, "An analyst who knows his industry inside out can tell you which private companies in it are mulling over an initial public offering, or what public companies might need some financing, and who might be talking merger. Given the fees of investment bankers, it may well be that any such business brought in by the analysts would represent a superior return on all that expensive analytical talent."[2]

Fortune also related that "some firms, predictably, don't see why security analysts shouldn't handle both functions—pick stocks and target investment banking business too." John Hindelong, at the time head of research at A.G. Becker Paribas, said, "You like to have a quarterback who can pass and run." Subsequently, Hindelong became managing director-head of research at Dillon Read. Then, in the spring of 1985, he jumped to Smith Barney where he analyzes hospital management stocks. According to one report, "Hindelong said he made the move in order to devote more time to research and deal-making. He pointed out that Smith Barney's institutional sales force of some 50 U.S. producers will give him more investment banking support than Dillon Read's force of four producers."[3]

A good write-up and recommendation for that clothing chain, fast-food operation, steel company, or electronics firm might fetch a reward, in the form of its management asking the investment banker to underwrite its next issue of stocks or bonds or perform some other function, such as arranging a merger.

Some Wall Street houses are startlingly frank about this. Prudential-Bache's research chief, Greg Smith, noted that this was one of the ways his analysts earn their fat salaries. "Quite honestly, you can't pay securities analysts the kinds of compensation that are competitive today and think you'll make any money on brokerage at pennies a share. It's naive to think that clients expect to get execution and research at that price."[4]

Analysts must earn their keep by being on good terms with the firms they cover, and that usually means pressure for supportive commentaries. Keep this in mind the next time you receive a glowing report on one or another company, with that disclaimer saying, "The information contained herein is based on sources believed to be reliable, but is neither all-inclusive nor guaranteed by our firm . . ." but ends with words like this: "We have been an underwriter, manager, or co-manager, or have previously placed securities of the company within the last three years, or were a previous underwriter of this company."

Perhaps that recommendation was honest enough, but I have seen precious few sells for companies with which the underwriter has such a relationship. So it was in 1983, when most of the investment community was recommending high tech stocks, and this at a time when many of them were planning underwritings. Then the balloon burst, as earnings began to come in under expectations. What accounted for this divergence? In the view of Chicago-based *Zacks Investment Research*, which tracks earnings estimates, it wasn't because profits were all that bad, but rather the failure of forecasts. "The analysts just started out way too optimistic, possibly because they are pushing stocks or have investment banking relationships with their companies." Zacks also notes that during the 1981–1984 period 86 percent of brokerage house recommendations were either neutral or buys, 12 percent were sells, and 2 percent strong sells.[5]

Little wonder, then, that most write-ups are positive, even in negative investment environments. "If I had 200 securities reports on my desk, 175 of them would be 'buy' recommendations," wailed one money manager, but under the circumstances, what else can be expected? This is one of the greatest pitfalls investors must guard against, which is why a knowledge of how the fraternity (and in recent years, sorority as well) operates.

Richard Hoffman, former chief investment strategist at Merrill Lynch who left to form his own advisory firm, has long been critical of this approach and aware of the problems involved. R.J. Hoffman & Co. set up a subsidiary in early 1985 called *Veritas* (Latin for truth), which does nothing but issue sell recommendations, this in an attempt to rectify the imbalance. "We're in a position to be a lot more objective than the Wall Street houses," said David Katzen, who is in charge of the operation. "Neutral on a stock is about as bearish as *they* get."[6]

The pressure upon analysts to "be positive," particularly when writing up firms which the investment banking part of the firm is wooing, can be intense. This is especially so when the analyst has earlier been positive on the stock. Being negative makes enemies of managements; switching positions can be murder on the brokers and institutional salesmen, those people and fiduciaries with whom customers deal. "If you put out a negative on the stock, people who own the stock hate you. Management hates you. And the people who don't own the stock don't care," was the conclusion of one analyst, while another, who claims never to have issued a sell recommendation in his 20 years of experience in the business, added, "It's very, very difficult to go before fifteen or twenty salesmen at 9 a.m. Monday morning and tell them to sell something you were recommending." Perfectly understandable, since to follow through, the salesman might have to call a client to tell him that the stock he thought wonderful on Friday should now be dumped.[7] In such a case the broker may ask the analyst to telephone the client and hold hands for a while because important accounts appreciate this kind of access. "I can't always be *right*," a prominent oil analyst whose fame is eclipsed only by his recent poor calls once told me, "But I can always be *there*. And that's my rule: when I'm right, I'm not there, and when I'm there, it's probably because I haven't been right."

Another problem securities analysts have to guard against is the tendency to fall in love with the firms they are following. Over the years they form close relationships with the executives and PR people there, who often provide them with tips, hints, or other information which makes the job all that easier and gives them bragging rights in the office. Why jeopardize a good thing with a sell recommendation? When asked to comment on the poor record of some forecasters, Raymond DeVoe Jr. of Legg Mason Wood Walker Inc. observed that "most analysts depend upon the company as their prime source of information. Often they reheat the data and pass it on as original thinking."[8]

Perhaps this explains the generally mediocre record of the profession over the years. "Performance in this business isn't good from the buy side or the sell side," conceded a rueful William Gillard, director of investment policy at Kidder, Peabody, who talked of "torpedo stocks—ones you don't see coming until they blow a hole in your portfolio." The reason, he suspects, is analyst–company relations. "The way we've been contacting companies is absurd. Everybody talks to the investor relations guy, who feeds them the same numbers." And what if those numbers turn out to be wrong? All the institutions which rely upon information put out by advisors dump at the same time, resulting in the kinds of selling panics which accompany so many adverse news releases.[9]

Of course, every field has its share of incompetents or hard-working journeymen whose records are spotty. What one must seek, be it in a heart surgeon, auto mechanic, lawyer, accountant, or securities analyst, is a person with a superb record over time, and then entrust that individual with one's life, car, or money.

The trouble is that locating such a person isn't easy. One might think, for example, that the "all star" analysts singled out each year by the prestigious *Institutional Investor* would be individuals worth following. After all, this magazine has become the bible of the profession and should know what it is talking about. Not necessarily. Several years ago another journal, *Financial World*, attempted to review the predictions of these superstars and encountered strong opposition from several of the brokerage houses for which they labored at from $150,000 to $500,000 per annum. The reason became evident once *Financial World* assembled the material on its own. Only one-third of the all stars performed better than the Standard & Poor's 500. According to money manager David Dreman, "For well over a decade one of today's top photography analysts has had a nearly unblemished record of recommending buys near major tops and sales near major bottoms."[10]

Such a person can be quite valuable. Any time you can find a person who is *consistently* wrong, all that remains to come out a winner is to do the opposite of what he recommends.

Part of the reason for this is the herd instinct which is keenly alive at most brokerage houses, a force which if transgressed can cost the individual heavily.

Consider the situation of Daniel Meade, a leading household products analyst who went through the mill. Meade recalled a time when the entire investment fraternity was bullish on Mattel, and he put out a sell recommendation. "Everyone dumped on me. They accused me of being short the stock and characterized my analysis as perverted." Then the company refused to talk to him, and his firm's clients complained about his lack of contacts "because they were getting more information than I was." Subsequently Mattel fell out of bed, declining from 38 to less than 2, making Meade look like a genius and boosting his career. But had this not happened Meade would have been in deep and very hot water.[11]

This isn't as uncommon as might be expected. When Lee Isgur, who follows leisure time stocks for Paine Webber, wrote disparagingly of Showboat Inc., that firm "cut him off," according to Isgur. Isgur also claimed that Showboat's management instructed its PR firm, Mallory Factor Associates, to withhold press releases and had even forbade it to read the releases over the telephone to Paine Webber analysts. Isgur also claimed that his calls to Showboat president, Joseph Kelly, were not returned.[12]

Take the cases of James Chanos, an analyst then operating out of Guilford Securities, and George Salem who worked for Becker Paribas. Each was subjected to the kinds of pressures discussed, each tried to buck the system and suffered for his rashness, but happily managed to come out smelling like roses.

In 1982 Chanos, who was then only 24 years old, thought there was something fishy in the reports issued by Baldwin-United, a piano company tranformed into a $4 billion financial conglomerate by Morley Thompson, one of the whiz kids of the time. Thompson had just been eulogized by *Fortune* magazine, as a more imaginative shuffler of paper than ever surfaced in a corporate suite. Thompson was very charming, and given to entertaining analysts and other Wall Streeters in positions to recommend the stock, which they obligingly did with frequency and passion.

Chanos, who rarely talks with management, had no such personal involvements. "I don't even go to visit companies I'm bullish on," he said. "It's too easy to get blindsided by management."[13] His method (and mine) is to study the information the company has to provide the SEC.

Chanos' sell recommendation on Baldwin was greeted with pressures from the financial community, threats, and blasts from Thompson, all of which is standard operating procedure in such matters. Merrill Lynch was one of many Wall Street brokerage houses that vigorously supported B-U, and its diversified companies securities analyst was among those whom Thompson wooed most assiduously.[13a] Merrill Lynch's Carol P. Neves was especially strong defending her bullish recommendations, claiming the only trouble at the firm was a bad press. Robert W. Back of Prescott, Ball & Turben, who also recommended purchase, telephoned Chanos to warn him against "ruining your reputation at such a young age," and later charged him with leading a smear campaign.[14]

When Ray Dirks, who blew the whistle on several companies, showed an interest in the situation, he received an invitation to talk with Morley Thompson, at which the Baldwin chairman told him, "I hope you aren't going to do what Mr. Chanos is doing, because he is going to be in trouble with our lawyers."[14a] But Chanos stood firm in reference to his negative research stance on B-U. Then came investigations by state regulatory agencies which substantiated much of what Chanos had claimed. B-U fell from a high of 50 5/8 to under 5, and in the autumn of 1983 filed for voluntary reorganization under Chapter 11 of the Federal Bankruptcy Code.

Chanos went on to bigger things, and now is one of the highest paid analysts in the field, at the same time becoming the subject of sour grapes remarks from those on the other side. One critic observed that B-U was an easy call. "It was a perfect opportunity for the guy. Now he is trying to set himself up as a picker of impending disasters."[15]

Not necessarily. Chanos has also made timely buy recommendations, but he remains best known for blowing the whistle on the flawed operations supported by others. When still working on B-U he noted that Waste Management was overvalued considering its *true* (as opposed to purported) earnings and balance sheet. Once again there were indignant outcries from the firm's fans, especially A.G. Becker Paribas and Kidder, Peabody. And once again Chanos came out looking good; Waste Management slipped from 46 to 27,[16] before subsequently recovering in price.

George Salem's story is not as dramatic, but in many ways tells us even more about the problems faced by independent minded analysts who dare buck the trend (and their own firm's investment banking staffs). Salem, then a bank analyst at Prudential-Bache, became troubled about money center banks in 1982, considering their foreign loans questionable and their accounting procedures deceiving. He noted that if they established just a 10 percent loss reserve for these low-quality loans their earnings would drop by close to 90 percent, and he was having nothing to do with them. Because of this and despite howls from his bosses he refused to recommend big city bank stocks, and this cost him his job.[17]

"If you put a 'sell' on a bank, people equate it with the bank going under," said Salem, trying to understand the attitudes of those who insist upon favorable reports. Salem wound up at Becker Paribas, where he continued his negative reporting on the major banks. By then he had learned the lexicon one must use when trying to signal readers the stock should be dumped. "Sell is a four letter word," remarked one analyst, "and not to be used in polite company." So you employ euphemisms, like, "we are lowering our intermediate term rating," "the stock is not likely to outperform the market," "this stock is for patient investors," and "defer action." Hoping to do just that, Salem rated Continental Illinois a "weak hold," and soon after saw his negative opinion vindicated by that bank's debacle.[18]

None of this is meant to suggest that investors must always look for clouds under every silver lining, that truly knowledgeable people wind up as bears, or that the techniques discussed in this work will only help you to avoid disasters (important as this is) but not how to pluck out winners from the dross. Just as a careful investigation of available documents can be used to spot losers and overvalued situations, so it can be utilized to uncover undervalued, overlooked ones. Today's truly successful operators, such as Warren Buffett of Berkshire-Hathaway, will tell you that this is the way they do it. But it does take some learning and time, and the confidence to say "no" to that broker peddling the recommendations put out by his firm's researchers. "My problem is I don't get 50 great ideas a year," said the self-effacing Buffett. "I'm lucky if I get one or two." He gets them not by reading analysts' reports, but by poring over the documents.[19]

Think of the brokerage house as a store and the investment advice as wares to be sold. The message is *caveat emptor*—let the buyer beware—especially when you, on your own, can do a better job of research and often with surprisingly little effort, once you get the hang of it.

CHAPTER 2

And Don't Trust
Your Auditor

So you can't really trust your analyst, because he may have a stake in his bullishness, his employer may have some kind of arrangement with the company discussed, or for a variety of other reasons. How about the independent auditor, who is paid by the firm to go over its books and issue an opinion as to their veracity? You might think such a person or company, operating under professional guidelines, could certainly be trusted. One analyst might differ from another regarding whether a company is going to make $2.00 or $2.50 per share next year, but how could two qualified auditors arrive at different conclusions regarding the toting up of assets and liabilities? So it would appear that if anything in the annual report is to be accepted at face value, it would be the auditor's opinion.

The investment house of Drexel Burnham Lambert certainly thinks so. In its pamphlet, "A Look At Annual Reports," Drexel says: "Probably the first item to check is the auditor's opinion to see whether or not it is a clean one—'in conformity with generally accepted accounting principles consistently applied'—or is qualified in regard to differences between the auditor and company management in the accounting treatment of some major item, or in the outcome of important litigation." Abraham Akresh, national director of auditing for Laventhol & Horwath, agrees, adding that short and sweet opinions are the best. "If that's all there is, it means as a reader I can assume that everything that is supposed to be disclosed has been disclosed, that the numbers are not materially in error. It doesn't mean they are perfect or 100 percent right, but that there is not a major error in there and that I can go ahead and read the financial statements and [know] that somebody had taken a look at them."[1]

All well and good. Drexel and Akresh are saying that if the auditor finds items that smack of deceit he can—indeed, must—say so in the opinion. In fact, there are four categories of opinions that might be awarded, in order of occurrence: (1) "clean," which is unqualified acceptance and is usually presented in two short paragraphs; (2) "subject to" in which the auditor accepts the financials subject to pervasive uncertainty that cannot be adequately measured such as relating to the value of inventories, reserves for losses, or other matters subject to judgment; (3) "except for" meaning that the auditor was unable to audit certain areas of the company's operations because of restrictions imposed by management or other conditions beyond his control. (It should be noted that the SEC generally will not permit publicly owned companies to get away with an "except for" opinion); and (4) a statement from the auditor disclaiming any opinion regarding the company's financial condition which is in effect a disclaimer of opinion.[2]

Most opinions are clean, and I have rarely seen a disclaimer. But I have come across many "subject to" and "except for" opinions. For example, Coopers & Lybrand, auditors for Manville Corp., noted in their 1984 opinion that the company and "certain of its subsidiaries are defendants in a substantial number of asbestos-health legal actions and may be liable for asbestos removal property damage claims and other claims." This is hardly surprising, since the asbestos situation had been plastered across the financial pages for months. Yet it is nice to know that Coopers & Lybrand has been doing its job. Also, note that the qualified opinion doesn't challenge the accuracy of the report, or offer an opinion regarding Manville's health and future prospects. It is all very scientific, precise, and legalistic. Or so it would seem.[3]

Unfortunately this is not always so. Reading on in the Drexel Burnham Lambert pamphlet we come across this: "Largely due to the growing incidence of shareholder suits in recent years, auditors have begun issuing more and more qualified opinions. In essence, the auditor's opinion provides a good indication of the reliability of the company's financial statements." Now this is a non sequitur if I ever saw one. Drexel is saying here that on the one hand there have been many shareholder suits alleging that the auditors haven't been doing their jobs as well as they might, while on the other claiming that the opinions remain a good indication of the accuracy of financial statements.[4]

Which of the two is more accurate? The answer is the former: the auditors haven't been doing their jobs as well as they might. Indeed, as of the summer of 1985 the Big Eight accounting firms have been obliged to pay almost $180 million in settlements of audit-related suits, and because of this their insurance premiums increased by as much as 200 percent that year.

"The outside auditors are complaining that the public doesn't understand that a clean opinion on an annual report isn't a guarantee against all future problems of the company," says John C. Burton, former chief accountant for the SEC and presently dean of Columbia University's Graduate School of Business. He goes on to observe that auditors are "going to point to any uncertainty," even in borderline cases, in the future.[5]

Dean Burton would have us believe that the profession is becoming more careful because the public is uneducated as to the meaning of the auditor's statement and needs help. In fact, it is the other way around; it is the auditors who have failed, not the public, as those whopping settlements indicate.

The evidence is blatant. For example, Baldwin-United, Penn Square Bank, and Continental Illinois all failed. They also have something else in common: All received clean opinions in the most recent report prior to collapse.[6] And these are only the more spectacular cases.

There are a multitude of other examples. Ernst & Whinney gave a clean opinion to United American Bank in Tennessee a month before it went under.[7] Fox & Co. had to defend itself in a civil action brought by the SEC for its audits of Alpex Computer, Flight Transportation, and Saxon Paper. The Commission alleged that Fox "aided and abetted" Saxon in making misleading financial statements. In its defense Fox claimed to have been the victim of "massive, if not unprecedented management fraud." But the SEC charged that the auditor "recklessly allowed Saxon to limit the scope of its audits in 1979 and 1980 by delaying the commencement of the onsite audit until mid to late March when Fox knew that Saxon's consolidated financial statements were due on March 31 of every year."[8]

But why go on? That these incidents are out of the ordinary is certainly true. But that can hardly console stockholders in the failed companies who thought the clean auditor's report meant that everything was as represented.

Don't think you can count on the SEC to monitor all of these activities. If anything, in recent years the agency has become less effective. From 1962 to 1984 the number of filings to be reviewed by the division of corporate finance increased from 18,000 to 66,000, while the professional staff was cut from 146 to 134 in the same period. In 1984 the SEC conceded that it was barely able to review ten percent of the 8,832 10-Ks filed the previous year. As *Forbes* has observed, "There are just far more crooks around than there are cops."[9]

The accounting profession claims that its imprimatur on a report is a sign that careful auditing has been performed, and that a clean opinion is a sign that all is as represented. Indeed, Congressman John D. Dingell (D, Mich.), who chairs the House Commerce Committee's Subcommittee on Oversight and Investigations, has noted, "It is extraordinary that literally two days *after* the SEC closed down ESM [a failed government securities dealer] because of massive fraud and accounting abuses, the Commission and the American Institute of Certified Public Accountants' Public Oversight Board were telling the Subcommittee that the system is working just fine. That is why our inquiry—begun nearly a year ago and well before the recent failures—is so important and timely."[10]

The reason for this is not necessarily incompetence, though like doctors and lawyers auditors have their share of such practitioners. Rather, its roots are in the unusual relationship between auditors and their clients.

The client pays the bill to have an independent audit and will be displeased if the auditor discovers irregularities sufficient to prevent him from offering a clean opinion. Putting that in writing might mean the loss of an account in an industry marked by intense competition, in which raids for clients and price slashing have become the rule. A full audit for a large corporation can cost from $1 million to $6 million and can open the door for other services and fees. "Many of our clients are treating the audit as a commodity, like shopping for cheaper gasoline," complained Eugene Bertorelli, partner in charge of the San Francisco office of Oppenheim, Appel, Dixon.[11] The result is lower fees and more pressure upon the auditors to comply with client demands. Peter R. Scanlan, chairman of Coopers & Lybrand, has warned that "CPA firms that do audit work for low fees cannot sustain quality work. If a company only wants to pay peanuts, it may get monkeys looking at its business instead of thoughtful professionals."

In April of 1985, the SEC issued a warning to registrants and independent auditors attempting to engage in "opinion shopping." The practice of "opinion shopping" involves a corporation that attempts to obtain reporting objectives by following questionable accounting principles and a pliable auditor willing to go along with the desired treatment.

Professor Abraham Briloff of Bernard M. Baruch College, one of the more acerbic critics of the accounting profession, tells the story of a corporation shopping for an auditor: "The president figured he'd make the rounds, asking CPA firms how much is two plus two. Invariably, they all said four. Finally, when he gets to the last firm on his list, he poses the question again: How much is two plus two? This time the response is more to his liking, 'What did you have in mind?'"[12]

As has been suggested, the entry of what were once purely accounting firms into other areas may have made those auditors' statements even more suspect. Syndicated columnist Mark Stevens has written in a penetrating fashion about the evolution of auditors into what he calls "a hybrid: part professional firm, part supermarket. They became—with Peat Marwick, Arthur Andersen, and Coopers & Lybrand leading the way—purveyors of a varied smorgasbord of financial services. The marketers among them saw, quite clearly, that the rich veins to be tapped were in general consulting, taxes, small-business consulting, government work, executive recruiting, feasibility studies, and actuarial services. Put simply, whatever clients requested, providing it was remotely related to the CPA's role, The Big Eight provided it."[13] And always for fat fees, with the audit often the opening wedge. "Of course, they could sign up clients for a host of services," added Briloff. "They were already part of the family under the guise of independent auditors. It's easy to capitalize on this privileged position. The point is, is it right?"[14]

The stakes are clearly tremendous. From 1983 to 1985 revenues at the Big Eight firms from audits grew by only 14 percent, while those for management consulting were up by 33 percent and for tax practice, 28 percent.[15] The dismissal of an auditor usually means that the non-audit work is also lost.

Robert Israeloff, former president of the New York State Society of CPAs and managing partner of Israeloff, Trattner, who is involved in management operations himself, believes that "any time fees from non-accounting/auditing/tax engagements become very substantial—and this can be less than 50 percent of the total—the firm may no longer deserve its professional standing." As Professor Robert Chatov of the State University at Buffalo put it, "If one were starting from point zero today, I think that it would be judged madness to invent a system where the one to be audited hired the auditor, bargained with the auditor as to the size of the fee, was permitted to purchase other management services from the auditor, and where the auditor in turn had the prime responsibility for setting the rules and for enforcing them and applying sanctions against themselves."[16]

Here is one example of how the system can work—or to be more accurate, fail. Arthur Young & Co. was auditor for the Penn Square Bank in 1980. Young qualified its report for that year, because it was "unable to satisfy [itself] as to the adequacy of the reserve for possible loan losses, due to the lack of supporting documentation of collateral values of certain loans."

Out went Young and in came Peat Marwick. Peat Marwick's report which came out March 19, 1982—three and a half months before the bank's collapse—removed the qualification. "It should be understood that estimates of future loan losses involve an exercise of judgment," the report said. 'It is the judgment of management that the allowance is adequate at both December 31, 1981 and 1980.'

It should be noted that at year end 1981, Penn Square's provision for loan losses totaled $6.3 million compared with $1.4 million at year end 1980. The substantial increase in the loan loss reserves resulted in both Peat Marwick and the U.S. Comptroller of the Currency commenting favorably upon Penn Square's boost in the provision for loan losses.

Peat Marwick officials allowed that the firm believed that its positive report on Penn Square was accurate at the time, even though the bank collapsed shortly afterward. "They had a new management team and had improved the situation over the year before," said Dean Cook, an audit partner for Peat Marwick in

Oklahoma City. "We really don't know what happened" to alter the bank's financial position.[17]

After investigating Penn Square, the Comptroller of the Currency concluded that the audit by Peat Marwick was "unacceptable," and in 1983 the Michigan National Bank filed a suit against the large accounting firm asking $41 million in damages. Peat Marwick is now defending itself against suits by five Penn Square creditors.[18]

On February 20, 1985, Professor Briloff testified before the Subcommittee on Oversight and Investigations, Committee on Energy and Commerce, United States House of Representatives. In his testimony, the professor even went so far as to suggest that there be a requirement for a skull and crossbones logo next to the independent auditor's opinion. Within this context, the professor testified as follows:

> If these hearings do nothing else, if they make known to the public that fact that there are enormous risks that are implicit and impacted into the audit reports and the financial statements, and possibly require that there be a skull and bones associated by way of a logo next to the CPA's opinion as he writes it, so that they will understand the fact that it might be risky if they were to take it internally, something like the legend that is on cigarette packages. Maybe no one will read it, but at least our consciences would be clear.[19]

The analogy is fitting. Approval by the Pure Food and Drug Administration of a prescription drug is taken by most to mean the product has undergone rigorous testing and has been deemed reasonably safe for use. Likewise, many investors believe a clean auditor's opinion signifies that a reputable outside agent has gone over the books in a dispassionate fashion and is prepared to say that everything is as indicated. But as we have seen, "It ain't necessarily so."

The average investor probably never even looks at the auditor's statement, and after what we have seen here, might be forgiven if he doesn't do so in the future. But recent blunders, misstatements, and law suits may be changing the situation, though I am not optimistic. What I do find discouraging is the low rating investment professionals—money managers, analysts, and the like—assign to such matters. As will be seen in the next chapter, they rank "statement of accounting policies" in the eighth slot in ranking importance of various segments of the annual reports, behind the puffery of management's review of the year.

We opened by suggesting that you can't trust your analyst, and now we have seen why you can't trust the auditor hired by the company to certify its books. So we come down to a reiteration and reenforcement of the message presented earlier: Intelligent and informed investors have to do the job themselves. The care and feeding of investments requires time and effort. There is no more a simple way to manage your portfolio than there is a painless and quick way to shed 30 pounds.

We start out with this in mind. Most preconceptions regarding individuals who are supposed to help in formulating investment decisions should be looked at with askance. I will try to show in the rest of this book just how you can find information and learn about those stocks before making the commitment to buy or sell. At times it will seem like hard work. It is. But then consider how much time and effort went into earning those thousands you have invested, perhaps on an analyst's recommendation or a quick read of the annual report—along with that clean opinion. Think of losses incurred because of lack of knowledge, and reflect on the fact that the facts were there to be seen and analyzed, if only you knew where they were and the techniques to be applied. Do this and you will appreciate that whatever it takes to understand the often arcane material is worth it. This might not make you a millionaire, but the knowledge could save you from many stock market catastrophes.

CHAPTER 3

Person to Person:
A Shareholder Letter

IN WHAT'S AHEAD you will read and learn to analyze several key documents, such as the 10-K, the 10-Q, and the proxy statement, all of which public corporations have to prepare and file with the Securities and Exchange Commission. Between the lines of these bland, legalistic, and too often overlooked filings are to be found stores of information. Sometimes the facts are released reluctantly, in order to conform with the law, in the hope that they will be overlooked or ignored, and occasionally the company will blunder and reveal more about its operations than it cares the stockholders and general public to know.

All of these filings are readily available, either direct from the company or from two private concerns: Disclosure Inc. (5161 River Road, Bethesda, MD 20816, 800-638-8241) and Bechtel Information Services (15740 Shady Grove Road, Gaithersburg, MD 20877-1454, 800-231-DATA), which are in the business of providing them to interested parties. But the best place to start would be with a more accessible document, one every shareholder knows will arrive in the mail, usually in the early spring. These are the annual reports, which are sent out by more than 10,000 companies.

One of the reasons companies issue annual reports is to comply with the mandate set down in Rule 14a-3 of the Securities Exchange Act of 1934, which sets down the specific financial information which must be revealed, but not the form in which it is to be presented. Several years ago a handful of companies experimented with sending shareholders a short statement wrapped around a copy of the 10-K filing, this both to save money and impress them with a no-nonsense attitude. The idea is spreading.

Over the years public relations experts have gone to work to turn what was once a rather drab recitation of facts and numbers into what often appear akin to art books, more suited to the coffee table than the analyst's desk. These can be lengthy, expensive productions. The full-scale annual report can run to more than 100 pages, costs the company as much money to turn out as the price of a slim paperback novel (the range is estimated to run between $2 and $6), and of course is much more lavish, printed on heavy, glossy paper, dotted with many illustrations, and artfully conceived. Taking all costs into consideration, including overheads, and dividing them by the number of copies printed, the cost to deliver such a report to a stockholder can often be as high as $8. If many firms could in some way eliminate them their per share earnings might be a few cents higher. This is hardly a likely happening, even if the law were changed, since the annual report is one of the firm's most important public relations offerings. As Bennett Robinson of Corporate Graphics, a firm which designs reports put it, "many corporations make a big effort with the annual report because it's essentially the main communication a company has with the public."[1]

Obtaining annual reports presents no problem. A telephone call or letter to the company is usually all that is required (addresses and telephone numbers can be obtained by referring to the Standard & Poor's manuals available in many public libraries). In addition, each spring the leading newspapers and business magazines, such as *The Wall Street Journal, Barron's, Business Week, Forbes*, and the business section of *The New York Times* carry several pages offering free annual reports of more than a hundred companies to anyone who asks. Select those that interest you or scrawl the word "all" across the coupon, mail it in to the box number indicated, and you'll be getting a steady stream of them for several months.

Annual reports come in many shapes and sizes. All contain some basic statistical material and ancillary information; most go quite a bit further. With all those pages one can always learn *something* about the firm, since the longer the report, the greater the chance that management will inadvertently slip in something which can be dissected by astute readers.

In fact, a gold mine of information can be gleaned from a proper reading of the reports, partly because managements are obliged to release the material, though they often do so hoping that it will be overlooked by stockholders to whom it resembles arcane mysteries. However, the annuals shouldn't be read in a vacuum. Often they refer to developments of the past few years which should be checked by referring to reports of that period and, if possible, the quarterlies as well. Serious investors should consider looking these up in the libraries or getting them from Disclosure. What it comes down to, then, is that the annual report, with its glossy pictures, upbeat prose, tables, and notes, should be looked at as one might a possible mine field. Before you is a verdant meadow, but you know there *might* be explosives under all of that greenery. The trouble is that you can't be sure if indeed there are some mines, how many of them are there, and where they are located. Again, what I want to do is give you a mine detector. If the numbers are all in place, the outlook pleasing, and there are no surprises, the stock might be a buy. If not, perhaps you should hold back, or if you own the issue, sell.

Many shareholders suspect this to be the case and walk the field anyway, hoping against hope they won't be unpleasantly surprised. These people are skeptical of the glossy renderings, perhaps because they are so glitzy. A 1984 survey by the public relations firm of Hill & Knowlton came up with the unsurprising findings that 73 percent of individual investors agreed that the reports either play down bad news or hide it in the back of the statement, 58 percent thought them too promotional, 32 percent agreed with the statement, "I don't trust what I read in annual reports," and 27 percent said it was sometimes difficult to tell from the reports what business the company was in.

Here are some more numbers. Half the recipients said they only skimmed the reports or didn't read them at all, a third of H & K's respondents said they read them, and 18 percent claimed to have "studied" them. Most important for our purposes, while 55 percent find them useful in making investment decisions, most gave them low ratings in assisting them in buy and sell decisions, ranking the reports next to last among all available information.

But this survey was made of the general shareholder population. When it came to serious investors one obtained a different picture. All of these in the study considered the report "essential" to their analysis, unanimously agreeing with the statement, "As a professional investor, corporate annual reports are essential to me," with most saying that the general level has improved in recent years.

Among the more important criticisms were that the reports are too oriented to the past; the pros would prefer something about where the company is heading. In the professional sample 56 percent agreed that "Annual reports all too often fail to clearly present management's goals and strategies." "Annual reports should try to look forward, instead of backward. I'd like to see more discussion of strategies and how a company did in relation to the rest of the industry and the economy," was one comment, and another said, "Discussing the goals of the company and management's strategy for achieving those goals would be very helpful. Also, comments on how close the company came to achieving its goals and why it fell short or exceeded them would be good."[2]

The typical annual report contains more than a dozen segments. Asked to rate them in order of importance, the investment professionals came up with the following:

Section	Importance Rating
1. Financial Statements	95 percent
2. Business Segment Information	93
3. Financial Review	87
4. Five or Ten Year Financial Summaries	87
5. Management's Analysis	81
6. Review of the Year	78
7. Quarterly Summaries	74
8. Statement of Accounting Policies	73
9. Financial Highlights	70
10. Letter To Shareholders	69
11. Dividend Payments (two years)	54
12. Stock Price History (two years)	43
13. Inflation Accounting (effects of changing prices)	39

Source: Hill & Knowlton, The Annual Report, p. 13.

Except for a handful of items, the ranking isn't all that surprising. I would strongly object to the low esteem inflation accounting seems to enjoy, for these figures (adopted in 1979 by the Financial Accounting Standards Board) which display earnings, assets, etc. adjusted for alterations in the price level, can show that what at first blush seem respectable advances were really declines, and indicates that the pros haven't learned to respect these numbers as much as they might.

Hold that annual report in your hand and look at the cover. Perhaps there is a picture of happy employees and/or customers, a montage of the firm's products, a view of the countryside or a cityscape which in some way is connected with the firm's major business, a realistic or abstract drawing—or just a simple, unadorned logo, indicating either the designer's infatuation with minimal art or lack of imagination. Sid Cato, publisher of *Sid Cato's Newsletter of Annual Reports*, suggests you might want to start off by flipping through the report, reading at random, and asking, "Do I feel good about these people?" Then turn to the specifics. If the financials are not displayed prominently be prepared for trouble. Does the company mention problems, and if so, are possible solutions discussed? Cato says to beware of firms that dismiss these by blithely saying, "We're confident we can overcome the situation."[3]

Consider the IBM 1984 Annual Report, one of the classier examples, selected because it is quite typical and the firm is familiar to virtually all investors. In this case the cover picture is that of an attractive woman, identified on the inside cover as an IBM marketing representative, explaining products to a man (a customer?). Behind her is a case filled with IBM programs. The inside caption explains that program products are increasing at the rate of 30 percent per annum, and that industrywide revenues from them will come to more than $150 billion by 1994. "Customers can choose from more than 2,500 different IBM programs to extend the usefulness of systems from the largest 308X computer to the smallest desk-top PC."

"Hackers" will recognize that the programs behind the marketing rep are all designed for the PC, indicating that in 1984 IBM intended to draw attention to that highly successful product, and that the use of the picture instead of abstract drawings and photos of high tech items, which IBM often utilized in the past, is yet another sign of the company's recent switch to the kind of marketing more identified with consumer goods than capital goods. IBM signaled this change on the cover of its 1982 report, which pictured a young boy happily banging away on the keyboard of his PC.

A minor point, but one worth noting.

In any case, the report is the product of the firm's in-house or

hired public relations firm, which serves the corporation in somewhat the same way a fashion designer does an auto company,
namely to make the product appear enticing and interesting. What's
under the hood may be far more important—in our analogy these
are the statistics and footnotes, provided by corporate management
and support personnel—but the designer is responsible for providing the company with its image, and that's what often sells cars
and companies to prospective buyers. Ten years ago IBM cared little what the run-of-the-mill shareholder purchased, since its customers were almost exclusively government agencies and corporations. All of this has changed and is reflected in the cover of IBM's
annual report.

Turn the page and you'll find the Financial Highlights, a summary of the company's performance over the year. It is worth a
quick skim, because you'll encounter the information in far more
detailed form later on, at which time you'll recognize that while
the earlier figures may be interesting (and in the case of IBM for
1984, pleasing), they aren't adequate for diagnosis. It's as though
your doctor tried to discover the state of your health by a quick
glance and perhaps a chest thump or two.

Turn the page again and you'll find the first meaty part of the
report, the Stockholders' Letter, which in the case of IBM is called,
"To the Stockholder." Some of the letters in annual reports are random and rambling thoughts of the CEO (Chief Executive Officer);
Harold Figgie of Figgie International will write at great length of
the need to reduce debt—not only his company's, but that of the
Treasury as well, and Peter Grace of W.R. Grace & Co. uses the
letter as a springboard for his thoughts on federal spending. Union
Carbide offered a cautious explanation of the Bhopal, India gas
leak tragedy; a few years earlier Procter & Gamble wrote almost
nothing about its troubles with Rely tampons and ignored Pringle's
potato chip failure. Firestone Tire & Rubber wins some sort of prize
for vagueness, says Cato. In its 1984 Report the company wrote:
"Sales in the U.S. of replacement tires and automotive services are
increasing at a rate of about $3 billion to $4 billion annually." Even
nowadays, a billion dollars up or down is hardly small change.

Warren Buffett was delightfully frank in his 1984 Berkshire
Hathaway letter, which runs a full 19 pages. He noted the firm's
excellent showing for the year, but added, "This sounds pretty good
but actually it's mediocre," and then went on to indicate why, get-

ting away with it not only because he has a good record, but also because he owns a controlling interest in the company. In fact, if all CEOs followed his example, this book would be much thinner than it is. Buffett once explained his rationale this way: "I just assume my sister owns the other half of the business and she's been travelling for a year. She's not business ignorant, but she's not an expert either." As for frankness, consider this from Parker Drilling: "Parker experienced another tough year in 1984. . . . Nothing has happened that indicates the coming year will be any better. . . . It is not fun to be in the drilling business at this time."[4]

The low ranking afforded the shareholders' letter in the Hill & Knowlton survey is puzzling, for in this can often be found the very material the pros indicate elsewhere they would like to have, namely discussions of successful and failed strategies. Also, the stockholders' letter is usually jargon-free, and so quite accessible to novice investors. Clearly such letters are of less importance than "the back of the book," namely the financials, but a well-crafted letter can provide insights into operations which may not only illuminate activities but also serve as a guide to reading and analyzing the statistics. But remember, there is no general format for these letters; unlike profit and loss statements, balance sheets, and other "number items," these essays are individualistic. In a way they are minor works of art, and have to be approached that way. Don't look for formulas from me in this instance, but rather some examples of what to look for, what I consider good, bad, and indifferent letters, and the reasons for these judgments.

Finally, without meaning to do so, in the letter managements often provide information of great value to indicate cover-ups and blunders which can be masked by fiddling with the numbers. The trouble is you have to read them slowly, carefully, and with a critical eye, especially those parts of the letter which can be verified by reference to the statistics contained elsewhere in the report or in earlier messages from management to stockholders.

Most of the letters for the bigger firms include smiling pictures of the top management team, and the words indicate those smiles are there for a reason: everything looks pretty good, since you can count on the firm putting its best foot forward. If the company has had a bad stretch, the letter will tell you improvement is in sight. If things are proceeding swimmingly, count on the letter to spread the credit all around, and indicate more of the same might be expected, while warning of the risks inherent in doing business in highly competitive environments—doesn't do to be too complaisant, you know, and such caution indicates that management is on the ball, preparing itself for any and all eventualities. There may be discussions of new products, expansion into new markets, ongoing research and development, or mergers, and if the firm has been in the news recently, reference to these items as well. All of this can be found in the IBM letter.

Read it and learn, but also realize, as must be obvious, that while the letter is signed by the chairman and president it usually is written by those PR fellows. It is designed to serve as the veil for a striptease dancer, namely, to offer a hint of what is underneath, indicate shape and form, but not to permit too much insight. Also, the letter is the first of the legendary seven veils to be seen.

But not quite. Most letters refer obliquely to past years and developments, always in such a way as to be upbeat. Those managements seeking to appear progressive and on the ball will do so in the safe and sure knowledge that most investors don't hold on to their old reports, and that newer ones won't go to the trouble of looking them up in nearby college or university libraries or getting microfiches of them from Disclosure. It's always helpful to be able to look over letters in reports of the past few years. Are they contradictory? Overly optimistic? That could be an indication they're on shaky ground. Sid Cato suggests you compare the reports to see if there were many charts and graphs during good years and none or few in bad ones. "If that's the case, I'd say they're phonies."[5]

Investors should always take the time and trouble to make these comparisons. Nine times out of ten little will come of it; the tenth occasion could save you a bundle.

Perhaps the best and most dramatic illustration of this is the case of International Harvester (HR), an $8.4 billion firm as recently as 1979, whose stock was a component of the Dow-Jones Industrial Average. In that year the stock sold for as high as 45 1/2. It is my opinion that the 1980 International Harvester letter is one of the most flagrant examples of attempts to minimize difficulties I have seen. So it is not typical, but it contains many elements of letters which should be read as warnings to stay away from the stock.

HR had some rough sledding in 1980, when CEO Archie McCardell reported a revenue dip to $6.3 billion, red ink covered the ledger, and the stock's price was shaved in half. As might have been expected McCardell's letter in the 1980 report was chock full of hope, which could have led investors to assume the worst was over and HR was a buy at its price that spring in the low 20s. In this case and others to be discussed, the poetry of the letter should be compared with the prose to be found in statistics presented elsewhere in the report, which can be read without much difficulty by almost anyone with a modicum of knowledge of what those numbers stand for. For those who don't fall into this category, I will offer some guidelines and hints in subsequent chapters. What follows may be considered an introduction to such matters as well as a dissection of a most interesting letter, which is reproduced here in full. Read it and reflect on the sunny outlook, the optimistic tone, the "future lies ahead" prose—a pretty meadow with several mines underneath, ready to explode.

To Our Stockholders

SUCCESSFULLY meeting challenge is a 150 year tradition of this Company.

In 1831, Cyrus McCormick and his reaper were tested and proved themselves in the market place. Today, the people, products and strategies of the Company which started with McCormick's reaper are successfully meeting the new challenges of our second century and a half as a world leader.

International Harvester enters 1981 following a tightly focused long-term strategy to improve our cost structure, advance IH product and market superiority and make maximum use of company resources—both human and financial.

Our accelerating progress toward these goals was dramatized in the contrasting markets of the last two years. In 1979's expanding markets, we stretched our productive capacity, gained market share, cut excess operating costs, increased investment in the future and earned record profits. In 1980, we met the challenges of sharply lower demand in our industries, escalating interest rates and a strike which idled most U.S. plants the first six months of the year and increased Company debt.

INTERNATIONAL HARVESTER'S performance in the last half of fiscal 1980 proved again the basic strengths of this Company, and the effectiveness of its long-term strategy.

IH forged a strong recovery of market share that had been eroded by inventory shortages during the strike. Agricultural Equipment Group set an all time quarterly sales record the last three months of the year. Truck Group resumed leadership in U.S. medium and heavy duty registrations during the same period. The newly created Diversified Group increased its market share in both its financial services operations and most turbo machinery models.

This market recovery reflects the established and growing customer preference for IH products and services. It also clearly proved the strength of our dealer and distributor organization, now some 5,800 strong. This sales network quickly moved product to our customers once U.S. manufacturing was resumed in May.

Our strategy to maintain lean dealer inventories during the declining market strengthened our sales network by helping IH dealers avoid the high interest costs and the price-cutting which penalized our competitors' dealers.

YOUR COMPANY continued its strategic drive to improve the use of financial resources. Despite reduced manufacturing volume, IH exceeded its cost improvement targets for the last six months of the year. Today, International Harvester's annual operating costs are more than $400 million lower than they were three years ago. By better use of financial resources, we need significantly less working capital today to operate our business than we would have at our current level of business five years ago.

During the fourth quarter, International Harvester Company reduced its short term debt by $562 million and total debt by $488 million from the peak third quarter levels caused by the strike.

Your Company continued to protect its future while meeting these short-run challenges. New records were set by the $255 million invested in research and development and $384 million for more efficient plant and equipment. The Company continued programs to upgrade current management through training and to recruit the best talent available.

WE PIT THESE STRENGTHS against unparalleled challenges. Most of our markets appeared to have bottomed out during the last quarter of 1980, and North American agricultural equipment market began to show improvement. However, new rises in interest rates are again putting pressure on customer demand in all the industries we serve.

IH's long-term strategic plan accepts these conditions as inherent factors in the cyclical markets we serve. Our 1981 plan calls for slowing the rate of investment in many areas during the downturn. To maintain financial flexibility in a period of economic uncertainty, the dividend on common stock was reduced in the first quarter of 1981 from 62 1/2 cents per share to 30 cents per share. The on-going program to reduce operating costs has been intensified. We will closely monitor demand, but maintain lean inventories of both our dealers and the Company until signs of an upturn are detectable.

Declining interest rates and revival of market demand expected later this year will coincide with introduction of a record number of new IH products and new technology in updated products impacting more than one-third of the Company's normal sales volume. Some of these new models are in areas of traditional IH leadership such as heavy duty trucks, tractors, and combines. Others are designed to establish profitable new market niches.

THE IH ORGANIZATION brings new strengths to fiscal 1981.

Our earning power is unmatched in recent IH history, and growing. Our advance in market share, interrupted by the strike, has resumed its upward trend.

Customer preference for our products, a traditional IH strength, is the highest in decades. Products like our heavy and medium duty trucks, the 2 plus 2 farm tractor, Axial-Flow combines, Mars turbines, and 466 diesel engines are acknowledged standards of their markets.

Intensive effort to upgrade our distributor organization has given us the strongest sales networks ever in our key markets, particularly the North American truck and the North American and European agricultural equipment markets.

With these strengths, International Harvester operations are well positioned to continue riding out the economic downturn and to take full advantage of the recovery in our markets. It will be a difficult task, requiring aggressive effort from the entire organization. We expect to achieve it.

Successfully meeting challenge is a 150 year tradition of our Company. And we intend to confirm it as part of our heritage for the next century and a half as well.

Archie P. McCardell
Chairman of the Board
and Chief Executive Officer

Warren J. Hayford
President
and Chief Operating Officer

Note that McCardell began his message with a review of the company's 150-year history, and its current "tightly focused long-term strategy to improve our cost structure," such words being a clear warning flag of troubles. He went on to say that "International Harvester's performance in the last half of fiscal 1980 proved again the basic strengths of this Company, and the effectiveness of its long-term strategy." And what lay ahead for fiscal 1981? According to the CEO, "Our earning power is unmatched in recent IH history and growing. Our advance in market share, interrupted by the strike, has resumed its upward trend."

Elsewhere in the report we learn that the *first half* results were heavily penalized by the aforementioned strike, so that the second half, during which old orders were filled, was bound to appear strong. In the Statement of Operations at the end of the report HR reports earnings from continuing operations of $2.65 per share for the 1980 second half versus $6.98 for the same period in 1979, hardly a strong performance, and one which was even worse than that, since for the last 1980 quarter earnings came to $0.64 per share compared with $4.79 for the 1979 fourth quarter. From this we may assume McCardell was whistling in the dark and hoping readers wouldn't compare the letter with the statistics. Although McCardell may have believed what he was saying, and did not deliberately intend to mislead his readers, the obvious discrepancies between the prose and the statistics should have alerted readers that more inconsistencies might be expected.

And so it comes a few paragraphs later, when the letter says, "During the fourth quarter, International Harvester Company reduced its short term debt by $562 million and total debt by $488 million from the peak third quarter levels caused by the strike." Now it's usually nice to see debt shaved, especially so dramatically, but one is justified in asking how HR managed to pull off such a coup with its limited earnings. And it's all there in the financials. From these one learns that between 1979 and 1980 HR increased its short-term debt from $682 million to a whopping $1.13 billion, and that during the same period long-term debt plus preferred stock rose to $1,257 million from $758 million, for a total increase of $948 million, all of this at high interest rates. The combination of the strike, soaring interest charges, and a recessionary economic environment caused havoc with the company's finances. The recovery enabled HR to cut back a portion of the debt, but the fact remained that total debt was $948 million higher at the end of 1980 than it had been at the end of 1979, this hardly being the message sent out by the shareholders' letter.[6]

That's about as far into the report as investors might have cared to go. An analysis of that much of the letter, compared with some of the basic statistics, would indicate the firm was still in deep trouble and the stock should be avoided.

Two years later HR sold as low as 2 3/4. A preview of what was in store could have been obtained by a careful reading and analysis of that stockholders' letter in the 1980 report.

Andrew Corp., a highly regarded telecommunications company, offers a clear example of how one can be misled by optimistic statements in annuals and quarterlies. The firm's earnings had risen smartly in fiscal 1981–1984, and there seemed no reason to believe the string wouldn't be extended further.

In the report for the first quarter ended December 31, 1984, Andrew reported $0.42 per share vs. $0.38 for the same period the previous year, which was not as good as analysts had been anticipating. Andrew's management conceded there were some troubles. "Results in the first quarter of fiscal 1985 present a mixed picture," began the stockholders' letter, which went on to note that while net sales had increased by "a healthy 27% over the first quarter of 1984" new orders were 1 percent below the previous year's figures. Then followed an analysis, ending with this: "All things considered, we believe that subsequent quarters will bring substantial improvements in profitability. . . . We are currently expecting a strong second quarter, with the result that orders in the first half should be 20% or more above the first half of 1984."[7]

On revenues of $49.6 million Andrew recorded profits in the second quarter of $0.15 per share versus $48.8 million and $0.41

for the same period in fiscal 1984. Profitability had declined, not risen, and one might have expected that Andrew's management had at least an inkling of this at the time the stockholders' letter for the first quarter was being composed. This is the explanation offered in the second quarter's Letter:

> Following our customary, usually reliable procedures we had planned FY 1985 for a sales increase of 20% or more, with a corresponding increase in expense budgets. Results of the first fiscal quarter were a bit disappointing, but not enough to suggest a significant shortfall from the plan.
>
> *By the end of February* [emphasis added], it became clear that two of our largest common carriers—MCI and GTE Sprint—were deferring or cutting back their large construction programs, and that in consequence orders and sales in 1985 would fall substantially short of the planned increases.[8]

There followed news of additional problems, declines in the work force, and other retrenchment measures. And even this: Vice Chairman Robert E. Hord resigned "to devote more of his time and attention to the philanthropic activities of the Aileen S. Andrew Foundation," and another director, Juanita A. Hord, also resigned (no reason given). August Grasis II announced his retirement as vice president after 20 years of service. "He will continue to serve the company as a consultant."

Andrew thought the third quarter might be difficult, but expected a strong fourth quarter.

Notwithstanding all of this, you should note that a sudden shift in gears is usually indicative of a situation that will not turn around nearly as fast as the company would have the shareholders believe.

When I read Andrew's Letter to Shareholders for the third quarter ended June 30, 1986, I chuckled over the company's comment that, "Because our recent forecasting performance has been less than illustrious, we have decided to remain silent on the subject of future sales and earnings until we regain our confidence."

Apple Computer, the wunderkind of the microcomputer industry, sent its stockholders a lavishly illustrated, multicolored, multipaged report for the first quarter of fiscal 1985 ended December 31, 1984. The numbers certainly were impressive: Earnings were $0.75 per share versus $0.10, on revenues of $698.3 million against $316.3 million. The prose in the Letter was on the purple side—"innovative new marketing programs . . . great new products

. . . phenomenal results . . . "—and so forth. But given those numbers some boasting was perhaps not out of line. Apple went on to talk of "the two-horse race for leadership in the personal computer market," and so without coming right out and saying so suggested it was a titanic struggle between itself and IBM—everyone else was pretty much out of the running. "We will keep pushing," the company promised, "and leading."

One of the pictures, occupying two full pages, was of the new highly automated plant in Carrollton, Texas, where the Apple IIc's "roll off the production line as fast as one every ten seconds." The workers there seemed quite pleased, as well they might: Carrollton was being portrayed as at the cutting edge of technology, an example for the rest of the industry—IBM included.[9]

The second quarter ending March 29 wasn't so hot; in fact, it was extremely disappointing. On revenues of $435.3 million Apple earned $0.16 per share, against $300.1 million and $0.15.

The letter was more subdued this time; instead of talking about leading Big Blue (IBM), management said "we have announced a strategy to *coexist with IBM* [emphasis in the original] in the office. Moreover, Vice President of Finance and Chief Financial Officer Joseph A. Graziano left the firm to "pursue other interests." There was also a general reshuffling of personnel, duly noted but played down.

> The rapid growth and change in our industry can produce tremendous tensions, [said management]. Nevertheless, Apple creates an environment in which innovation can flourish, an environment that attracts the *very best people* [emphasis in the original]. Our employee turnover is among the lowest of any Silicon Valley company and, in fact, among the lowest of the Fortune 500 firms. Apple does more than attract the best—we *keep* the best, and provide them with the resources that allow them to contribute their best.

As befitted the somber news and tone, this quarterly was done in monochrome. In place of a picture of the plant, there was a striking portrait of Alan Greenspan, the well-known economic advisor, pictured with an extremely skeptical look on his face (or is that my imagination?).[10]

The second quarter ended on March 29, 1985, and the quarterly shareholders' report came out more than a month later. On May 5, the company announced it would lay off 75 employees in

San Jose, and another 100 at Carrollton (the same facility featured in the first quarter report) because the Macintosh XL had been discontinued. Also, in late May, Apple eliminated approximately 80 jobs. A San Jose facility that produced Winchester disk drives was shuttered. On June 14, Apple announced that it was firing 1,200 workers, or 21 percent of its work force, closing three plants, and would incur a loss in the third fiscal quarter ending June 30. One of the three was the Carrollton showplace. Finally, Apple related that another restructuring was taking place, with Chairman Steve Jobs, one of Apple's founders, stepping down from active day-to-day operations.[11]

No one can take any satisfaction from this, but I have to observe that Apple must have had its share of troubles which *were not previously revealed to its stockholders* while they were developing. This situation suggests that the left hand did not know what the right hand was doing.

Apple's report to shareholders, for the nine months ended June 28, 1985, discussed the closing of three of the company's manufacturing sites; the adoption of a new organizational structure; and the laying off of 1200 Apple workers.

After devoting considerable dialogue in reference to having the right organization, the shareholders' letter which was signed, as usual, by President and CEO John Sculley and Chairman of the Board Steven Jobs, succinctly commented that Steven Jobs continues to be involved with Apple's success in his role as chairman of the board. However, I found it interesting that the front cover of the Apple shareholders' report, which featured a picture of "Apple's senior management team—architects of the new organization" did not include Jobs.

The enormous shakeout at Apple, for all of the pain that it caused, actually turned out to be a major turning point for the organization. Subsequent shareholders' communications went on to illustrate this fact. The Apple annual report, for fiscal year ended September 27, 1985, related that after ceasing to hold management responsible for the Macintosh Division when it was absorbed into the Products Operation Group as part of the major reorganization in June, Jobs had subsequently resigned as chairman of the board. Even a casual reading of the Apple annual report made it clear that Apple was now a much more lean and more competitive company.

Sculley had worked over Apple Computer. The reorganization

had proved costly in the short run, but, for the long run, Apple was much more clearly and efficiently organized. This success of the cost cutting was documented by the first quarter report dated December 27, 1985. The company had a record first quarter, earning $56.9 million, or $0.91 per share, versus $46.1 million, or $0.75 per share the previous year, while, amazingly, a look at the income statement showed a decrease in sales. Cost cutting and restructuring had boosted profit margins and improved inventory control. Inventories dropped from $261.2 million on December 28, 1984 to $108.3 million on December 27, 1985. During the same time span, Apple's sales declined to $533 million from $698 million.

For the six months ended March 28, 1986, Apple again exhibited striking profit margin improvement. In a *Quality of Earnings Report* dated June 16, 1986, I conveyed the following commentary on Apple to my subscribers:

> *APPLE COMPUTER, INC.*—For the six months ended March 28, 1986, AAPL earned $1.40 a share compared with $0.91 for the six months ended March 29, 1985.
>
> *Background Information:* The following data is statistically striking. For the six months ended March 28, 1986, AAPL's sales declined to approximately $943 million from about $1.1 billion for the six months ended March 29, 1985. During the same time span, AAPL's cash and cash equivalent investments soared to $518 million from $194 million and inventories declined to only $102 million from $260 million.
>
> One key result of AAPL's reorganization is that the company's cost of sales as a percentage of sales has dropped dramatically, as illustrated by the following table, which provides data regarding AAPL's net sales and cost of sales as a percentage of net sales for the six month period ended April 1, 1983 through March 28, 1986.

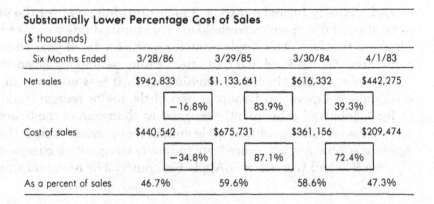

Substantially Lower Percentage Cost of Sales
($ thousands)

Six Months Ended	3/28/86	3/29/85	3/30/84	4/1/83
Net sales	$942,833	$1,133,641	$616,332	$442,275
	−16.8%	83.9%	39.3%	
Cost of sales	$440,542	$675,731	$361,156	$209,474
	−34.8%	87.1%	72.4%	
As a percent of sales	46.7%	59.6%	58.6%	47.3%

Interpretation: The preceding table illustrates that between March 29, 1985, and March 28, 1986, AAPL's net sales declined by approximately 17 percent whereas the cost of sales plummeted by almost 35 percent. During the same sequel, cost of sales as a percentage of net sales dropped to 46.7 percent from 59.6 percent. The percentage decline was equal to $0.94 a share, after tax.

In the third fiscal quarter ending June 30, 1986, AAPL will again be the beneficiary of a considerably lower percentage cost of sales. The moment of truth for AAPL, on an operating basis, will be in the fourth quarter of the fiscal year ending September 30, 1986, and fiscal year 1987 when AAPL will no longer be the recipient of a substantially reduced percentage cost of sales.

Remember the great Coleco runup? Adjusted for a 2–1 split the stock went from 3 to 65 in less than a year, and, at its peak, in the summer of 1983, it seemed destined for even greater things. A leader in home entertainment with ColecoVision video games, Coleco had announced its Adam Family Computer System, a low-cost product which was supposed to go against the likes of Atari and Commodore International. Management, headed by Chairman Leonard Greenberg and his brother Arnold, who was president, was hailed as aggressive, feisty, and imaginative, having taken Coleco from a $71 million swimming pool and toy manufacturer in 1975 to a half-billion dollar glamour company eight years later, with some analysts predicting that the billion dollar level would be reached in several years.

Those investors who purchased Coleco in 1982 and sold the summer of the following year did amazingly well. I am the first to admit that anyone following my analytical method would have steered clear of the stock. But on the other hand, such individuals would have been spared one of the great sell-offs of our time.

An analysis of the balance sheet in 1983 would have indicated trouble ahead, since Coleco had an abnormally large inventory— one of the most certain signs of trouble ahead. But I first became suspicious of Coleco's veracity by a comparative reading of management's letters to shareholders.

In the 1973 letter the Greenbergs said: "We are confident we will enjoy a year of significant progress in 1974 both in terms of sales and earnings." Nothing unusual about this; managements often make such predictions, and in precisely these words. But, in fact, earnings fell more than 50 percent, coming in at $0.07 versus $0.16 the previous year. And the experience was to be repeated; management predicted "an increase in earnings" for 1975. Alas, Coleco reported a penny a share, but the brothers remained confident, calling it "a year of both disappointment and progress for Coleco."[12]

Better times were ahead, indeed. Coleco's revenues rose by 65 percent and earnings advanced to $0.34 in 1976. The 1976 letter spoke glowingly of the acceptance of video games, which supplanted pools as the firm's leading product line, much needed improvements in the balance sheet, and a credible inventory situation. "We foresee another year of record operating results in 1977, with substantial increases in both sales and earnings," was the Greenbergs' verdict. But it didn't turn out that way; in the words of management, "Coleco experienced a difficult and disappointing year in 1977," this attributed to a strike and production delays. Earnings fell to $0.12, and another red flag was waved: Coleco's independent auditor, Price Waterhouse, put out a qualified opinion on its report, and in May of 1978 resigned the account.[13]

A note of caution now appeared: "It is . . . appropriate that 1978 be a year of consolidation." Some consolidation! Coleco racked up a loss of $22.3 million, which came to $1.62 per share, this blamed on "deteriorating prices" and a host of other problems. As usual management was cheery on prospects.[14]

Of course, not many people were following Coleco in those days, but the reports were on file and available to those who awakened to the firm's potential soon after.

Investors came alive to the video game mania which was rolling across the nation soon after. Revenues and earnings rose nicely in 1979 and 1980, and the letters became positively euphoric. But there were troubles ahead. Perhaps aware that more eyes than ever were on them, the Greenbergs turned wary in March, 1981, when they wrote their stockholders' letter. Conceding that the first quarter's business had been "somewhat more moderate" than the previous year, they went on to predict that "the last nine months will be even stronger than the comparable year-ago period." Off mark once again. Earnings were down 45 percent for the year, coming in at $0.51, on revenues of $178 million. The excuse: reduced sales volume for electronic games.[15]

One might by now have concluded that the Greenbergs' record as prognosticators left much to be desired and so cast a skeptical glance at their prediction of $300 million in sales for 1982, this based upon record backlogs and a good response to new products. Once again management erred badly, but this time, to stockholders' delight, they were off base on the upside: revenues came to $510 million, earnings were $2.90 a share, and Coleco had become the darling of Wall Street.

If you were on the investment scene in 1983 you might recall how the Street was touting Coleco. The stock split 2–1 early in the year and took off into the stratosphere on heavy volume. Donkey Kong, the leading video game, was a Coleco product, as was the old favorite, Pac-Man; more than three million units of these and other company products were sold. Coleco was the only company producing home video game software for three systems—its own, Atari, and Mattel. There was talk of the Adam home computer, which the company said would be on sale for the Christmas rush. The 1982 Coleco shareholders letter predicted revenues of $800 million for 1983 and, as one might infer from this, record earnings as well.

Investors might easily have been drawn to Coleco common in this period. Stock prices were rising, video games were the vogue, and Coleco was the darling of the group. So you read the newspaper columnists, went through a few brokerages house and investment advisory reports, saw some television business programs, talked it over with your friends, and placed an order for a few hundred (or more) shares. Your broker congratulated you on getting in on a good thing, and you got into the habit of calling regularly for updates.

I have no quarrel with any of this but suggest you might have gone through some of the old annuals and read the letter to stockholders (and also taken a careful look at the balance sheet). Had you done so you would have taken anything the Greenbergs predicted with a grain of salt.

In the first nine months of 1983 Coleco earned $1.71 against $1.93 the previous year, and by early autumn the stock's price had been halved to around 30. Never fear, said the bulls; Christmas sales will bail out the firm and make good the earlier prediction. Every week there were new rumors about the Adam computer, but few had ever seen it, certainly not the retailers who had been promised it for the Christmas rush. Angrily management denied stories of production foul-ups and poor quality control and reiterated pledges to have 500,000 Adam units in the stores for Christmas sales.

By early December the company conceded that it had produced only 140,000 Adams, but retailers said they still hadn't seen many of them. Now management lowered its shipment prediction to 400,000. Arnold Greenberg told reporters that his Amsterdam, N.Y., plant was producing Adams at a rate of 2,500 a day, which would be upped to 7,500 a day by mid-January. Perhaps there wouldn't be many of them in the stores for Christmas, but watch our smoke in early 1984, said Greenberg, and he forecast profits on the machines "during the first quarter, certainly in the first half, of 1984."[16]

For 1983 Coleco posted a loss of $0.48 per share. At that time I told syndicated columnist Dan Dorfman, "The question is, 'How can you believe anyone who has been wrong so often?' The answer is you can't."[17]

The bloodbath occurred soon after. ColecoVision fizzled and Adam proved a dud, which resulted in a $119 million writeoff. In 1984 Coleco reported a loss of $4.95 per share, and the stock traded as low as 9 5/8.[18]

The International Harvester and Coleco letters illustrate the pitfalls that can await investors, and what to look for when assessing these communications. This isn't to suggest that you might not want to take a flyer in stocks whose managements you recognize are involved in hype; after all, stocks can move on dreams as well as reality. John Maynard Keynes wrote that if you want to discover which contestant will win a beauty contest analyze the judges, not the entries, and there is something to be said for that. In other words, if you concluded a management was deceptive but felt the public hadn't caught on, you would be justified in thinking that its stock would rise with the next bit of fluff from corporate headquarters, and you might want to buy. Keynes, who in addition to being one of the century's great economists was an uncommonly successful investor, did buy. But if you do so, knowing the credibility of management, make your purchases with the knowledge that once investors catch on it all could fall apart; nowadays that can be within a single trading session, or even less.

Likewise, honest, intelligent, and forthcoming letters shouldn't prompt a purchase, since the information contained in these might indicate that just the opposite strategy is called for. What you are seeking, after all, is the best information, which once in your possession would lead to an investment decision. And often this can be gleaned from well-crafted, credible letters, but you have to know how to recognize them.

I would not only look for projections but also ascertain why management believes them reasonable. One expects hyperbole, optimism, and "the future lies ahead" rhetoric so often identified with these letters, which most managements appear to believe shareowners and analysts find soothing, but behind all this (and perhaps in front of it as well) should be something of more substance. Above all, difficulties should be dissected, not hidden or ignored. A frank discussion of problems, along with thoughts of proper solutions, is the mark of a management which can be trusted—that is, not necessarily should it come up with excellent results and so cause the price of a stock to rise, but rather it should provide you with the kind of material to make intelligent investment decisions. Keep in mind, too, that capable managements are the kind that *do* solve problems, recognize opportunities, and more often than not turn in results superior to others in the same industry.

One of my favorite companies when it comes to letters is Koppers Co. Inc., the $1.6 billion Pittsburgh-based diversified manufacturing complex, whose operations tend to follow the business cycle. Koppers had a rough time of it in 1984 and in the letter went to great pains to inform shareholders of its problems and the methods for dealing with them, all of which made its projections more convincing than otherwise might have been the case.

"This was a mixed year," CEO Charles R. Pullin opens. While optimistic (who isn't in these reports?), he adds, "We still have a good distance to go before any of us can be proud of our performance, but we did move in the right direction." Yet the bottom line appears quite pleasing—$1.46 per share versus $0.42 in 1983. But Pullin clearly states that this wasn't as good as it seems: "The real operating gains appear only after looking past the fairly heavy one-time charges we took at the close of 1984," which brought 1984 income from continuing operations down to $0.97, against an adjusted $0.78 for the previous year. All of this is clearly stated in an accompanying box, under which are two columns, the first labeled "Problems" and the second "Solutions," in which Koppers offers a rather detailed analysis of its difficulties and means of resolving them. These range from the familiar (a strong dollar) to the discontinuation of several units and an unfavorable jury verdict in a case under appeal.[19]

Pullin's candor extends to the inevitable group picture, which accompanies the letter. It shows him at a desk, surrounded by four people who appear to be executives. At first glance Pullin seems deeply troubled, but on further examination it becomes evident he merely is straining to listen to something one of the people is saying. It's comforting to know that this chairman at least is eager to let his shareholders know he is open to ideas, and I would be to his ideas whenever he speaks or, in this case, writes.

Will this kind of approach boost Koppers stock, and does it indicate readers should go out and place buy orders? Not necessarily, but it does instill confidence, and I'd rather have that than the euphoria most communications are intended to create.

A business lifetime of plowing through documents makes one suspicious of motives and ever-willing to piece together the jigsaw puzzle that they often resemble. So I should note that Koppers has gone to great pains to provide an extensive breakdown of operations by divisions, complete with statistics. A thorough examination reveals that what the company has done is to incorporate virtually all of its 10-K into the glossy annual report, thus offering shareholders as much material here as they might obtain from that SEC filing.

Occasionally I come across letters which communicate problems and possibilities clearly, in such a way as to simultaneously illuminate the situation at the firm and provide guidance for the probing of the rest of the report which necessarily must follow. In fact, this is the prime purpose of these letters. For example, consider the case of AMP, a major manufacturer of connectors used in the electrical and electronic industries, both of which are fast-growing and highly glamorous fields. These are the opening paragraphs from AMP's 1984 shareholders' letter:

> Our 1984 performance, when the year is viewed as a whole, was good and above our long-term growth trend. Sales were up 20% and earnings up 23%. In fact, if currency exchange rates had remained constant, sales could have been up 23% and earnings up 30%. However, it was a year of sharp contrast. The recovery that began in January 1983 gathered strength throughout 1983 and into the spring of 1984. Strong economic growth and booming electronics markets led to record orders of $549,000,000 in the first quarter and record sales and earnings of $477,200,000 and 54 cents per share in the second quarter of 1984. During the second half, however, an economic

slowdown and a significant correction in the U.S. electronics markets, combined with a weakening of foreign currencies against the U.S. dollar, resulted in declines to $340,000,000 in orders, $423,400,000 in sales, and 37 cents per share in earnings in the fourth quarter.

The declining sales put profit margins under pressure. We had added 2,400 people in the first half and 800 more in the early part of the third quarter, mostly domestic manufacturing employees, before imposing hiring constraints in the fall. To reduce expenses and activities in line with lower sales, one-week furloughs were required of most domestic production workers in the fourth quarter and the Company closed during the year-end holiday week. This reduction in employment costs, plus substantial tightening of general expense budgets, limited the decline in pretax margins from a peak of 22% in the second quarter to 17.1% in the fourth quarter, despite $53,800,000 less in sales and over 1,300 higher average employment.

As our domestic business slowed during the summer, we continued with capital spending projects already underway, but began to scale down and postpone new commitments. As a result, capital spending peaked in the second half. Expenditures doubled to $255,700,000 in 1984 from $127,600,000 in 1983. The total for 1985 may approach $200,000,000. A continued high level of spending is needed for tooling for new proucts, equipment for productivity and quality improvements, and preparation for future growth.[20]

One should keep in mind that while many of us derive pleasure from reading annual reports, as investors we should look upon them as sources of information, and not as literary masterpieces or wellsprings for inspirational prose. I confess to enjoying myself while curling up with a stack of annuals, but, unless I come away from a reading with a much improved picture of the company's true prospects and a feeling as to where its stock might be headed, the exercise must be put down to recreation, not research.

CHAPTER 4

Differential Disclosure

DON'T LET the title of this chapter throw you. Differential disclosure simply refers to the possibility that what the company says in one document is markedly different from what it says in another. Or, there may be more complete information on a particular topic.

I'm not referring here to press releases and interviews by reporters, but rather to those mailings stockholders and other interested parties may easily obtain, the aforementioned annual and quarterly reports and the 10-Ks and 10-Qs.

Caution should be exercised when you encounter any significant divergences between annuals and quarterlies and the government-mandated documents.

The reason for differential disclosure is obvious. The annuals and quarterlies are meant to be read by stockholders, most of whom in the opinion of managements tend to be more impressed by glossy presentations and hyped writing than statistics and footnotes. The 10-Ks and 10-Qs are official reports filed with the SEC. No chief executive officer will go to jail if, in the face of declining business and stiffer competition, he predicts a rosy future in the stockholders' letter (though in recent years some critics have recommended that such projections be included in SEC reports). But he could be in trouble if the 10-K and 10-Q do not conform to SEC guidelines. Generally speaking, the narrative portion of annual reports is put together with the assistance of public relations experts whereas the financial part of the annuals is compiled by the accounting staff of the company and reviewed by the external auditors. The 10-K is the direct responsibility of accountants and lawyers.

If this is the case, you might be thinking, why bother reading the annuals and quarterlies at all? Why not go straight to the 10-Ks and 10-Qs if that is where one can get more accurate statements? The answer has in part been provided earlier, namely that only in the stockholders' letter can one discover the ideas and rationale behind management actions and decisions. It is there where CEOs talk about their strategies, defend past actions, and, if you are fortunate, disclose plans. Moreover, as noted, a comparative study of these statements can indicate their credibility.

Other reasons to study the annuals and quarterlies will be discussed later on, but at this point consider that almost anything the corporation provides by way of information is worth perusing—always assuming it is done with an educated eye. Moreover, occasionally you will spot contradictions between one section of the annual report and another.

A prime example of this can be found in Procter & Gamble's 1984 Annual Report. For the fiscal year ended June 30, 1984, P&G earned $5.35 per share versus $5.22 in 1983, hardly an earth-shattering advance. Moreover, the company revealed that part of the improvement came from changes in its corporate tax rate, which declined to 37.6 percent from 44.1 percent in 1983, this equal to $0.56 per share. Finally, the 1984 figure included an $0.18 per share special item against one of $0.10 in 1983, both resulting from swaps of stock for debt. So the company actually experienced an operating earnings decline in 1984, a fact which is noted elsewhere in the Analysis and Discussion section—located in the back of the report.[1]

In the letter, management explained that the "modest earnings increase . . . reflects the cost of broadening the Company's product base and augurs well for the long-term health and vitality of the business." So it would appear that P&G believed it would reap a bountiful harvest from the investment in new products somewhere down the line. All's well and good, for this is a sign of vigor and health. As will be seen, in some new product areas increased marketing expenses can be an indication that better bottom-line results are in the offing. This will be discussed in some detail in Chapter 5. But it hasn't been the case recently in toiletries and related items.

Changes in family structure had something to do with it. Says an advertising executive who once worked at P&G, "There is no way the traditional housewife, who is generally a smart shopper, is going to go for something like a toothpaste pump. Today's consumer will [go for such gimmicks], however, and that's the kind of thing P&G might not see."

Given the breakdown of the nuclear family, two-job families, women's liberation, and related social changes, men do more of the shopping than they used to. Studies show that husbands select different brands than their wives 43 percent of the time. So it was that P&G's Crest toothpaste, long an industry leader, was being seriously challenged by Colgate. Tide was threatened by Wisk, and Pampers, which once had 75 percent of the disposable diaper market, was down to less than 33 percent in 1985.

Increased advertising budgets, which in the past had enabled P&G to increase market share, weren't doing the job as well. "The old disciplines haven't been as successful as they were in the past," wrote Cliff Angers, a senior vice president at Ogilvy & Mather in a report on P&G.[2]

None of these basic problems is discussed in the P&G annual report—I wouldn't expect them to be. But in the analysis and discussion section we encounter this explanation: In addition to the aggressive investment program there was "the highly competitive climate faced by many of the Company's established brands in the U.S. consumer business." Which is another way of saying that rivals have turned in a remarkable job of "catch up." That this would be a long-term problem could be seen in the fact that for the fiscal year ended June 30, 1985, P&G's earnings dropped for the first time in three decades.

Convergent Technologies (CVGT), once one of the hottest stocks of the microcomputer age, also offers a good example of differential disclosure. For 1983 the company reported earnings of $0.40 a share compared with $0.42 in 1982. CVGT's Annual Report and letter were both optimistic, but the 10-K provided a somewhat different picture.

Among CVGT's more important products were multiprocessor superminicomputers known as the NGEN work stations and the MegaFrame, upon which the company had pinned much of its hopes. The letter started out by noting that "1983 was a year of progress and challenge for Convergent Technologies." Now this word "challenge" always puts me on guard; managements often use "challenge" to mean "trouble."

The rest of the letter was relatively upbeat, however, though there were exceptions. For example, NGEN shipments were below and costs above expectations. The reason: "Slow manufacturing start up and disappointing performance by some suppliers." There were words of praise for WorkSlate, a powerful portable micro-computer which can also function as a terminal. "These machines were sent as 'high tech stocking stuffers' to initial customers order-ing through the American Express Christmas catalog," with a good reception.[3]

Some of the numbers weren't at all pleasing. Revenues rose from $96.4 million to $163.5 million, net income went from $11.9 million to $14.9 million, but CVGT earned only $0.40 per share compared with $0.42 in 1982 due to a substantial increase in the number of shares outstanding.[4]

Despite this the letter ended on a note of triumph. "Upon re-flection, 1983 was a year of investment and a year of rewards. . . . We have retained our tough operating culture and entrepre-neurial spirit, and will continue to set demanding goals for our-selves."[5]

The 10-K presented quite a different picture, one of the clearest examples of differential disclosure recently seen. In that document we learn that there was only one supplier for the ad-vanced microprocessor upon which MegaFrame is based, and one for the disk drives. "To date the disk drives have been manufactured in limited quantities and the microprocessor is on allocation from its manufacturer." The report went on to claim that this had no material impact upon the business, but later in the 10-K we read that "with the increased demand for certain components in the computer system industry the Company believes that there is a greater likelihood that the Company will experience such delays." Further, "some of these new components have yet to be manufac-tured in volume by their suppliers. The Company's ability to man-ufacture these products may be adversely affected by the inability of the Company's vendors to supply high quality components in adequate quantities."[6]

A similar situation existed for WorkSlate. The company stated that production and shipments increased in the first quarter of 1984, "but have not reached anticipated levels." The problem? Availability of components, "and the development and management by the Company of retail channels of distribution, an area in which the company had no prior experience."[7] (It should be noted that CVGT discontinued the WorkSlate in 1984, resulting in an after-tax charge of $11 million.)

What this amounts to is a concession that the failure of a single supplier could bring to a halt one of the most important parts of CVGT's business, and that there were no alternate sources of supply. Moreover, the firm lacked experience with some of its new products, and so failures might easily have developed—hardly the kind of situation to create confidence in the hearts and minds of customers—or investors.

Suppose everything turned out as well as might be hoped. Components arrive on time, and they are flawless. The market for WorkSlate and MegaFrame exceeds expectations, and the company has no trouble marketing its products. What then?

There were approximately 36 million shares of CVGT outstanding at that time, this for a firm whose revenues came to $163.6 million. The 10-K notes that approximately 46 percent of its total revenues came from Burroughs Corp., which sells CVGT products under its own labels; the Annual Report calls this "more than 10 percent of consolidated net sales" and lets it go at that.

The loss of this business would have a very negative impact upon CVGT. Notes accompanying the Annual Report observe that Burroughs owns warrants to purchase 1.5 million shares of CVGT at $6.53 or 1.6 million at $6.67, based upon purchases of workstations. The 10-K elaborates upon this. Under certain circumstances Burroughs could obtain licensing from CVGT and go into the field on its own. Is this a possibility? "The Company believes Burroughs intends to commit to the volume purchases necessary to exercise the manufacturing license and will exercise the manufacturing license for the NGEN and MegaFrame products. Such exercise could have a material adverse effect on the Company's future revenues. . . . "[8]

In July, 1984, the SEC issued a bulletin dealing with warrant accounting for the issuance of stock. In the future, common stock warrants would have to be valued on a different accounting basis from that previously employed by CVGT. In its 1984 Annual Report the company observed that it was unlikely that additional warrants would be granted in connection with future Original Equip-

ment Manufacturer Agreements. CVGT added that it had granted
Burroughs a license to manufacture some of its products and that
Burroughs had commenced doing so.

The bottom line for CVGT in the summer of 1984 was that
there was a good chance the company would come in for its share
of troubles in the year ahead, and that if it avoided the shoals it
could either be dominated by its major customer or come under its
wing. What might the investor have gathered from this situation?
He would have seen the importance of looking at a company's 10-K
report as well as the annual report for what I call differential disclosure. CVGT had some major problems; the stock should have
been avoided.

The situation at Academy Insurance Group (ACIG) was more
complicated. This is an aggressive concern established in 1968 to
develop and provide insurance for military personnel. Academy
marketed the forerunner to the popular Universal Life policies and
created its own agency structure from scratch, training former
commissioned and noncommissioned officers to become insurance
salesmen. The results were impressive; in its 1983 Annual Report
the company noted it had racked up 22 consecutive quarters during
which earnings increased at least 35 percent. *Financial World*
named it the number one growth company in the insurance industry and gave it an "A" rating based upon its financial condition.

Academy also expanded into other fields, purchasing the Ami-
stad Savings & Loan and a resort complex in the Poconos which it
was converting to time sharing. More of the same was promised for
the future.[9]

As might be expected, Academy captured the attention of the
cognoscenti; on an adjusted basis its stock rose from 1/4 to 17, and
seemed headed for even better things.

Then the facade cracked. In December, 1983, *Barron's* ran an
article in which agent misrepresentations were noted in the sale of
the company's Estate Conservation Plan Insurance. The magazine
also observed there could be a write-down due to problems that
had developed within Academy's conservation plan insurance division. In the 1983 Annual Report President Alvin H. Clemens denied some charges, conceded others were partially true, and attempted to minimize the problems.

Now we come to the matter of differential disclosure. In the first quarter of 1984 earnings per share rose from $0.24 to $0.27, nice enough but hardly up to the level of earlier periods. Poring over the 10-Q, I noted that Academy reported revenues of $2.2 million and after-tax earnings of $600,000, or $0.04 per share, from sales of Poconos units. Now this element was not present in the first quarter of 1983. Thus, earnings from insurance operations were actually down on a year-to-year basis. My interest piqued, I went back to the 1983 10-Qs and Annual Report and discovered that 40 percent of the increase in earnings for the 1983 fourth quarter had come from time-sharing sales.[10]

Later on we will see how anyone equipped with the proper analytical tools could have arrived at this conclusion, but we are now concerned with differential disclosure, and how it applies in this case.

Stockholders in Academy would have noted that the annual played up the importance of this activity, but it was not even mentioned in the 1984 first quarter report. One can't read the minds of management, but the quality of earnings from insurance is better than that from time-sharing sales. A dollar of earnings from an insurance policy is usually part of a continuing stream, while one from real estate sales can be a one-shot addition to the bottom line (a matter which will be discussed and analyzed in some detail in the next chapter). The mass marketing of time-sharing units is a volatile, hard sell business, and companies in that area generally command a low price–earnings ratio from investors. This may explain why Academy now chose to downplay this activity, even though it was contributing to revenues and profits.

Executive Vice President and Treasurer W. Benjamin Weaver offered this explanation. While conceding that the Poconos venture had become "more important" for Academy, he said it wasn't a "major element." He went on to say that "I guess we probably should have emphasized time-sharing more in the first quarter report," but he thought it best to concentrate attention on moves taken to rectify problems in the firm's insurance business.[11]

As might be expected, companies like to put their best foot forward. And this example of differential disclosure should have warned investors away from the stock. Writing in *Quality of Earnings Report* on June 11, 1984, I observed that "this factor could continue to affect ACIG's price earnings ratio over the next several years."

First Boston analyst David Seifer, who had been close to the situation and a bull on Academy, disagreed strongly with my analysis, not unexpectedly since he had been putting out buy notices with some regularity. Seifer thought the insurance business would expand significantly, and that the stock would outperform the market in 1985. "If ACIG comes through with earnings and return on equity the multiple will take care of itself."[12]

But it didn't come through. In 1984, Academy incurred a loss totaling $12.8 million or $0.81 per share. This loss was primarily attributable to problems within the company's estate conservation plan division. That year Academy's time-share resort segment of business wound up with an operating loss of $431,000 compared with operating income totaling $1.9 million the previous year.[13]

Academy's problems continued into the following year. In the first quarter of 1985, its time-sharing business incurred a pre-tax loss of $2.9 million. This was partially due to two charges totaling $1.6 million for doubtful accounts for prior sales and for the costs of closing a sales office.[14]

Another excellent illustration of substantial differential disclosure was the 1984 Annual Report and proxy statement for Texas Commerce Bancshares. Cast your mind back to the situation in Texas in March of 1985, when the proxy was mailed. Texas was going through its biggest banking collapse since the Great Depression, with dozens of institutions in trouble due to failed loans to energy companies and wildcatters as well as to speculators in the booming real estate market. One could go through the state and see rows of drilling rigs in the parking lots of many banks, repossessed due to failed loans. "In Texas, we've been having hard times in both energy and real estate," said Joseph Grant, vice chairman of Texas American Bancshares, but the worst seemed over. James J. McDermott, banking analyst for Keefe, Bruyette & Woods observed that "Texas banks have to be among the most heavily examined in the country. These guys from the [Comptroller of the Currency's] office have pitched tents in Houston and Dallas."[15]

With all of this there seemed little to worry about regarding Texas Commerce Bancshares (TCB), a regional powerhouse which with Morgan Guaranty Trust was one of the two American bank holding companies with the highest S & P rating.

Texas Commerce had grown rapidly, its deposits rising from

under $3 billion in 1974 to more than $13 billion ten years later. Part of this was accomplished through mergers; by 1985 there were 66 member banks under its wing, with offices in the Southwest, but also in such places as Brazil, Bahrain, Venezuela, and Mexico. Most of the business was in Texas, however, with close to 60 percent in commercial loans and leases. In 1984, TCB earned $5.64 per share versus $5.50 the previous year. Included in the TCB 1984 annual report was an interesting footnote under the caption Loans and Lease Financing which read as follows:

> Certain related parties (directors and officers of Texas Commerce and Texas Commerce Bank-Houston and their affiliates, families and companies of which they are principal owners) were loan customers of Texas Commerce and its subsidiaries in the ordinary course of business. *Such loans were made on substantially the same terms, including interest rates and collateral, as those prevailing at the same time for comparable transactions with unrelated parties and did not involve more than a normal amount of risk* [emphasis added].

The total came to $545 million, up from $522 million at the same time the previous year.[16]

Now there isn't anything wrong with this. In fact, the directors and officers might have been complimented for having brought their business to TCB rather than some other financial institution. After all, they were paying the going rate, weren't they? At least that is what the Annual Report indicated.

On March 16 or a day later, depending upon the mails, stockholders in Texas Commerce received their proxy statements, and most doubtless discarded them or filled out the enclosed reply card and sent it on. Such is the ordinary practice. But as I suggest, you should read everything the company puts out, because while some of the material is puffery, other reports and statements contain information management would rather you didn't know, but must release to comply with the law. And such was the case with the 1985 proxy.

The notice opened with a letter inviting shareholders to the annual meeting which was scheduled for April 16. Then there was a brief agenda—little of consequence—followed by twelve pages of pictures of directors, along with their occupations, years of service, and age. As befits an institution of TCB's status, they are a prestigious lot. Among their number are T. Boone Pickens, former Secretary of Energy in the Carter Administration Charles Duncan, and former Congresswoman Barbara Jordan.

On page 22 was an item, entitled: "Certain Transactions with Directors, Director Nominees and Executive Officers," this mandated by law, and it was here where prudent stockholders could have discovered information of some significance.

TCB stated it had made loans to John Duncan, R. W. Moncrief, and Pat R. Rutherford for assorted real estate deals. Additional loans went to other Board members. The notice reiterated the statement made in the Annual Report, namely that all loans were made at prevailing interest rates. But it then went on to say that:

> In connection with an examination by representatives of the Comptroller of the Currency, Texas Commerce Bank-Houston has been informed that certain actions taken by it . . . may have constituted violations of the Financial Institutions Regulatory and Interest Rate Control Act of 1978 (FIRA). *This law requires that any loan to a director of a bank or bank holding company or a related entity be made on substantially the same terms, including interest rates and collateral, as those prevailing at the time for comparable transactions with other persons and further requires that these transactions not involve more than the normal risk of repayment or present other unfavorable features. Texas Commerce Bank-Houston is of the opinion that there were no such violations*[17] [emphasis added].

In mid-March of 1985, TCB announced that it expected earnings of only $0.92 per share for the first quarter. A month later, the bank came in with a figure of $0.90 compared with $1.41 in the same period in 1984, this a 36 percent falloff. The decline was TCB's first year-to-year quarterly drop since 1968.

TCB's common stock declined by approximately 30 percent between January and April, and some might have thought it a bargain. Even so, I would not go out of my way to own shares in TCB. This is because TCB revealed that its related party loans, which totaled $545 million at the end of 1984, included $76 million (or 14 percent) that were either classified as nonperforming or considered to be potential problems. Yet, the bank also had stated that the insider loans were made on substantially the same basis as those with unrelated parties, and did not involve more than a normal amount of risk. So one must be concerned about the quality of loans that TCB makes with unrelated parties as well.

In reference to insider loans, TCB announced in August 1985 that an investigation by the Comptroller of the Currency regarding allegations that it gave preferential treatment on loans to two directors "were not supported by facts and are therefore being totally dismissed."[18]

Years ago Speaker of the House Sam Rayburn told a reporter that he never lied, not so much because he was an innately truthful person, but rather that he had a hard time keeping track of just who it was he told which story. This isn't a prelude to a suggestion that corporations are duplicitous or chronic deceivers. Rather, they hire scores of public relations experts to enable them to present their best sides and play down the bad, much in the way a man with a weak chin might grow a beard or a woman with wide hips dress to achieve an illusion of slimness.

The trouble is that often these attempts backfire—astute observers discern that weak chin and those spreading hips. But to do so takes a trained intellect and keen powers of observation, neither of which is innate, but rather learned. In this chapter I have discussed differential disclosure. We have seen how materials in the Annual Report often contain the equivalent of that beard and dress, and that materials filed with the government or buried in the backs of annual reports reveal what is under them. Investors ignore these things at their peril.

CHAPTER 5

Nonoperating and/or Nonrecurring Income

IF YOU BELIEVE Standard & Poor's *Stock Reports* and *Moody's Handbook of Common Stocks,* those two reference bellwethers, in 1982 Pepsico (PEP) reported $2.40 per share which rose to $3.01 the following year, for an increase of 25 percent. But subscribers to *The Value Line Investment Survey,* an equally reputable publication, were informed that the 1982 earnings did not come to $2.40, but rather to $3.24 and 1983's to $3.01, for a decline of 7 percent.

This is hardly a minor difference; according to which set of figures was accepted, PEP was either roaring ahead or stagnating. Nor was it a matter of typographical errors; S&P and Value Line maintained that 1982 statistic in subsequent reports.

The explanation for this divergence involves the matter of nonoperating and/or nonrecurring income (NO/NR), a subject which accountants debate with the kind of passion and zeal usually witnessed at political conventions and in barroom discussions of the merits of one team or player over another, though their language may seem arcane to those outside of the profession. It is a technical issue which, depending upon the stance you take, can result in the kind of disagreements seen in the case of PEP.

While the debate can become quite sophisticated, as will be seen, the principles involved aren't all that difficult to comprehend. More to the point, it is a matter which in some cases can be quite crucial when it comes to investment decisions. But before turning to the abstractions, let us see what is behind this difference regarding Pepsi's earnings.

In 1982 PEP reported an "unusual charge" relating to the write-down of overseas bottling assets, which previously had been overvalued due to the application of improper accounting techniques. The charge amounted to $79.4 million, or $0.84 per share.

It would appear that such things are unusual and so might be considered nonrecurring. This was why Value Line decided to exclude the item from PEP's earnings, and so reported the higher figure. S&P and Moody's, on the other hand, opted to include the charge, and so came up with the lower figure.

This is a fairly recent problem. At one time accountants would almost automatically classify any charge or earnings not resulting from operations as nonrecurring. Thus, profits or losses from any one-time deal or from any source other than the company's prime business were placed in this category. But in the 1970s the profession decided to cut back on the use of this convention, which opened a can of worms. Pepsi's accountant, Arthur Young & Co., holds that companies, in general, have write-offs of assets on a regular basis, which is to say they are not extraordinary, and so should not be reported as such. Another accounting firm might take a different view of the matter. "Does this situation make sense?" asked *Forbes* reporter John Heins, who answered his own question. "To the accountants, maybe, but not to us."[1]

Most of the time the differences between operating and nonoperating income are quite clear; the problem comes on close calls. One can readily agree that some charges are unusual, such as the expropriation of assets by a foreign government or a loss due to a natural disaster such as a fire when destroyed properties are uninsured. On a more individual level, a million dollars won in a lottery drawing could be seen as nonrecurring.

Take the example of a company that sells a property on which it makes a $1 million profit. Is that nonrecurring? It probably is if the firm is a small manufacturer of electronic parts moving to a new location after a couple of decades in one place. However, what about a real estate operator who engaged in this transaction on a regular basis? What for the electronics firm is unusual is bread-and-butter for him.

Intent is another matter that clouds the issue. In the 1960s many conglomerates purchased casualty insurance companies—

ITT acquired Hartford, Leasco took over Reliance, and Avco obtained Paul Revere, to name just three instances. There were many reasons for this interest, one of which being the nature of the business and the way it functioned under law. All casualty companies are obliged to maintain large reserves. The funds are invested in stocks, bonds, mortgages, and other holdings which generate substantial investment income.

When ITT Chairman Harold Geneen, an accountant himself, purchased Hartford, he was reported to have remarked to an aide, "Well! The Hartford acquisition is going to give us the opportunity to have *programmed* earnings!" There would be serious problems in the future with Hartford. Nonetheless, as another former executive put it, "The Hartford portfolio was played like a violin."[2]

By this he meant that whenever ITT wanted to report higher earnings, it could have Hartford sell part of its investment portfolio to show a profit—just about whatever number was required, it could produce.

At the end of 1974, Hartford's equity security portfolio had a cost of $879 million. However, the market value of the portfolio was only $638 million. The difference between cost and market was an unrealized paper loss of approximately $241 million. Yet, in 1974, Geneen was able to run through approximately $22 million in after-tax net realized gains from Hartford's equity portfolio.

Of course this can't go on indefinitely. In time a good portion of profits may be realized, and portfolio gains taper off. For example, in 1983, ITT's insurance and finance subsidiaries generated pre-tax net realized investment gains totaling $74 million. At year end 1983, ITT's insurance and finance subsidiaries had investments in equity securities at a market value of $502 million, with unrealized gains of $77 million. In 1984, these subsidiaries recorded pre-tax gains totaling around $118 million. At the end of 1984, however, the subsidiaries carried their equity position at a market cost of approximately $185 million—with an unrealized loss of $1 million! Clearly it will be difficult to generate substantial additional profits from this portfolio. So it is evident to me that over the next few years, barring a spectacular stock market, ITT's equity security gains would sag.

Still, the question remains: Should these earnings be considered nonrecurring? Keep in mind that all of the insurance companies purchase and sell securities every year, which brings up the matter of motivation. So it comes down to this: Would you call the sale of a large amount of the holdings that produces a substantial profit for any particular year nonrecurring?

Consider the following dramatic ploy, which market veterans will find familiar. An old administration fallen on bad times is replaced by a fresh new one, which takes an accounting "bath," thus showing a large loss. The slate wiped clean, profits tend to rise in the following years. Now management goes before the stockholders and analysts and says, in effect, "We took over a company with a loss of so many millions of dollars and transformed it into one which had huge profits." Of course, management does not indicate that the losses were nonrecurring—as are the profits. Thus, the matter is clouded, but this need not mean investors' eyes need be the same.

Here is how one expert on the subject, Professor Leopold A. Bernstein of Baruch College, puts the matter:

> By "operating" we usually identify items connected with the normal and usual operations of the business. The concept of normal operations is more widely used than understood and is far from clear and well defined. Thus, in a company operating a machine shop, operating expenses would be considered as those associated with the work of the machine shop. The proceeds from a sale above cost of marketable securities held by the company as an investment of excess cash would be considered a non-operating gain. So would the gain (or loss) on the sale of a lathe, even if it were disposed of in order to make room for one that would increase the productivity of the shop.[3]

Former U.S. Supreme Court Associate Justice Potter Stewart once said that while he couldn't define pornography with a great degree of precision, he knew it when he saw it. Something like that might be said of nonoperating and nonrecurring income. As in the case of pornography, one person's operating income may be another's nonoperating, as seen in the Pepsi case.

Not only is the distinction difficult to make, but unlike many other items we will be discussing there is no single place in the annual report or quarterlies in which the items are isolated and analyzed in just these terms. Astute investors have to be prepared to ferret the information out of the shareholders' letter, the management and discussion segment, and footnotes, as well as the profit and loss statement. Occasionally one can learn of developments which impact upon whole industries, or individual corporations, from the front pages or business sections of the daily press. Alterations in the tax laws provide one clear example of this, which will soon be illustrated.

Keep in mind too that it is necessary to consider the magnitude over the years of increases or decreases in nonoperating income. By observing this factor on an *incremental* basis one can better look ahead to determine if future earnings will be impacted positively by nonoperating and/or nonrecurring earnings, and make investment decisions accordingly.

Finally, a thorough understanding of NO/NR matters, while helpful in appreciating the quality of earnings, is no panacea. Often the stock can go north while the Q of E goes south, and vice versa. It is just one additional technique investors can employ to enable them to be better informed prior to taking action.

Now to see the matter in the context of a specific case.

In late 1984 rumors flooded the Street that Sears, Roebuck would have a poor fourth quarter, due to losses at its Dean Witter Reynolds subsidiary, indifferent results at Allstate, and a less than exuberant Christmas season. For the first three quarters the giant retailer had earned $2.47 per share versus $2.15 for the same period in 1983. In that year a robust $1.65 in the last quarter enabled it to turn in a record $3.80. The consensus among analysts seemed to be around $1.20–$1.30 for the 1984 fourth quarter, with a few saying it could be lower. Sears would do well to match the 1983 figure, they thought, and some institutions started selling the stock in the fall.

Imagine the delight on the part of stockholders and the stock's fans when Sears reported earnings of $1.54 per share for the fourth quarter, for a new yearly record of $4.01.

The trouble is that some $468 million of Sears' earnings that year, or $1.31 per share, came from earnings which to my mind could be construed to be of the NO/NR variety.

To be fair, for the previous year Sears had $208 million in NO/NR earnings, which worked out at $0.59 per share. One way to take account for this would be to lower Sears' 1984 reported earnings by $1.31, bringing them to $2.70, and then subtracting the $0.59 from Sears' 1983 earnings would take them down to $3.21. This indicates that on an *operating* basis Sears had a decline of 16 percent instead of a gain of 5 percent. (See Table 5.1, p. 60.)

All of this information could have been gleaned from the 1984

TABLE 5.1
Selected Figures for Sears, Roebuck, 1984 and 1983

For the Year Ended	12/31/84		12/31/83	
	Amount ($million)	Per Share	Amount ($million)	Per Share
Allstate tax credits	$152.0	$0.42	$104.9	$0.30
Allstate capital gains	71.4	0.20	41.8	0.12
Reduction in deferred taxes, Allstate	60.0	0.17	—	—
Gain from sales of property (Coldwell Banker)	64.7	0.18	46.7	0.13
Swing to other income from loss (merchandise group)	67.3	0.19	—	—
LIFO inventory credit (merchandise group)	52.7	0.15	15.1	0.04
Total	$468.1	$1.31	$208.5	$0.59

Source: Sears, Roebuck, 1984 and 1983 *Annual Reports*.

Annual Report, but as noted it takes some digging. Here's how it is done.

From the annual reports we learn that Sears Allstate Insurance Unit had an income tax benefit from current operations of $152 million in 1984 against $104.9 million in 1983. The number of shares outstanding in these two years were 359.3 million and 353.1 million, respectively. Divide the tax benefits by the outstanding shares and you get $0.42 per share and $0.30 per share.

The Allstate capital gains figures are derived the same way. They were $71.4 million for 1984 against $41.8 million the previous year, which comes to $0.20 and $0.12 per share respectively.

Now for the reduction in deferred taxes for Allstate. This was due to the changes brought about by the Tax Reform Act of 1984, which that year's annual report tells us was $60 million and so works out to $0.17 per share.

From the reports we learn that the gains from the sale of property in the two years were $64.7 million in 1984, $46.7 million in 1983, or $0.18 per share versus $0.13 per share.

The swing to other income from losses is a little bit more complicated. The report informs us that Sears' pre-tax income in 1984 was $1.695 billion, on which it paid taxes of $810.4 million. These figures are equal to a tax rate of 48 percent. By the way, in 1983 pre-tax income was $1.440 billion and taxes $687.8 million, which works out to 48 percent as well.

In the reports for both years we learn that the benefits from a swing to other income from a loss in the merchandise group was $129.4 million in 1984, on which taxes of $62.1 million were paid. Subtract that from $129.4 million to get $67.3 million, divide by the shares outstanding, and you arrive at $0.19 per share. In the previous year the loss was $9.0 million, by the way.

In 1984 Sears had a LIFO credit of $101.3 million, and using the now familiar way of adjusting for taxes this came to $52.7 million or $0.15 per share. LIFO credits in 1983 were $15.1 million which, as you can easily see, was $0.04 per share. It should be noted that the increase in Sears' Merchandise Group LIFO credits was mostly attributable to a lower rate of inflation than anticipated in reference to the application of the Bureau of Labor Statistics index. I think it reasonable to conclude that each of these items could be construed to be of the NO/NR variety.

Sears' chief financial officer, Richard M. Jones, differed with this interpretation, noting that Sears "consistently" sells securities and real estate. Only an "extremist" would call these dealings "one time" gains, and as noted there are those who would agree with him. But then Jones added that one might say that $0.41 of the reported $4.01 figure might be classified as being nonrecurring.[4]

In 1984 Beatrice Cos. (BRY), then a $9.3 billion food-based conglomerate whose more familiar brands were Tropicana, Samsonite, Culligan, and Steiffel, paid $2.7 billion for Esmark Inc., a firm which at the time was in the process of digesting Norton Simon, a conglomerate it had taken over the previous year. Such are the ways of modern capitalism, in which takeovers are as commonplace as a small fish gobbling a smaller, only to be swept into the maw of a still bigger one, providing yachts and limos for squadrons of attorneys, accountants, and investment bankers.

At the time it seemed like a pretty good move, one which made Beatrice about as large as Procter & Gamble. Into the Beatrice collection came the likes of Avis, Hunt tomato products, Wesson oils, Peter Pan peanut butter, and the Swift meat business. Most important was the premier Esmark grocery distribution operation which Beatrice CEO James Dutt hoped would enable him to take national several of his regional brands, such as La Choy Chinese foods and Country Line cheeses.

Some analysts seemed less than enchanted, however, observing that, largely as a result of having to borrow heavily to pay for the purchase, BRY had increased its total debt from $991 million to $5.1 billion, much of which was financed at rates ranging from 12 to 14 percent. Dutt lightened the load by selling off $1.4 billion in companies which no longer fit the pattern he hoped to establish at Beatrice, but he had a long way to go before paring the debt to manageable levels.[5]

Some of these doubts were dispelled when Beatrice released its quarterly and annual figures. For the fiscal year ended February, 1985, BRY recorded fully diluted earnings of $4.77 a share versus $3.99 for fiscal 1984, this a close to 20 percent advance. Soon after, as though to silence critics who were troubled about the sanctity of the company's $1.70 dividend in the face of all that debt, Dutt upped it by a dime to $1.80.

The trouble with all of this is the matter of NO/NR earnings. For example, the 1985 Annual Report revealed that those divestitures brought in sizable profits—$220 million after tax, which came to $2.20 per share. (This sum is net of other charges for the integration and restructuring of businesses.) In fiscal 1984 BRY recorded "Business Realignment Program" profits amounting to $99 million, or $0.91 per share.

Beatrice had purchased and sold companies in the past, but never before on such a widespread basis. Would you call the 1984 divestitures NO/NR? And how about the restructuring operation, which isn't the kind of thing one does every year; is that to be considered NO/NR? My answer to both questions is "yes." Remove these figures, and BRY's fiscal 1985 earnings would be $2.57 a share.

Now for another matter which complicated the Beatrice report, one which benefited a majority of American companies and which no one could possibly consider a recurring addition to earnings. Under the terms of the Tax Reform Act of 1984, companies with domestic international sales corporations (DISCs), a device granted to encourage exports, were forgiven taxes deferred through DISCs. Well, the footnotes to the BRY report indicate that it took in an additional $17 million, or $0.17 per share, from this source. Take that away from the $2.57, and you have $2.40.

Finally, we learn from the footnotes that in fiscal 1985 BRY recorded a gain totaling $19 million from the annual realignment of a portion of its outstanding sinking fund debentures in exchange for shares of a convertible adjustable preference stock. A lot of that was going on in 1984, as firms swapped debt for equity and vice versa in attempts to improve their balance sheets, and investment bankers like Salomon Brothers, Goldman Sachs, First Boston, and other imaginative houses were coming up with new wrinkles every week or so to delight corporate treasurers and confuse wretches like me who tried to figure out what the *real* earnings had been. As common as this was, it is hardly the kind of play that will be adopted every year or so. Because of this I would classify the re-alignment as NO/NR. It came to $0.19 per share, bringing the earnings figure down to $2.21 per share.

In all, these three items accounted for $2.56 per share, equal to 54 percent of BRY's fully diluted earnings for the 1985 fiscal year.

Doing the same kind of calculation for the fiscal 1984 figure, I came up with $0.91 per share. Comparing the two, one can see that without NO/NR income, BRY had an earnings decline of $0.87 per share, which works out to 28 percent.

What kind of NO/NR figures would BRY report for fiscal 1986? I couldn't say, but even though Dutt sold Beatrice's chemical operations to Imperial Chemical for $750 million in March, 1985, I found it difficult to believe they would be as high as those for fiscal 1985. Certainly these gains couldn't last beyond a year or two at the most. Hence I thought that BRY would report lower per share earnings than the Street was forecasting.[6]

Value Line agreed, lowering its per share estimates for fiscal 1986 from $2.90 to $2.60 on May 3, and then to $2.40 on June 1.[7] By then quite a few financial analysts had removed BRY from their "buy" lists, and S&P had lowered its rating of the company's securities from AA to A.

Yet the stock hadn't done as badly as these developments might suggest. It was in the low 30s in July, 1985, when a sharply critical article of the company appeared in *Fortune*, this being a trifle above where the stock had been the previous August when the merger went into effect. The reason? A vogue for the stocks of food companies. Still, I expected little by way of good news out of BRY and would have avoided the stock. By the way, as I relate in Chapter 9, entitled "Debt and Cash Flow Analysis," I made a mistake in taking a negative approach with BRY.

Sometimes a company can generate a significant amount of interest income from the investment of available cash, a common example of an NO/NR situation. Such was the case at Rolm in the fiscal year ended June 29, 1984.

In the first quarter of that fiscal year this highly regarded man-ufacturer of rugged computers and private branch exchanges re-ported earnings of $0.12 per share versus $0.47 for the same quarter the previous year. This wasn't completely unanticipated; the firm's stock, which had peaked at 80 that summer, had declined by more than 20 points by the time the quarterly figures were released. But the picture was much worse than it appeared, since the 1984 quar-ter's figure had been distorted by NO/NR items.

In February, 1983, Rolm had a public stock offering that raised $172 million, and in July it sold 3.9 million shares of its common stock to IBM for $229 million, for a total of $401 million. This sum was partially offset later on by Rolm's tender offer for 4 million of its common stock, which cost $124 million. At the end of Rolm's 1984 fiscal year, cash and equivalents totaled $237 million com-pared with $213 million a year earlier, but during most of the pe-riod the amount available for short-term investments was quite a lot higher than that.

During fiscal 1984 Rolm earned $36.2 million in interest and $26.5 million pre-tax from operations; in the previous year the in-terest income came to $7 million, the pre-tax operating income to $54 million. We can see that in fiscal 1984 Rolm was earning more money on its short-term investments than on operations. Rolm's investors probably purchased their stock so as to participate in the growth of a high tech company; in fiscal 1984 they got more on the bottom line from the investments officer than from the technicians and scientists. (See Table 5.2.)

Many Rolm-watchers were unaware of this. As I told *Forbes* columnist John Heins in May, 1984, "Apparently some analysts lumped all the income together." Rolm hid nothing, and the atten-tion drawn to the situation may have been partially responsible for this condition's being spelled out in the Annual Report. But those who followed the stock earlier and didn't peruse the report with sufficient care may have obtained the wrong view of what was hap-pening at the company. This was confirmed by Gerald White, chairman of the Financial Analysts Federation's Financial Account-ing Policy Committee. "From an analyst's point of view, the geo-graphic location of the items on the income statement doesn't really

TABLE 5.2
Rolm's Income Before Taxes and Before Interest Income, 1983–1984

(figures in millions of dollars)

	Fiscal Year 1983		Fiscal Year 1984	
	Total Pre-Tax Income	Excluding Interest Income	Total Pre-Tax Income	Excluding Interest Income
First Quarter (Sept.)	$14.9	$14.5	$ 5.2	$ (3.3)
Second Quarter (Dec.)	15.8	15.1	22.0	10.7
Third Quarter (Mar.)	14.6	12.6	16.6	7.0
Fourth Quarter (June)	15.7	11.7	19.0	11.9
	$61.0	$53.9	$62.8	$26.3

Source: 1983 and 1984 Rolm Annual Report, p. 32.

matter." To which Heins replied, "But that's just the sort of thinking you would expect. If the numbers in the annual reports were all crystal clear, who would need analysts to interpret them?"[8]

The Rolm example isn't all that unusual. In 1983 and 1984 scores of companies with high-flying stocks rushed to the capital market to supply eager investors with additional shares, using the funds obtained from the flotations to purchase high-yielding short-term securities, and the augmented financial income made their results look that much better.

However, it turned out that Rolm's shareholders did very well because in November, 1984, the company was acquired by IBM, which paid $70 per share in convertible debentures due in 2004. And that too, I might add, is a nonoperating/nonrecurring item.

Subsequently, *Fortune* related that in the year 1985, Rolm, under the aegis of IBM, lost $100 million or more.[9]

TIE/Communications was a market star in this period. As the name indicates, TIE is one of those telecommunications companies which grew, proliferated, and prospered in the wake of antitrust decisions culminating in the breakup of American Telephone & Telegraph. It grew faster than most, in part by establishing new units such as Technicom, which markets telephone equipment to small businesses and residences. In addition, TIE had a large short-term investment portfolio, from which it derived dividend and interest income and gains on sale of securities.

As recently as 1976 TIE reported revenues of only $13 million; by 1983 it was up to $324 million. Institutions were taking large positions in the stock, which rose from $1 a share in 1980 to over $40 in the summer of 1983. The earnings picture was also quite pleasing: TIE reported $0.18 per share in 1980, $0.43 in 1981, $0.61 in 1982, and in 1983, $1.13. But it wasn't that clear-cut, due to NO/NR.

In 1983, TIE had a public stock offering by which it raised $61 million, and an additional $46 million was generated through stock offerings of subsidiary companies. At the end of 1983, TIE had a short-term investment portfolio which totaled $93.4 million, compared with $21 million in 1982. Included were marketable equity securities amounting to $70.7 million compared with only $7.3 million at the close of 1982. It should be further noted that as of the end of 1983, TIE also had unrealized marketable equity security gains of $8.2 million.

As noted, TIE reported earnings of $1.13 per share before extraordinary items, compared with $0.61 in 1982. However, the company's pre-tax income was substantially bolstered by financial income, net, which was $16.5 million compared with an expense of $1.2 million in 1982, all of which was clearly disclosed in the notes in the Annual Reports. The swing from financial expense to financial income accounted for 54 percent of TIE's 1983 pre-tax income, which totaled $61 million versus $27 million in 1982. (All of this was derived from dividends, interest, and gain on the sale of securities after allowing for interest expenses.)[10]

The fact that there is nothing underhanded about any of this bears repeating; the information was published in the 1983 Annual Report. But there was that erosion of Q of E to worry about. I first warned readers about TIE in my *Quality of Earnings Report* of April 27, 1984, soon after receiving their 1983 Annual Report. By then TIE had fallen to the low 20s. Much of its loss was ascribed to the general pounding being meted to the high tech section; TIE still had plenty of boosters on the Street.

Things seemed to have changed by June, 1984, by which time the stock had gone to around 15, due in part to what seemed a declining growth rate—$0.34 for the first quarter versus $0.25 for the same period in 1983. But the situation was worse than it appeared due to a NO/NR item—financial income which included $3.6 million, or $0.11 per share from the sale of TIE's holding of

Nitsuko Ltd. stock—and interest and dividends. Consider the following comparisons shown in Table 5.3.

TABLE 5.3
Comparative Statistics for TIE/Communications, 1982–1984

(figures in millions of dollars)

For the three months ended:	3/31/84	3/31/83	3/31/82
Pre-tax income	$18.9	$12.5	$4.1
Financial income	8.2	4.2	(0.4)
Pre-tax income excluding financial income, net	$10.7	$ 8.3	$4.5

Source: *Quality of Earnings Report*, June 11, 1984, p. 102.

In the first quarter of 1984, TIE's pre-tax income rose 51 percent over the same period in 1983. But when the financial income is subtracted, leaving the operating income, the advance is lowered to 29 percent. Compare this to the increase in operating income of 84 percent from 1982 to 1983, and you will see why TIE still ranked as a sell in June, even as some brokerage firms were recommending it as a depressed special situation.

The situation turned sour in 1984, when TIE's earnings sagged to $0.47 a share from $1.13 in 1983. On a pre-tax basis the company recorded a $77,000 loss compared with pre-tax income of almost $61 million in 1983. It is interesting to note that between 1983 and 1984 TIE's net financial income plummeted to $2 million from $16.5 million.

In its 1984 Annual Report TIE related that a key reason for the decline in financial income was

> net realized losses on the sale of marketable securities of $3,455,000 in 1984 versus net realized gains of $9,972,000 in 1983, due principally to the result of the unanticipated liquidation of short term investments during the third and fourth quarter in order to fund the cash obligations of Technicom International Inc. to its banks and suppliers.

In the first half of 1985, TIE reported an operating loss and in the summer of 1985 sold for as low as 4 1/8 per share.

Now for one of the more intriguing and dramatic examples of NO/NR income, which will provide an insight into its most blatant use by a highly skilled practitioner, who managed to fool some of the district's most astute analysts, and whose collapse caused a rash of red faces in the financial district. I won't go so far as to say they could have been spared the anguish if only they had read the company's report with some care, for considering their positions they must have done so. Rather, see for yourself and wonder with me as we did in Chapter 1 about the value of expert opinion.

The company is Baldwin United (BDW), a financial holding company cobbled together by Morley P. Thompson. Baldwin's most important "product" was the single premium deferred annuity, offered by its National Investors Life subsidiary, and sold by some of the nation's most prestigious brokerage houses, including Merrill Lynch and Prudential-Bache.

In March of 1982 BDW purchased MGIC Investment Corp. for $1.2 billion. Of this sum BDW borrowed about $600 million. MGIC is the nation's largest nongovernmental insurer of home mortgages. Wall Street seemed to think well of this takeover, since the price of BDW stock rose substantially in the first 11 months of 1982. So did the reported earnings, making it appear that perhaps Thompson's own "magic" was working. For the third quarter ended September 30, 1982, BDW's fully diluted share earnings, before net realized gains, totaled $1.22 per share compared with $0.82 in the comparable 1981 quarter, continuing the upward trend established in the first half of the year. For the nine months ended September 30, BDW recorded fully diluted share earnings before realized gains of $3.85 versus $2.19 for the 1981 period.

As might have been discovered by a careful study of the BDW 1982 nine months report, all of this was done with accounting mirrors. BDW reported nine months earnings of $86.1 million, but in fact its operating income absent NO/NR income before taxes and security gains really came to $2.3 million.

Where did that earnings increase come from? As I stated in the *Quality of Earnings Report* for November 29, 1982, "During the nine months ended September 30, 1982, BDW had income tax *credits* totaling $83.8 million, equal to $3.70 a share with income tax *credits* of $2.2 million, equal to $0.09 a share, during the nine months ended September 30, 1981." So you can see that $3.70 of that $3.85 in nine month income ($86.1 million minus $83.8 million) was derived from income tax credits.

By the same reasoning, BDW's third quarter figures, minus these NO/NR items, would have shown a *loss* of $9.3 million, because the company claimed income tax credits of $36.7 million and reported pre-tax income of $27.4 million. This led me to observe that

> We believe that the vast majority of BDW's income tax credits are in the nature of "paper" transactions and do not represent *cash flow* to the Company. On an interim basis, BDW does not segregate its provision for current and deferred federal income taxes. However, because we believe that BDW is incurring *losses* for *Federal income tax purposes*, the Company should provide investors with data segregating current and deferred income taxes. BDW should also provide investors with an itemized list by category and dollar amounts of all items attributable to the Company's income tax *credits* totalling $36.7 million, and $82.8 million for the third quarter ended September 30, 1982 and the nine months ended September 30, 1982, respectively.[11]

Now "paper" income tax *credits* are nice things to have if you need an earnings booster, but you can't pay the rent or buy food with them. More to the point, they can't be used to pay interest on that large debt incurred by the MGIC purchase, or dividends on BDW common and preferred. On this point, the April 18, 1983 issue of *Fortune* comments that, "Trouble was in the making before the MGIC purchase, however. Those handsome earnings gains Baldwin has booked since 1979 have largely been paper tigers, in the form of tax credits, hiding serious shortages of cash flow." Also, *Fortune* related that "about 70% of the tax credits Baldwin books as current income are merely credits against future income. 'Tax credits' observes a security analyst, 'are fine for impressing shareholders, but they are not real money. You can't pay the bank with them.'"[12]

Going through the BDW reports led me to recall an old Betty Grable movie, "The Shocking Miss Pilgrim," in which a poet and a musician enter into a deal. The poet admired one of the musician's tunes, and purchased it for $5, whereupon the musician allowed that he was a great admirer of one of his friend's poems, which he promptly purchased for $5. Each man felt rewarded, each could claim a profit, but in fact no money really changed hands. Then I remembered John Anderson's 1980 comment on how he thought candidate Ronald Reagan could balance the budget while cutting taxes and raising military spending. You may recall that Anderson said it would be done "with mirrors."

Well, Morley Thompson had a fine set of mirrors at BDW in 1982. He revealed to some extent what was behind some of his 1982 nine months report. Not enough for my liking, but sufficient for me to ring an alarm.

As noted in Chapter 1, the BDW situation did attract the attention of James Chanos, who in late 1982 was quite lonely in observing the paper edifice Thompson had created. Then state regulatory officials were moved to question his procedures and BDW unravelled, with the brokerages withdrawing their support for his SPDAs. Law suits proliferated. BDW, which sold as high as 50, collapsed to the teens and then below 10. In 1982 it reported a pre-tax operating loss totaling $123.9 million. The following year BDW filed for Chapter 11 bankruptcy, Thompson was out, and the stock finally bottomed out at 2 1/8.

The calculation of nonoperating income requires digging into the reports and looking into some nooks and crannies in the notes. It's all there to see, laid out in front of you, but all too often ignored by readers. As Sherlock Holmes once said, it is hidden in plain sight, and investors must behave like detectives in ferreting out the information.

CHAPTER 6

Declining
and Increasing Expenses

DECLINING AND INCREASING EXPENSES IS a simple enough concept. Suppose that in order to obtain $100 in revenues a company had to spend $90 on such things as wages, interest, raw materials, administration, marketing, taxes, and other cost items. If this were the case, the company would report a profit of $10.

Imagine a situation in which expenses are reduced due to a one-time change. This could be due to the introduction of a radically different production method which slashes labor costs, a decline in interest rates which enables the company to refinance its debt at a lower rate, a decline in raw materials prices, a restructuring at headquarters to eliminate staff positions, lower distribution charges, or a lower tax rate. Any or all of these could be translated into higher earnings which might continue to benefit the firm in the future, but not necessarily result in ever-higher earnings.

It works the other way too. Let the tax rate rise, labor or raw materials costs advance due to shortages, or expensive advertising campaigns be waged to introduce new products, and earnings could come in lower than they otherwise might have been.

There are scores of examples by which earnings are increased or decreased through one-time changes, and others in which earnings remain the same, but their quality can be altered by perfectly simple, honest, and straightforward changes not appreciated completely by analysts and investors. Rather than catalogue them, it might be best to offer specific examples to demonstrate the points.

Take the earnings reported by IBM in 1983 and 1984, which were $9.04 and $10.77 per share, respectively, for an increase of 19 percent. Right on target, said analysts. But a careful analysis of the 1984 IBM Annual Report would have indicated that while Big Blue had higher earnings, the true increase was nowhere near 19 percent.

The IBM situation was due to the presence of several items which increased earnings, but not through any spectacular breakthrough in sales. But before doing this, remember that it works both ways, that these items can penalize as well as inflate earnings.

So let's begin by noting an item which compromises IBM's earnings. The dollar was strong against all foreign currencies in 1984, and since IBM derives around half of its revenues from overseas, this meant that the yen, mark, pound sterling, franc, etc. were translated into fewer dollars. If the 1983 ratios had existed in 1984, IBM would have reported an additional $0.54 per share—which would have brought it to $11.31.

In 1983 IBM's pre-tax earnings were $9.94 billion and the provision for income taxes was $4.455 billion, or 44.8 percent. The following year's pre-tax figure came to $11.62 billion, and the tax rate was 43.4 percent, which is 1.4 percent lower. Now suppose IBM's 1984 earnings had been taxed at the 1983 rate. The arithmetic is simple enough: multiply the $11.62 billion by 0.014 and you get $162.722 million. In 1984 IBM had 611.4 million shares outstanding. Divide the $162.722 million difference by the number of shares outstanding to arrive at the per share figure, which is $0.27. (See Table 6.1.) Finally, subtract that from the $10.77 and you get $10.50.

Now for something more subtle. Due to a cost-cutting program in effect for several years, IBM was able to reduce its selling, general, and administrative expenses (SGA) from 26.4 percent of gross sales income to 25.2 percent. One key reason for this decline was the absence of incentives that were offered to IBM employees in 1983 with 25 years or more of service to leave the company voluntarily. So an increase in costs in 1983 resulted in a decrease for the following year. This can be a one-shot deal, not necessarily repeated. The lower percentage amounted to another $0.51 per share, bringing the year's total down to $10.26.

Here is how I arrived at the figure. As you will see, the method

TABLE 6.1
Calculation of IBM Corporate Tax Rates, 1983–1984,
and Their Impacts upon Income

1984		1983
$\dfrac{\$5,041 \text{ B}}{11,623 \text{ B}}$	Provision for Income Taxes Earnings before Income Taxes	$4,455 B 9,940 B
43.4 percent	Corporate Tax Rate	44.8 percent
	$\begin{array}{r} 44.8 \\ -43.4 \\ \hline \end{array}$	
	1.4 percent difference in rates	
$\dfrac{\$11,623 \text{ B}}{\times 0.014}$	Earnings before taxes (1984) Difference in tax rates	
$162.722 M	Income due to difference in tax rates	
611.4 M	Shares outstanding	
$162.722 M divided by 611.4 M shares = $0.27 per share		

B = billions.
M = millions.

was not too different from the one used to calculate differences due to changes in the tax rate.

SGA for 1983 came to 10.614 billion, which is 26.4 percent of the gross sales income of $40.18 billion. In 1984, as a result of the aforementioned factors, SGA rose more slowly than gross sales income—$11.587 billion out of $45.937 billion, or 25.2 percent.

The difference between the two years is 1.2 percent. Multiply that by the 1984 gross sales income and you get $551.244 million, this being the savings resulting from SGA. This figure is, of course, pretax, and so must be multiplied by the corporate tax rate, which it will be recalled was 43.4 percent in 1984, in order to find how much in the way of taxes would have had to be paid.* Do this to

---

*An alternative, simpler method would be to consider that if taxes took 43.4 percent, then the post-tax would have been what remained, or 56.6 percent of the $45.937 billion. But for the purposes of illustrating the technique, I will calculate the rate this way.

obtain the taxes on that savings, and you'll get $239.293 million, which is now subtracted from that income due to the SGA difference ($551.244 million) and you'll arrive at $312.005 million, which now should be divided by the number of shares (611.4 million). And this is how that $0.51 figure was derived.

There is also an interesting little item regarding changes in the IBM pension plan. As the real return on invested assets rose, most pension plans have upped the assumed rate of return on their holdings. Prior to 1984, IBM had utilized a very conservative 5.5 percent figure; in that year the company raised it to 7.5 percent.

IBM puts a specified amount of money into the plan each year which, together with assumed earnings, will cover pensions. The assumed higher rate of return meant that in 1984 IBM could place less money into the fund. And since the support of the pension fund is an expense item, it would lower that cost, in this case $1.180 billion in 1983 to $1.096 billion, or by $84 million, which works out to $0.08 per share, after taxes.

This figure is derived as follows, and once again, all of the material can be found in the Annual Report. The contributions to the pension plan declined from $1.180 billion in 1983 to $1.096 billion the following year, a difference of $84 million pre-tax. Taking account of the 43.4 percent tax rate as we have in the earlier examples ($84 M × 0.566) we get $47.544 million in earnings added due to the drop in costs after taxes. Divide this by the shares outstanding, and the figure comes to $0.08 per share. Subtract that from the $10.77, and we come to $10.69 per share.

Changes in the way IBM calculates depreciation is a final item. In 1984 the company adopted a more liberal method of depreciation for rental machines, plant, and other property. It was all there to see in the Annual Report:

> On January 1, 1984, for financial reporting purposes, the company adopted the straight-line method of depreciation for rental machines, plant and other property capitalized subsequent to December 31, 1983. Rental machines capitalized prior to January 1, 1984, continue to be depreciated using the sum-of-the-years digits method. Plant and other property capitalized prior to January 1, 1984, continue to be depreciated using either accelerated methods or the straight-line method. In the opinion of management, this change will result in a more appropriate matching of costs with revenue for these new assets

as a result of evolving changes in our operations, maintenance costs, and technology. The new method conforms to prevailing practice in industry.[1]

This clear statement ends with: "This change did not have a material effect on 1984 earnings." However, in reference to materiality, accountants usually do not consider an item to be material if it approximates 3 percent to 4 percent of earnings. But, many investors would consider an item to be material if the incremental impact upon earnings growth is significant. With IBM in the year 1984, this was the case. In 1984, IBM's depreciation expense dropped to $2.987 billion from $3.362 billion in 1983. But this means nothing unless related to percentages of rental machines and plant and other property. Figure this out from the numbers given by the company, and it comes to 10.15 percent for 1984 versus 11.52 percent for the previous year. Thus, IBM was charging less to depreciation in terms of percentage of rentals and the like in 1984—around $0.37 per share. This adjustment would reduce 1984 reported earnings from $10.77 to $10.40 per share.

By now the method applied should be quite familiar, and you might ask yourself how the number was derived before reading ahead. (See Table 6.2, p. 76.)

Let us go back to where we began. The casual reader of the Annual Report saw an increase from $9.04 per share in 1983 to $10.77 in 1984, a 19 percent advance versus the 14 percent increase in revenues. But the adjustment figure of $10.08 per share, reflecting the cumulative effect of the five adjustments above, represents an 11.5 percent advance—indicating that IBM's profit margin on *operations* was declining. It was reason enough to suspect that IBM was slowing down.

I will return to the IBM case later on, since there were additional things in the Annual Report (and in the 10-Q for 1985's first quarter) which were troublesome. For the moment note that through all of this CEO John Akers remained optimistic. He conceded the first quarter and then the second might be disappointing, but announced there would be a turnabout in the second half. As will be seen, these other items cast some doubt on this, but my attention to the situation was first awakened by making these one-time adjustments to the 1984 figures.[2]

TABLE 6.2
Contributions to IBM Earnings Made by Reduced Depreciation Expense for Rental Machines, Plant, and Other Property, 1983–1984

	1984	1983
Rental machines and parts	$ 6.375 B	$ 9.201 B
Plant and other property	23.048 B	19.986 B
Total	29.423 B	29.187 B
Depreciation charged to costs and expenses	2.987 B	3.362 B
Depreciation as a percentage of rental machines and parts, plant, and other property and expenses	$ 2.987 B	$ 3.362 B
	$29.423 B	$29.187 B
Equals	10.15 percent	11.52 percent
Difference: 1.37 percent		
Total rental machines, plant, etc.		29.423 B
		× 0.0137
Gain due to difference in depreciation expense on these items		403.095 M
Tax rate (1984)		× 0.434
Taxes on gain		174.943 M
		403.095 M
		− 174.943 M
Gain, net of taxes		228.152 M
Shares outstanding		611.4 M
$228.152 M divided by 611.4 M shares = $0.37 per share		

B = billions.
M = millions.

Church's Fried Chicken (CHU) is a fast-food operation which, as the name indicates, specializes in fried chicken at 1,500 restaurants in 33 states.

CHU's former management was not a strong advocate of advertising. Therefore, the company had been skimping on these expenditures. However, CHU's new management decided to reverse field in this area and embarked upon an aggressive and expensive ad campaign during the first nine months of 1984 (see Table 6.3).

TABLE 6.3
CHU's Advertising Expenses, Nine Month Periods, 1980–1984

(figures in millions of dollars)

	1980	1981	1982	1983	1984
Expenses	$4.3	$4.3	$4.0	$3.6	$12.0

Source: *Church's Fried Chicken*, 10-Q Report.

The increase in advertising expenses over the same period in 1983 came to $8.4 million, and since CHU had 19 million shares outstanding, this came to $0.44 per share pre tax. Since CHU was in the 43 percent tax bracket, this came to an additional expense of $0.25 per share for the nine months.

A glance at CHU's quarterly earnings for the period between March, 1983 and September, 1984 (Table 6.4), would have provided a good indication that the company's ambitious advertising campaign was starting to pay off.

TABLE 6.4
CHU's Quarterly Per Share Earnings, 1983–1984

Quarter	March	June	Sept.	Dec.
1983	$0.43	$0.56	$0.35	$0.32
1984	0.36	0.58	0.55	

Source: *Moody's Handbook of Common Stocks*, Winter 1984 ed.

For the 36 weeks ended September 2, 1984, CHU earned $1.49 a share versus $1.34 in the same period of 1983. I regarded the $1.49 figure as impressive in the face of those higher advertising outlays. Also, earnings were beginning to pick up momentum with CHU turning in $0.55 a share in the September quarter of 1984 compared with $0.35 in the 1983 quarter.

It was apparent that CHU's additional advertising expenditures were starting to generate the incremental sales that would translate into additional earnings. On the basis of this, I anticipated that earnings in the fourth quarter of 1984 and into 1985 should hold some pleasant surprises for the stockholders.

There was another factor which reinforced this conclusion. Like all fast-food operations, the price of raw materials plays a large part in determining profits. This is because labor costs and overheads are lower there than for full-service restaurants, and prices tend to be stickier. A decline of a penny a pound at the wholesale chicken market can do wonders to boost margins and profits per share. The CHU 10-Q report quite handily presents wholesale chicken prices, indicating further help was on its way from that source (see Table 6.5).

TABLE 6.5
Wholesale Chicken Prices, Chicago Average, 1982–1984

(figures in cents per pound)

	1982	1983	1984
First 12 Weeks	43.79	42.39	57.64
Second 12 Weeks	43.81	42.10	53.04
Third 12 Weeks	44.65	49.16	50.14
Final 16 Weeks	40.81	50.99	

Source: Church's Fried Chicken, 10-Q Report.

Table 6.5 indicates that wholesale chicken prices trended upward between June, 1983, and March, 1984. Then prices started downward. I concluded that CHU's per share earnings in the fourth quarter of 1984 and after would be aided by a lower comparative percentage cost of goods sold because of the decline in wholesale poultry prices.[3]

As it turned out, CHU earned $0.77 per share for the fourth quarter, an increase of approximately 46 percent over the same period in 1983. CHU, which was selling at 28 when I wrote it up in November, 1984, advanced to almost 40 before splitting 2–1 in early 1985.

There was a similar situation at that old warhorse, Campbell Soups (CPB). The stock of this superbly managed company went nowhere until late 1981. That year it reported revenues of $2.8 billion, earned $4.00 per share, and paid a $2.05 dividend. Sixteen years earlier, in 1965, CPB earned $1.54 per share and had an $0.08

dividend on revenues of $713 million. Yet in both years the stock sold in the mid-30s. So CPB had gone absolutely nowhere in seventeen years. Then it started to rise steadily, and in the summer of 1983 the stock was above 50. The reason: increased earnings made possible by acquisitions and newly aggressive marketing both in the United States and overseas, combined with the tonic of a hungry new management.

The consensus view on Wall Street regarding earnings was that CPB would show a nice increase for the fiscal year ended July 1983, perhaps $5.00 per share against $4.64 in 1982, and go on to post $5.50 the following year—not bad for a company which only a few years earlier had been stranded in the Sargasso Sea insofar as the stock was concerned.

In my opinion these estimates did not sufficiently take into account the matter of declining costs and other special items. Specifically, the company had mounted aggressive marketing programs with the initial impact of increasing costs, but which, as with CHU, promised to increase future profits. At least this had been the situation in earlier years, and I saw no reason to expect anything different this time. Looking at the nine months figures as found in CPB's 10-Q, I found that marketing and sales expenses as a percentage of net sales for the nine months reporting period ending April 27, 1980 through May 1, 1983, came to 8.19 percent in 1980, 8.82 percent in 1981, 9.77 percent in 1982, and in 1983, 11.23 percent.

The main reason for the increase in 1983 was substantially higher advertising expenses, which in the nine months of 1983 totaled $112 million against $61.3 million in the previous year; thus, expenses in this area almost doubled. (For the nine months ended May 2, 1982, CPB's comparative advertising expenditures rose by only 36 percent.)

Campbell reported nine months earnings in fiscal 1983 of $3.98 per share versus $3.70 for 1982, which was a 7 percent advance, hardly anything to shout about. Using the same methods as with IBM, I calculated that the higher marketing and sales expenses were equal to $0.62 per share net of taxes. In other words, without the increase in marketing expenses Campbell's earnings for the nine months period in fiscal 1983 would have been $4.60, and this would have been a 24.3 percent advance, more than three times as great. Quite a difference—and reason to consider buying the stock.

The drill is as follows. During the nine months ended May 1,

1983, CPB incurred marketing and sales expenses of $283.8 million on net sales of $2.527 billion, which worked out at 11.23 percent of sales. For the same period in 1982 marketing and sales expenses came to $222.6 million on revenues of $2.278 billion, or 9.77 percent of sales. The difference represented an increase of 1.46 percent in marketing expenses. And 1.46 percent of the 1983 sales of $2.527 billion comes to $36.9 million. CPB's tax rate was 45.9 percent and 45.9 percent of $36.9 million comes to $16.9 million in taxes. Subtract this from $36.9 million and you get $20 million. At the time CPU had 32.2 million shares outstanding, so that $20 million represented $0.62 per share.

In its 10-Q for the nine months ended May 1, 1983, CPB noted that the company continued to emphasize marketing and minimized price increases. I concluded that CPB's substantial increase in marketing and sales expenses in relation to net sales was very bullish for future operating results. I doubted that Campbell's earnings for the same nine months in the next fiscal year would be penalized to the same degree by such expenditures. Thus, I concluded the Street's estimate of $5.00 per share for fiscal 1983 and $5.50 for 1984 was probably too low.[4]

As it turned out, Campbell earned $5.12 in 1983 and $5.93 in 1984, both figures higher than anticipated. The stock continued to rise, ending the year about 60, and it added another dozen points the following year.

Let us next turn to Shaklee Corp. (SHC), which in the summer of 1983 was known to its customers as a major manufacturer and distributor of health and diet products sold door-to-door by a staff of dedicated, hard-working agents, on the pattern of Fuller Brushes, Avon Products, and Mary Kay Cosmetics. At that time Shaklee was outdoing them all, with sales, earnings, and profit margins expanding nicely. Wall Street was in love with the company; its stock was a feature in the continuing bull market, going from 7 in 1982 to peak at 42 1/4 that June before falling back, apparently to regroup.

The reason given by Shaklee's fans among the analyst fraternity was a decline in the growth rate which became apparent in the June quarter and worsened in the following one. Even so, they argued, SHC had posted impressive figures for the fiscal year ended September 30, 1983—$2.71 per share versus $1.90—and as always they expected more of the same to come. By November, however, when the September fourth quarter's figures became available, the stock was down to the low 20s, at which time buying programs were triggered, the thought being that at that level hardly any risk was involved. The bull's case was plausible; here was a true growth stock selling for little more than 8 times earnings, and at a time when the consensus view was earnings would rise to around $3.20–$3.50 in fiscal year 1984. It seemed reasonable. After all, 1982–1983 earnings were up by 42 percent, and for the fourth quarter by 13 percent (see Table 6.6).

TABLE 6.6
Quarterly Per Share Earnings, SHC, 1981–1983

Quarter	Dec.	March	June	Sept.
1981–1982	$0.38	$0.38	$0.51	$0.63
1982–1983	0.51	0.73	0.76	0.71

Source: Moody's Handbook on Common Stocks, Winter 1984 ed.

At the very least the bulls might have explored the company's Annual Report; obviously a number of savvy bears did so. Had they gone over it in some detail, they would have realized that a goodly portion of the company's earnings was derived from what could turn out to be one-time factors.

The 1983 Annual Report indicated that SHC's cost of goods sold as a percentage of sales revenues declined substantially in fiscal 1983, to 22.31 percent from 24.94 percent. Management noted this was attributable to "cost efficiencies from higher production levels, higher margins on several new products, and the reduced inflationary impact on raw materials costs." And all of these *could be* one-time benefits.

By itself this wasn't troublesome, for SHC had experienced declining cost of sales-to-revenues percentages for quite a while; in fiscal 1981 and 1980 the figures were 25.57 percent and 28.1 percent, respectively. What bothered me was that in the earlier periods earnings had expanded accordingly; not so in fiscal 1983, and in particular for the fourth quarter.

In the *Quality of Earnings Report* for November 25, 1983, I noted: "For the fourth quarter ended September 30, 1983, SHC's cost of goods sold as a percentage of sales revenues declined to 20.54 percent from 23.46 percent in the fourth quarter of 1982. (The similar figures in the fourth quarters of 1981 and 1980 were 25.32 percent and 26.78 percent respectively)."[5] As noted, the per share earnings in the fourth quarter came to $0.71. How much of that resulted from the decline in the cost of goods as a percentage of sales revenues? Following the procedure demonstrated in the examples of IBM and Church's Fried Chicken, I discovered that the lower costs of goods sold was equal to $0.14 per share after taxes, which brings the figure down to $0.57 per share.

But there is still more to come. In the fourth quarter SHC's corporate tax rate declined to 47.6 percent from 48.5 percent in the fourth quarter of fiscal 1982. Performing the necessary arithmetic, we get another penny a share, and so the fourth quarter's profits were down to $0.56.

In the 1983 fourth quarter SHC's other income rose to $1.5 million from $900,000 in the 1982 period. That extra $600,000, based on the 12.7 million shares outstanding, was equal to $0.03 a share, net of taxes.

I haven't provided the arithmetic in these cases because it might be fun to test yourself to see if you come up with the same numbers.

So we come down to $0.53 per share in the fourth quarter of fiscal 1983 versus $0.63 for the same quarter of fiscal 1982. For the year, these items totaled $0.55 per share, equal to 68 percent of SHC's year-to-year gain in earnings of $0.81 ($2.71 versus $1.90). It was evident to me that, in fiscal year 1984, Shaklee could not again count on these items to bolster share earnings.

To reiterate, there is nothing underhanded about any of this, or even unusual. But, it struck me then that the stock was in trouble, in the short term at the very least. The message was simple: sell.

Without the aid from the declining expenses, earnings per share declined in each of the 1983–1984 quarters. Within a year SHC was down to 13.

Followers of Texas Instruments (TXN) in recent years have become accustomed to sharp fluctuations in earnings, the most impressive of which occurred when, from a profit of $6.10 per share in 1982, TXN went to a loss of $6.09 in 1983, and then on to a profit of $13.05 in 1984. The swing was due to a one-time charge in 1983 due to TXN's withdrawal from the home computer business and the massive write-downs this entailed. Here we will consider the declining expenses aspect of the situation.

TXN's allowance for losses on accounts receivable as a percentage of gross receivables came to 10.18 percent in 1982. Due to the discontinuation of the personal computer operation, TXN increased the allowance to 19.33 percent the following year. In 1984 the allowance dropped to 13.05 percent.

Now let's see how this impacted upon earnings in Table 6–7.

TABLE 6.7
Calculation of Earnings Benefit from Substantial Reduction in Texas Instruments' Percentage Allowance for Losses on Accounts Receivable

	Dec. 31, 1984	Dec. 31, 1983
Gross receivables	$912.8 M	$823.8 M
Allowance for losses on accounts receivable as percentage of gross receivables	13.05%	19.33%

19.33%	
−13.05%	
6.28%	
$912.8 M	
×0.0628	
$57.32 M	Pretax difference
× 0.35	Tax rate
$20.06 M	Tax effect
$57.32 M	Pretax difference
− 20.06 M	Tax effect
$37.26 M	After-tax effect
÷ 24.2 million shares outstanding	
= $1.54 per share	

M = millions.

So the 6.3 percent decline in the percentage allotted for losses served to increase the company's after-tax earnings by $1.54, a sum equal to 12 percent of TXN's 1984 earnings. To go further, using the same method I calculated just how this impacted on earnings in the fourth quarter, and discovered that the lower percentage aided earnings by an incremental $0.64 per share. This was 26 percent of TXN's fourth quarter earnings of $2.64. (It should be noted that in the fourth quarter of 1983, TXN earned $3.23 per share.)

This significant item, coupled with TXN's inventories imbalance, led me to conclude that TXN would report lower share earnings for the year ended December 31, 1985, than Wall Street was currently forecasting.[6]

There is a scene in John Irving's *The World According to Garp* in which the hero and his fiancée consider the purchase of a house, and while looking one over an airplane plows through the top floor. Immediately Garp decides to buy, reasoning that while it is possible for a plane to hit a house once, the chances of its happening twice are almost nonexistent.

Of course, this is meant as a humorous commentary on how we interpret statistics. The same can't be said of declining costs. It is possible for companies to have a string of them over a period of time, and investors have to become accustomed to differentiating between them. It can be a delicate task, and for that reason you may want to reread this chapter to make certain the techniques are understood before turning to the next subject. You may also consider going through the quarterlies and Annual Reports of some companies whose stock you own to see whether or not they have any of these declining and/or increasing expenses and, in the light of your discoveries, reassess your views regarding them.

CHAPTER 7

Shareholder Reporting versus Tax Reporting

GO THROUGH investment advisories published by Wall Street brokerages and market services, and you'll realize they are an art form unto themselves. Most contain descriptions of the company, perhaps a few paragraphs about the industry and related political and social forces, and then go on to current operations and future possibilities. All contain earnings and other statistics, along with predictions about where they are headed.

Seasoned readers know that the prose might be shaded to the optimistic side, and those projections can be changed by unexpected developments within the company, industry, nation, or world. But the earnings might appear carved in stone. After all, how can you change earnings which have already been posted?

As we have seen, those numbers can be more complex than the vast majority of investors imagine, and the quality of earnings can vary by wide amounts. Now that you are properly skeptical regarding them, let us turn to a most important aspect of earnings statements which almost *never* appear in those advisories, but can alter your opinion of a company's prospects considerably.

I have gone through literally thousands of investment advisories over the past quarter of a century and have rarely seen consideration of shareholder versus tax reporting discussed in any of them. Let me go further, to suggest that only a small fraction of the 16,000 or so members of the Financial Analysts Federation possess *meaningful* knowledge of the fact that most corporations keep two sets of books, the familiar one for the shareholders, which is reflected in those advisories, and a second for the Internal Revenue Service.

Occasionally mention of this appears in the business press. For example, in discussing President Reagan's tax reform package in early June, 1985, Linda Sandler of *The Wall Street Journal* wrote, "Ironically, the reported earnings of many companies in both the manufacturing and service sectors could rise under the new tax plan. What complicates matters is that companies keep two entirely different set of books, one for shareholders, and another for the Internal Revenue Service."[1]

Even a *Barron's* interviewer was taken aback in the summer of 1985 when money manager Ronald B. Haave of R.B. Haave Associates said, "I try to determine what the company's tax books look like because that's more of a good indicator of what cash flow is, and on balance I like to pay no more than three times depreciation per share. . . . " "The company's tax books?" the interviewer asked, as though this was a new one for him. Haave replied, "Meaning, I look at how companies account for depreciation. Do they use straight line depreciation or accelerated methods? I look at the deferred tax position. Is the accounting more conservative for tax books than it is for shareholders' books? If you get into a recession, is the company actually paying cash taxes while they are showing losses to the shareholders? These are critical things to look at so I emphasize accounting and just what the cash position is. . . . " And after this, the interviewer chose to change the subject.[2]

If you don't know what Haave was talking about, relax. You will know by the end of the chapter, and see why along with him I consider this matter one of the more important items in evaluating stocks.

Can you get a peek at the tax books? Yes, but you would have to be a substantial shareholder to ask for and receive a copy of IRS Form 1120, which is the official designation for the U.S. Corporation Tax Return, on which this information is filed. How substantial? According to section #6103 of the tax code, which is reproduced below, you would have to own one percent of the outstanding stock.

(3) *Persons having a material interest:* Upon written request, the filing taxpayer; a spouse who filed a joint return; partners of a part-

nership; shareholder of an S corporation; *one-percent shareholders* and persons authorized by resolutions of the board of directors or by written request of a principal officer; the administrator, executor, or trustee of an estate (and the heirs with a material interest that will be affected by the information); the trust of a trustee (and beneficiaries with a material interest); persons authorized to act on behalf of a dissolved corporation; a receiver or trustee in bankruptcy; the committee, trustee or guardian of the estate of an incompetent taxpayer; and the attorney of the enumerated parties. (Code Sec. 6103(e)) (Emphasis added)

Presented is a schedule M-1 from Form 1120—U.S. Corporation Income Tax Return. This schedule requires a corporation to reconcile its income reported to the IRS with the income that is disclosed to shareholders in annual reports. This key schedule can be obtained by a one percent shareholder as noted below.

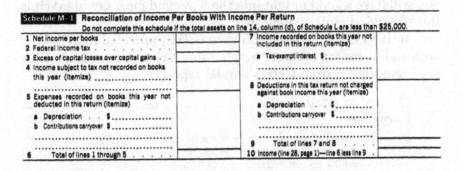

So if all that you have is a round lot of IBM, GM, or Exxon, forget about it. Such forms can be filed by the likes of T. Boone Pickens, Carl Icahn, Irwin Jacobs, or other major corporate raiders, but not by the ordinary investor.

It should be noted that many fiduciaries do own one percent or more of a particular stock which may be of only minuscule size in comparison to a *Fortune 500* company. Such a stock position is sufficient for a money manager to secure the actual IRS corporate tax report of his holding. Yet, I would wager that not more than one out of a hundred professional managers is aware of Section #6103 of the Tax Code. One reason for their lack of interest is the fact that they do not possess the skills to meaningfully compare the corporate tax return with a corporation's shareholder books.

In just about all Annual Reports there is a section entitled:

"Income Taxes," which does provide information with which an informed and trained investor can, to a surprisingly large degree, determine the difference between a corporation's tax books and shareholder books. It is a sad commentary that most securities analysts do not delve meaningfully into the corporate tax footnotes. I have seldom seen a research report generated on Wall Street that ever attempted to relay to the reader the difference between the two means of reporting when there was a sizable gap between them.

In all fairness, most corporations have a vested interest in presenting their income tax numbers and commentary in stilted accounting jargon fashion, and to compound the problem, neither the SEC nor the accounting professional requires much more than is offered, but that is no excuse for attempts to mask the true nature of annual results. Yet I hope that after you complete this chapter you will have a good insight into the ways and means of unraveling this somewhat esoteric material.

In 1984 Church's Fried Chicken (CHU) provided shareholders with an income tax footnote which is much clearer than most. Here it is, reproduced from CHU's annual report.

Income Taxes

Deferred Federal income taxes are provided for all significant differences between financial statement and tax earnings. The sources of these differences in 1984, 1983, and 1982 and the tax effect of each are as follows:

Sources	Tax earnings greater than (less than) financial earnings			Resulting in current taxes greater than (less than) reported tax expense		
	1984	1983	1982	1984	1983	1982
			(Thousands of dollars)			
Depreciation	$(2,610)	$(2,192)	$(2,289)	$(1,201)	$(1,008)	$(1,053)
Capital leases	(5,254)	(20)	(899)	(2,417)	(9)	(414)
Closed stores	(734)	1,581	—	(338)	727	—
Joint venture	—	(2,403)	696	—	(1,105)	320
Insurance and fringes	3,176	(92)	256	1,461	(42)	118
Other	1,232	(56)	(518)	567	(26)	(238)

What CHU has done in this table is to provide investors with the *sources* of the difference between tax earnings and financial earnings for the years ended December 31, 1982 through 1984. In the area of depreciation, the figures indicate that CHU's IRS tax reported earnings in 1984 were $2.6 million less than the company's financial (book) earnings. In reference to depreciation, the table also shows that in 1984 CHU paid $1.2 million less in taxes for IRS purposes (tax reporting) than it recorded as tax expense (shareholder reporting).

For example, in order to determine the impact of the difference between the tax and shareholder books for the depreciation expense item, we subtract $1.2 million of taxes computed at the statutory rate of 46 percent from the tax book differential for depreciation of $2.6 million.

The difference comes to $1.4 million, which was equal to $0.03 per share. This means that if CHU had utilized for shareholder reporting purposes the same fast depreciation write-off method it used for tax reporting, the company would have reported earnings of $1.10 per share or $0.03 less than the reported earnings of $1.13 per share.

If that were all there was to it, I would simply make the statement and let it go at that. Fortunately, however, the material can be gleaned from the Annual Reports augmented in some cases by the 10-Ks. But as you have learned by now, you have to know where to look. A clear and concise discussion of this topic can be found in Leopold A. Bernstein, *Financial Statement Analysis: Theory, Application, and Interpretation*, 3rd ed. (Homewood, Ill.: Irwin, 1983), Chapter 11.

Charles Vanik, a single-minded former congressman from Ohio, used to insert into the *Congressional Record* what he called the "Annual Corporate Tax Study," in which he would list corporations that paid little or no current federal income taxes. Vanik didn't question the legality or ability of many companies to substantially reduce and/or pay no corporate federal taxes, but rather the appropriateness of the situation insofar as public policy was concerned.

"Companies, just like individuals, take advantage of every tax provision they can to lower their taxes," he related. "They are foolish if they don't."[3]

The August 29, 1985 edition of *The Wall Street Journal* carried an article which was headlined, "No U.S. Income Taxes Were Paid in '84 by 40 Big, Profitable Firms, Study Says." The piece cited a report by a union-supported group called "Citizens for Tax Justice," which analyzed the Annual Reports of 275 major profitable cor-porations for the years 1981–1985. The organization contended that 40 of them had had combined profits of more than $10 billion in 1984 and did not pay a cent of federal taxes, and 36 others had sufficient credits and deductions left over to receive tax refunds for the previous year.

"The study noted that General Electric Co., which didn't have any federal income tax liability from 1981 through 1983, paid $186 million in taxes last year, on $3 billion in profits."

General Electric does it through the use of tax losses generated by its wholly-owned subsidiary, General Electric Credit Corpora-tion. It is difficult to locate information about GECC from the GE report. You won't find much detailed information regarding GECC in the GE annual reports. However, GECC does publish an annual of its own, which the company will send to you on request.

How would the average investor know about GECC's impact on GE's earnings? By two references that stand out like a windmill in a wheatfield. In its 1983 Annual Report, GE positioned GECC's revenues under "other income," and in its tax statement, there is an item entitled "Estimated amount recoverable (GECC—not con-solidated)" of $692 million, which more than wiped out the parent company's $657 million liability for the year. GE also provides a statement of why this is so.

General Electric's Total Tax Position for 1983, Including GECC

GE and GECC taxes (in millions)	For the year ended December 31, 1983
Provision for U.S. federal income taxes:	
Estimated amount payable (GE and consolidated affiliates)	$ 657
Estimated amount recoverable (GECC — not consolidated)	(692)
Net U.S. federal income taxes payable (recoverable)	(35)
Effect of timing differences and deferred investment tax credit	741
Total provision for U.S. federal income taxes	706
All other taxes (social security; foreign, state, and local income; property and franchise, sales and use	1,233
Total taxes payable currently or in the future	$1,939

In 1983, GE (including both consolidated and nonconsolidated af-filiates) provided an aggregate $1.9 billion for taxes of all types payable currently or in the future. The amount of U.S. federal income taxes recoverable by GECC *(which is consolidated for U.S. federal income tax purposes but not for financial reporting)* [emphasis added] arises primarily from its leasing activities. The leasing business continues to grow and provide a broad range of customer companies with attractive, cost-effective alternatives to direct purchase of plant and equipment. The leasing activities generating taxes recoverable in 1983 will result in taxable income in future years. This future obligation is included in the $741 million for the effect of timing differences. The net GE-GECC provision for recoverable taxes includes $25 million for taxes payable in 1983 and $118 million of tax credits earned in 1983 and generally recoverable as carrybacks against prior-year taxes paid.

What this means is that for 1983 GECC reported a pre-tax loss of over $1 billion for American federal income tax purposes. GECC's pre-tax loss, which was produced by considerable depreciation write-offs on leased equipment; plus investment tax credits, resulted in GECC receiving U.S. federal income tax refunds of $692 million. On a consolidated tax reporting basis, GE utilized GECC's tax recoveries to offset the company's estimated 1983 tax liability of $657 million. The difference between GECC's $692 million of recoverable taxes and GE's current U.S. tax liability of $657 million resulted in a tax refund of $35 million.

Table 7.1 (p. 92) shows the relevant tax data for GE and GECC, compiled from their annual reports for 1981–1983. Among the more interesting items is the fact that in these three years GECC generated a total of over $1.9 billion of income tax recoveries for GE, a sum equal to $4.23 per share. This alone should indicate the importance of understanding the difference between shareholder and tax books. The conclusion: GE was substantially understating its income to its shareholders.

Note the following regarding this table:

Items 1 and 2 indicate the net earnings and per share earnings of GE.

Items 3 and 4 illustrate GE's U.S. federal income tax refunds for *tax* reporting purposes and GE's zero corporate tax rate, for federal income taxes, in reference to U.S. operations.

Item 5 illustrates GE's current foreign taxes payable.

Item 6 discloses GE's total U.S. federal income and foreign

TABLE 7.1
Selected GE and GECC Statistics, 1981–1983

(m = millions, b = billions of dollars)

	1983	1982	1981
1. Net earnings	$2.024b	$1.817b	$1.652b
2. Per share	$4.45	$4.00	$3.63
3. U.S. federal income tax refunds	$35m = $0.08 EPS	$176m = $0.39 EPS	$104m = $0.23 EPS
4. Tax rate, U.S. payable for U.S. operations	0*	0*	0*
5. Current foreign taxes payable	$263m = $0.58 EPS	$301m = $0.66 EPS	$317m = $0.70 EPS
6. Total U.S. and foreign taxes payable	$228m = $0.50 EPS	$125m = $0.27 EPS	$213m = $0.47 EPS
7. % tax rate, U.S. federal and foreign	7.5%	4.5%	8.1%
8. GE earnings from GECC	$271m = $0.60 EPS	$205m = $0.45 EPS	$129m = $0.29 EPS
9. GE's U.S. federal refunds attributable to GECC	$692m = $1.52 EPS	$598m** = $1.32 EPS	$633m** = $1.39 EPS
10. Dividends GE received from GECC	$217m = $0.48 EPS	$163m = $0.36 EPS	$77m*** = $0.17 EPS
11. Total GE U.S. federal income tax refunds and cash dividends received from GECC	$909m = $2.00 EPS	$761m = $1.68 EPS	$710m = $1.56 EPS

* A zero corporate tax rate plus $35m, $175m, and $104m in U.S. federal income tax refunds for the years 1983, 1982, and 1981, respectively.

** Includes investment tax credits totaling $4.5m and $152m associated with tax transfer leases in 1982 and 1981, respectively.

*** After deduction of $25m income support payment by GE to GECC.

taxes payable for *tax* reporting purposes. In arriving at these figures, note that for these years U.S. federal income taxes *recoverable* were deducted from current foreign taxes payable.

Item 7 reveals GE's percentage corporate tax rate, for *tax* reporting. It should be noted that GE's tax rate for *shareholder* (financial) reporting purposes was 32.1%, 32.7%, and 36.2% for the years 1983, 1982, and 1981, respectively.

Item 8 indicates GE's reported earnings from GECC, utilizing the *equity* method of accounting for *shareholder* reporting purposes.

Item 9 reveals that in 1981 GE received substantial tax refunds from GECC.

Item 10 indicates the *cash* dividends GE received from GECC for the years 1981–1983.

Item 11 includes the total GE U.S. federal income tax recoveries (refunds) and cash dividends GE received from GECC in the years considered.

I was one of several who had observed for years the ways GE managed to dodge so much in income taxes. Gene Marcial of *Business Week*, in his "Inside Wall Street" column of April 26, 1982, wrote:

An Illuminating Note

The footnotes in a financial statement often yield valuable information for investors trying to assess companies whose stocks they own or want to buy. Sometimes, though, footnotes may be so obfuscatory that investors just skip past them. For instance, readers of General Electric Co.'s annual report would have difficulty detecting that its General Electric Credit Corp. subsidiary has been a bountiful "cash flow" contributor over the years. GE's credit subsidiary is among the most lucrative domestic "captive finance companies based on its role as GE's federal tax-refund cow," says Thornton O'glove, author of *Quality of Earnings Report*, which analyzes corporate financial statements for fiduciary clients. When investors and analysts come to better understand the significance of GECC to GE in regard to income tax refunds, GE's stock could reach at least a slightly higher multiple," says O'glove. At around $63, the price of GE's stock is about eight times earnings per share.

O'glove says that GE received a federal income tax refund of $104 million in 1981 mainly because of GECC. GE's annual report simply mentions that in 1981 GECC had "provisions for taxes recoverable"

of $633 million. In fact, O'glove asserts that in its consolidated state-
ment for tax purposes GE used the $633 million tax refund of GECC
to offset its 1981 federal tax liability of $529 million, thus getting a
refund. O'glove says that from 1979 to 1981 GE's fiscal situation arising from U.S. operations swung from a tax liability of $435 million
to a refund of $104 million. He estimates that swing as equal to $2.37
per share for GE, which reported net earnings of $7.26 a share for
1981.

Them's no small potatoes.

In 1982 there were approximately 1,500 companies listed on
the New York Stock Exchange. Out of these, I conducted a survey
of 704, in reference to their investment tax credits and depreciation
expense accounting practices. I learned that only 53 of them amortized (deferred) investment tax credits for shareholder reporting
purposes, in contrast to the much more liberal flow-through accounting method. Only 119 corporations, or a total of 17 percent
of those surveyed, utilized either partial or fully accelerated depreciation methods for shareholder reporting purposes.

While differentials between tax and shareholder reporting can
be found in several places in the annual reports, as noted the most
likely locations are in the tax reconciliation tables and related footnotes, and it is there where investors should do most of their digging. A classic case in recent years was that of Wang Laboratories
(WAN), the highly regarded office equipment manufacturer, which
went from a $75 million electronics company in 1975 to a multi-
billion dollar challenger to IBM in 1984.

Playing in the same league as IBM was never easy, as Wang
was finding out in the early 1980s. The company had impressive
strengths, but while continuing to grow was feeling pressures from
competitive machines and services in this highly volatile industry.
Yet earnings continued to rise along with revenues, going from
$107.1 million ($0.88 per share) in fiscal 1982 to $152 million ($1.16
per share) in 1983.

When I perused the Wang annual report for the fiscal year
ended June 30, 1984, I observed several interesting items in the
company's income tax footnotes, as shown in Table 7.2.

Table 7.2 has three items I flagged down, which are italicized
here for emphasis: certain customer lease transactions, spare parts,
and other. I then turned to the section of the report which delin-

TABLE 7.2
Wang Laboratories' Provisions for Income Taxes
and Deferred Taxes, 1982–1984

(in millions of dollars)

	1984	1983	1982
Currently payable:	$ 2.6	$ (6.2)	$ (0.9)
federal	14.7	7.2	7.5
state	3.7	3.7	2.2
	$21.0	$ 4.7	$ 8.8
Deferred—principally federal	30.0	33.0	20.2
	$51.0	$37.7	$29.0
Deferred taxes resulted from:			
Differences between tax and financial			
statement accounting for:			
Certain customer lease transactions*	$27.6	$33.8	$15.5
Spare parts*	59.0	—	—
Depreciation	8.3	9.3	2.2
Other*	9.5	4.9	7.9
Reduction of deferred taxes resulting from			
recognition of tax loss and tax credit			
carryforwards	(74.4)	(15.0)	(5.4)
	$30.0	$33.0	$20.2

*Emphasis added.
Source: *1984 Wang Annual Report.*

eates Wang's "Significant Accounting Policies" and there found the following:

> Income Taxes—*The provision for income taxes includes amounts currently payable and deferred income taxes arising primarily from different tax and financial statement accounting for certain lease arrangements, spare parts* and from the use of more accelerated depreciation methods for tax purposes. Investment credits are reflected in earnings as they are realized (the flow through method). The Company does not provide U.S. Federal income taxes on the undistributed earnings of its foreign subsidiaries since it intends to

permanently reinvest these earnings in the growth of the business outside of the United States. (Emphasis added)

The above figures in Wang's tax table have been computed at the corporate statutory rate of 46 percent, but for the sake of simplicity, let's assume the rate is 50 percent. We can conclude that in fiscal 1984 Wang's current tax liability benefited from a $27.6 million item attributable to certain customer lease transactions. With regard to spare parts, Wang charged off an additional $59 million for tax reporting compared to shareholder reporting. "Other" presumably comprises added expenses that were charged off for tax reporting compared to shareholder reporting purposes.

These three items totaled $96 million. Now recall that for the fiscal year ended June 30, 1984, Wang's *total* net earnings came to $210 million. Therefore, if one simply assumes a 50 percent tax rate, we find that if Wang's shareholder books had been kept on the same basis as its tax books for the above three cited items, the company's net income totaling $210 million for shareholder purposes would have been reduced by the aforementioned $96 million, bringing it to $114 million. On this basis, Wang Labs' earnings would have been slashed by about $0.69 per share from the reported $1.52.

Based upon my analysis of Wang's deferred tax timing differences, I concluded that the company was reporting a lower quality of earnings than previously had been the case, and that possible trouble lay ahead. So it did. For the fiscal year ended June 30, 1985, Wang's earnings declined to $0.11 a share compared to the reported $1.52 in fiscal 1984. Wang lost money in the fourth quarter, due in large part to inventory write-downs totaling $137 million pre-tax. A red flag was there to be seen in fiscal 1984—but only for those who appreciated the difference between tax and shareholder reporting.

The oil industry is a special case due to the nature of many of its operations, one of the most important being the way exploration is financed and reported. I shall start out this tale by raising a point familiar to those in the business, but not well known to others. A number of years ago Roland Harriman, then CEO of the Union Pacific, was asked to place a value on that company's extensive land holdings. Harriman said he had no idea of the figure. Believing him to be disingenuous, the questioner asked about oil and natural gas reserves under the soil, to which Harriman responded that he didn't

know what was there, since the company hadn't explored the most
promising regions and had no intention of so doing in the imme-
diate future. Why was this so? Because, as Harriman explained pa-
tiently, if the true value were known, the land would be taxed accordingly. Union Pacific was certain that the holding had mineral
wealth in abundance, but for the time being preferred not to know.

How much was Union Pacific worth? What was its *real* book
value at the time? The answer to both questions is the same: "Who
knows?"

Harriman might have gone on to note that in the oil and natural gas business there are two methods of accounting: full-cost and
successful efforts, the former being the more liberal variant. Under
the full-cost method all costs, productive and nonproductive, incurred in the search for oil and gas reserves, are capitalized and
amortized to income as the reserves are produced and sold. The
successful efforts alternative is that all costs which of themselves do
not result directly in finds should be expensed as incurred. This
means that companies utilizing the full-cost method will report
higher income than those employing the successful efforts approach. And this, of course, can result in quite a different picture
being presented to investors. What might that difference be? Consider the case of Texas Oil & Gas (TXO), a huge operator of gas
gathering pipelines in the Permian-Delaware Basin in Texas and
Anadarko Basin in Oklahoma, which utilizes the full-cost method
whereby all costs related to the acquisition and development of reserves, including failures, are capitalized. Like Wang, TXO had
racked up an impressive record, and in fiscal 1984, ended August
31, entered the ranks of $2 billion companies, in the process upping
its reported earnings from $1.41 per share to $1.65. Was this *really*
the case, however? Not if you consider that a substantial chunk of
those earnings derived from performing some deep drilling in the
tax code.

In my *Quality of Earnings Report* dated November 26, 1984,
I questioned the quality of TXO's earnings based upon an analysis
of the company's annual report for the fiscal year ended August 31,
1984. The critique was based upon a *subjective* intepretation of
TXO's federal income tax footnote which is reproduced here:

> Deferred federal income tax expense results from timing differences
> in the recognition of expenses for tax and financial reporting pur-

poses. A description of the differences and the related tax effect follows (in thousands of dollars):

	1984	1983	1982
Capitalized costs related to oil and gas properties and gas gathering and processing operations*	$191,572	$151,890	$154,644
Depreciation and depletion	(27,926)	(15,340)	(33,840)
Other	9,354	6,950	9,696
	$173,000	$143,500	$130,500

*Emphasis added.

TXO's letter to shareholders related that "Over the past two years, the surplus of oil and natural gas has resulted in weakening energy prices for producers. Reflecting these problems, our throughput and production levels have been substantially below capacity while our fiscal 1984 unit margins and prices declined." After this sober observation, the letter assumed an upbeat tone.

The red flag this time was in TXO's federal income tax footnote which revealed that between 1983 and 1984 the company's capitalized costs relating to oil and natural gas gathering and processing operations had risen from $151.9 million to $191.6 million.

My comment was that:

In 1984, TXO, for tax reporting purposes, incurred an additional $203 million of expenses, equal to $0.96 per share, than was expensed for book reporting purposes. In 1983, this sum amounted to $167 million or $0.79 per share.

In 1984, TXO's additional capitalized costs for book reporting purposes increased by $0.17 per share, compared with an earnings gain of $0.24, whereas in 1983 capitalized costs rose by $0.06 per share and earnings by $0.23 a share. . . .

Based upon an analysis of TXO's deferred tax timing differences, we question the quality of TXO's earnings.

On October 30, 1985, TXO and U.S. Steel announced a definite agreement providing for the merger of the two firms. All seemed to be proceeding smoothly, but by then a few analysts, attempting to understand the combination, started delving into TXO's books, and found what has been outlined above. In *The Wall Street Journal's* "Heard on the Street" on January 27, 1986, there was a quote from Kim Schnabel, a portfolio manager for the College Retirement Equities Fund, who was incensed by a proposed accounting change by TXO that involved a move to a more conservative method for capitalizing costs relating to property and plant. Schnabel was opposed to the merger, not only on the grounds that natural gas prices were soft, but the fact that TXO's "supposedly super earnings record" was now being called into question. Schnabel observed that TXO had deferred the cost of drilling dry holes. In switching to the successful efforts method, which recognizes these costs earlier, the company would have to write-off $624 million. "The net result," noted the *Journal:* "Texas Oil's retained earnings of $933 million will be marked down by $338 million."

This caused a flurry in the stocks of both companies, as analysts wondered whether U.S. Steel's management had done sufficient work on TXO's books before making their offer. The merger finally went through, as shareholders of both companies accepted the terms on February 12, 1986.

With the merger completed, it would be in the long-term interest of U.S. Steel shareholders to change TXO's accounting from the more liberal full-cost method to the conservative successful efforts procedure. This is because with oil and gas prices falling, TXO could have been facing a substantial write-off of capitalized costs. Now, under the aegis of U.S. Steel, the company can take an accounting "big bath" that will have the effect of enhancing future earnings. Also, it should be noted that the Marathon Oil subsidiary of U.S. Steel utilizes the successful efforts method of accounting and TXO's accounting will now conform to that of Marathon.

Consider the case of DSC Communications, a manufacturer of digital telephone switching systems, one of the more promising high tech areas. DSC's earnings had been growing rapidly; in 1984 they increased to $1.40 per share, compared with $0.89 in 1983 and only $0.23 in 1982—the very model of a modern major growth company.

But as is so often the case, there was more to it than met the eye at first glance. And in this instance, it was the growing gap between shareholder and tax reporting. DSC's accounting policies were as follows:

Revenue is generally recognized on switching systems when the Company has completed all manufacturing to customer's specifications, factory testing has been completed and accepted by the customer and the system has been delivered to the designated location.

Revenue is recognized on transmission and terminal products generally when the products are shipped to the customer, except that certain revenue from long-term contracts in years prior to 1984 was recognized using the percentage-of-completion method.

Reproduced below from the DSC 1984 Annual Report is an excerpt pertaining to the company's provision for deferred income taxes.

The provisions for deferred income taxes were as follows (in thousands):

	1984	1983	1982
Revenue recognition difference between book and tax return*	$31,403	$14,051	$ 2,648
Excess of tax over book depreciation	1,316	1,439	297
Excess of tax over book employee benefit costs	662	1,830	—
Warranty costs accrued	(1,710)	(1,149)	—
Inventory reserves	(1,009)	(130)	7
DISC	128	1,368	—
Tax credits	—	(1,929)	—
Other	1,270	(580)	101
	$32,060	$14,900	$ 3,053

*Emphasis added.

As we have seen, for reporting purposes, DSC recorded earnings totaling $1.40 a share in 1984, $0.89 in 1983, and $0.23 in 1982. During the same years, the company recognized an additional $31.4 million equal to $0.77 a share, $14 million equal to $0.37 a share, and $2.6 million equal to $0.09 a share in reference to revenue recognition for shareholder reporting purposes versus tax reporting purposes. (For simplicity's sake, these figures have been calculated on the basis of a 50 percent tax rate.)

Hence, it was evident that a goodly portion of DSC's earnings were the result of faster revenue recognition for book reporting than for tax reporting. This phenomenon is not necessarily unusual in the case of fast-growing high tech firms, but there is an added risk involved in investing in this kind of situation, because of the growing gap between tax reporting and shareholder reporting in the area of revenue recognition. Agreed, DSC does not have to spell everything out in fine detail, but shareholders and investors should be aware that quite legally, the company is, in effect, keeping two sets of books, one for shareholders, the other for the IRS.

On October 3, 1985, DSC announced it was restating its 1984 financial statement and its first and second quarter statements for 1985. It related that the previously reported earnings of $1.40 a share for the year ended December 31, 1984, were being restated downward to $1.08 per share, and that the 1986 six months earnings totaling $0.68 a share would be reduced to a *loss* of $0.11.

DSC informed shareholders that the restatement was being made

> to exclude previously reported revenues and earnings from shipments of current switching expansion ports for which a customer is now denying any obligation. Our restatements in 1985 exclude revenue and earnings attributable to sales switching systems to the customer which were reflected in the first quarter of 1985 and because of a recent change made by the Company in its revenue recognition policy for financial reporting in 1985.

In summary, DSC commented that

> the weakness in the long distance switching market, which became significant earlier in 1985, has caused the Company to change its revenue recognition policy for financial reporting in 1985. The policy as changed reflects current conditions wherein customer installation plans and programs are being changed or delayed frequently and provides that revenue from sales of the Company's equipment is reflected in its financial reporting only when the equipment has been shipped to the customer's final installation site.

A few days after this announcement, two shareholders filed separate class action lawsuits against the company alleging that its financial reports for 1984 and 1985 were "materially false and misleading." According to a newspaper report,

> The action was taken because of an accounting change and a customer dispute over a contract for long-distance switching equipment. The Company said one of the suits also names as a defendant three of DSC's principal officers and its auditor, Arthur Andersen & Com-

pany. DSC said it intends to defend itself against the suits. Arthur Andersen officials could not be reached for comment.[4]

If there is a moral to this—for stockholders, that is—one might say that a careful examination of DSC's reports, available for all to see, would have revealed a very wide gap between DSC's tax and shareholder books with reference to revenue recognition. Astute investors need not have worked out all of the figures: what was required was a knowledge that, of the two methods of calculating profits, DSC was utilizing the one that made it appear most favorable.

HBO & Co. was a rapidly-growing corporation in the hospital processing systems industry. Earnings for 1984 totaled $0.86 a share, compared with $0.61 in 1983 and $0.44 in 1982. The 1984 HBO Annual Report was a lavish document, including many color photographs of the firm's operations, along with a ten-page section entitled: "Investing in HBO & Company," devoted to testimonials regarding operations by financial analysts. And one of the testimonials in part praised HBO's conservative accounting.

What could the analyst be thinking of? After looking over the tax footnote section, it seemed to me that such was not the case, that here was yet another example of an important divergence between tax and shareholder reporting.

Start out by examining the following reproduction of that segment.

The provision for income taxes consists of the following components:

(000 Omitted)	1984	1983	1982
Current portion—			
Federal	$ 86	$1,165	$2,596
State	152	332	501
	238	1,497	3,097
Deferred portion—			
Federal	8,048	4,168	2,550
State	980	477	143
	9,028	4,645	2,693
Total provision for income taxes	$9,266	$6,142	$5,790

Deferred tax expense results from timing differences in the recognition of certain items for tax and financial statement purposes.

The tax effects of major timing differences are as follows:

(000 Omitted)	1984	1983	1982
Related to current balance sheet items—			
Gross profit on EPLAs and service agreements discounted*	$1,281	$ (125)	$ 300
Other, net	341	133	(230)
	1,622	8	70
Related to noncurrent balance sheet items—			
Gross profit on service agreements discounted*	5,924	3,979	740
Accelerated depreciation	1,637	528	521
Investment tax credit (Note 1)	(443)	(5)	1,304
Other, net	288	135	58
	7,406	4,637	2,623
Total deferred tax provision	$9,028	$4,645	$2,693

*Emphasis added.

Note that there is a significant difference between HBO's shareholder books and tax books having to do with gross profit on EPLAs (equipment purchase and software license agreements) and service agreements discounted. These items in total accounted for additional profits of $0.44 per share in 1984 and $0.24 in 1983 for shareholder reporting purposes than was recorded for tax reporting. These figures compare with HBO's reported earnings of $0.86 and $0.61.

HBO's accounting policies in reference to EPLAs and revenue recognition from Service Agreements as delineated in its 1984 annual report is as follows:

Equipment Purchase and Software License Agreement ("EPLA")

The Company receives a lump-sum fee for a renewable six-year license to use the software; the customer purchases the computer equipment from the Company. Fees under these agreements are included in service and fee revenue in the statements of income and amounted to approximately $4,824,000 in 1984, $10,083,000 in 1983 and $15,565,000 in 1982.

The significant accounting policies adopted by the Company in preparing the financial statements are as follows:

REVENUE RECOGNITION
Revenue from service agreements is recognized monthly, as billed, over the life of the agreement, beginning at the system installation

date or in full on the date the contract is discounted without recourse to a financial institution. Contracts discounted contributed revenue of $25,853,000 in 1984, $12,709,000 in 1983 and $3,288,000 in 1982. Revenue from EPLAs is recognized at the system installation date.

On January 16, 1986, HBO announced its preliminary 1985 results, indicating that earnings would be in the range of $0.90–$0.92 compared with $0.80 for the previous year. This was deemed rather disappointing since the Street had thought it would do somewhat better than that. For the first three quarters, HBO had reported earnings of $0.77 versus $0.61 for the same period in 1984, and the final quarter, if it came in at $0.13–$0.15, would look feeble when compared with the $0.23 in 1984.

In the preliminary report HBO commented that "net income and earnings per share in 1986 are projected to grow at slower rates than revenue due to management's goal to emphasize revenue from recurring sources rather than one-time sales." Management also related that it had "implemented a Company-wide cost cutting program and other actions to increase productivity and improve margins in the future."

I realize that shareholder versus tax reporting isn't the simplest thing to comprehend, but nonetheless it is of vital importance to investors who want to be better able to assess the additional investment risks associated with the important points I make in the following paragraph.

Under the umbrella of generally accepted accounting principles, a company can utilize accounting methods that accelerate revenues for book reporting purposes and/or limit expenses being deducted for financial reporting purposes. When a corporation does this, it may start out with less aggressive accounting policies and then change to more aggressive ones in order to maintain the facade of growth. When this occurs, investors may be forewarned only through careful analyses of tax versus shareholder reporting. In most cases due to the lack of meaningful disclosure, the figures presented are left to the subjective interpretation of the investor. Keep your eyes on those financial footnotes, however, for they may offer clues that, with proper interpretation, can prevent you from falling into many pitfalls.

On a closing note, I find it very significant that the U.S. Senate's tax reform bill includes a provision whereby a corporation's book (shareholder) income could become a factor in determining tax liability. Within this context, under the corporate minimum tax proposals, one-half of the difference between a corporation's book income—the profit it reports to its shareholders—and the profit reported for IRS tax reporting would become a "preference item" for purposes of determining its alternative minimum tax.

CHAPTER 8

Two Key Ratios: Accounts Receivable and Inventories

In 1931, WHEN STOCKS CONTINUED their dizzy plunge during the nation's most spectacular bear market, Bernard E. Smith, better known as "Sell 'Em Ben," was the king of the district. As the sobriquet indicates, Smith was a short seller who, as legend had it, ran from brokerage to brokerage on Black Tuesday, 1929, screaming, "Sell 'em all! They're not worth anything!" Two years later, this former longshoreman out of Hell's Kitchen was taking in more than $1 million a month, scorching the few remaining bulls.

According to one of many stories about him, Smith was monitoring the stock of a medium-sized industrial company which supposedly was bucking the trend and doing quite nicely. Because of this the stock was setting new highs almost daily, while the rest of the list was hitting bottom. Smith was puzzled, and one day motored to the factory where he asked to see management, only to be turned away at the gate. Undeterred, he walked around the plant, and noticed that only one of its five smokestacks was belching forth smoke. Smith took this to mean the other furnaces weren't operating, and so business was bad. Rushing to a telephone, he shorted the stock which plunged several weeks later when poor earnings were reported. This was how Sell 'Em Ben made part of that month's $1 million.

The investment world is far more sophisticated today, but such simple ploys still work better than the most baroque equations cooked up in the business schools for use on giant computer mainframes.

One of these simple ploys—the best method I have ever discovered to predict future downwards earnings revisions by Wall Street security analysts—is a careful analysis of accounts receivable and inventories. Learn how to interpret these, and you will have today's equivalent of Smith's smokeless smokestacks. In fact, had old Ben been able to go through that company's books, he probably would have found two things: a larger than average accounts receivable situation, and/or a bloated inventory. When I see these, bells go off in my head telling me to analyze that particular stock in a devil's advocate manner.

In the summer of 1985, I published a short paper on why accounts receivable and inventories analysis are so important. The work was presented in a question and answer format, and here are two of the more pertinent segments:

QUESTION: Why is accounts receivable analysis so important?
ANSWER: Conventional accounts receivable analysis involves running a ratio called days sales in accounts receivable. This ratio, which indicates receivable turnover, can illustrate the granting of more liberal credit terms and/or difficulty in obtaining payment from customers.

However, even more importantly, the analysis of sales and accounts receivable may provide a clue as to whether a company is merely shifting inventory from the corporate level to its customers because of a "hard sell" sales campaign or costly incentives. In such an instance, this type of sales may constitute "borrowing from the future." Within this context, it is important to note that in most instances, a sale is recorded by a company when the goods are shipped to the customer.

Also, there is an added cost to the company in carrying an above-average amount of accounts receivable.

QUESTION: Why is inventory analysis so important?
ANSWER: Obviously, higher trending inventories in relation to sales can lead to inventory markdowns, write-offs, etc. In addition, it is important to note that an excess of inventories, time and time again, is a good indicator of future slowdown in production. Within this context, it is important to analyze the components of inventories. If the finished goods segment of inventories is rising much more rapidly than raw materials and/or

work-in-process, it is likely that the company has an abundance of finished goods and will have to slow down production. Akin to accounts receivable, bulging inventories are costly to carry.

These are the essential ideas developed and illustrated in the following pages.

Let's start with the basics. Accounts receivables are monies due from customers for goods shipped and/or services performed. By itself this isn't a problem; just about every operation has accounts receivable. As a consumer you add to a company's account when purchasing a product and paying for it by check at the end of the month. A clothing retailer who takes delivery on a truckload of suits, with payment due in 30 days, is contributing to the accounts receivable of the company that sold them to him.

The difficulty comes when accounts receivable rise substantially over what they had been in the same reporting period during previous years. This can result from any of several factors. A spell of economic hard times for the country, industry, or region will often cause stretchouts in payments. A poor collection job might be another reason. Perhaps the retailer, his back against the wall and eager to make sales, has offered his customers liberal credit terms. This often happens in the auto industry during slack periods. In retail business, this is the equivalent of end-of-season sales and the dumping of unfashionable merchandise. One dramatic instance of this occurred at RCA just prior to that company's departure from the computer business, when mainframes were being leased literally on a "two for the price of one" basis simply to move them out of inventory prior to the news being released. Whatever the cause, major increases in accounts receivable is a danger sign.

An analysis of the relationships between sales, accounts receivable, and inventories may provide a clue as to whether a company is merely shifting inventory from the warehouses to its customers due to "hard sell" campaigns or costly incentives. In such an instance, these kinds of sales may constitute borrowing from the future or rectifying past errors. In this context it is important to recall that in most instances, revenues are recorded by a company when the goods are shipped to the customer. Also, there are the added money costs of carrying accounts receivable.

Now for inventories. These are stores of raw materials and finished and semifinished products. Manufacturing concerns may have very large inventories as a ratio to sales, while service companies have smaller ones. Indeed, the key distinction between the manufacturing and service sectors is just that: companies can stockpile inventory products, but not services.

For example, a stock market advisory service has an inventory of paper, back copies, postage stamps, and the like, which can be quite minor when set beside gross income. Knowing the inventory for such an operation isn't very useful. On the other hand, a furniture factory can have an inventory larger than annual sales. As I said, the specific amount of inventory is not particularly meaningful in and by itself. What matters is comparisons with the same reporting period in previous years.

Increases in raw materials inventories from reporting period to reporting period might mean the company had decided to stock up in anticipation of a price boost, but this is not very likely most of the time, since the company has to lay out money for inventory and wants to move it as quickly as possible. Indeed, one of the reasons the Japanese car makers are more efficient than those of Detroit is inventory management; Toyota does far better in this regard than General Motors. So an increase in raw materials inventories usually means business is speeding up, and this will be reflected in future revenues and profits.

More interesting are major changes in semifinished and finished goods. If business is sluggish due to economic conditions or the fact that our furniture manufacturer decided to produce Colonial when customers decided they wanted Scandinavian Contemporary, this figure could rise substantially. On the other hand, should we have targeted the market correctly, retailers would be pounding on his door pleading for sofas and cabinets and the manufacturer would be drawing down his finished goods inventories.

Examples abound of how considerable increases in inventory and/or accounts receivable can forecast downward earnings and surprises. This is especially true in those industries subject to rapid changes in products and taste. Expect to find them in companies dealing with high fashion, seasonal goods, and especially high tech. No investor seriously involved with stocks in these industries can afford to ignore accounts receivable and inventories.

Let me go one step further: had investors been monitoring these figures on a quarter-by-quarter basis, they could have predicted the collapses in the price of perhaps four out of every five stocks which occurred during the high tech washout in 1984–1985. Fast-growing industries are always subject to such shakeouts. As science writer Kathleen Sylvester put it, "Nothing recedes like success."

By the summer of 1985 Silicon Valley was reeling. As Regis McKenna, one of the Valley's marketing gurus, put it: "150 companies making PC clones created market share battles rather than market expansion battles." Some of the area's big names were laying off workers. Not surprisingly, most of my examples will be drawn from this segment.[1]

Let us start out with a classic example of a buildup in accounts receivable and inventories, and how it impacted upon the company involved. I will cover the example in some detail, because once you understand the fundamental methods involved, applying them will be easy.

What stock marketeer doesn't know the saga of Commodore International (CBU), the microcomputer operation that entrepreneur Jack Tramiel took from nowhere to the point where it became a billion dollar operation dominating its fast-growing field? Tramiel bragged that he could undersell and outperform even IBM by turning out most of the components for his machines rather than purchasing them from suppliers, as did many competitors. Of course, Tramiel had a reputation for poor relations with some of his retailers and played an aggressive game of corporate hardball when he felt the occasion demanded. But he did produce results.

For the fiscal year ended June 30, 1984, CBU reported revenues of almost $1.3 billion on which it realized after-tax earnings of $143.8 million and earnings of $4.66 per share. These figures compare with $681 million of revenues in 1983 and earnings totaling $2.86 a share. But there were troubles. After some squabbling, Tramiel left the company and soon would acquire Atari, which he swore would push his old operation out of its leadership position.

Partly for this reason the stock of CBU common declined from its 1983 peak of 60 5/8 and toward the end of 1984 was selling in the high 20s. Yet the outlook seemed pretty good. CBU had recently acquired the smallish Amiga Corp., and with it an advanced design machine that did everything the Apple Macintosh could and more, but could be sold for a lower price.

Keep in mind that this is an industry marked by innovation, rapid product changes, and price erosion, where a 30-year-old is deemed a veteran and a machine more than six months old can be obsolete. It is a prime candidate, then, for accounts receivable and inventory problems.

Table 8.1 illustrates CBU's net sales, accounts receivable, and inventories for the first fiscal quarters ended September 30, 1982 through September 30, 1984. Charts like this will appear throughout this chapter, so learn how to read it. Note that for the first fiscal 1985 quarter ended September 30, 1984, CBU earned $0.90 a share versus $0.79 for the same period in fiscal 1984.

TABLE 8.1
**Commodore International's Sales, Accounts Receivable,
and Inventories, 1982–1984**

(figures in millions of dollars)

	9/30/84		9/30/83		9/30/82
Net sales (3 months)	$244.2		$209.3		$103.3
		16.7%		102.6%	
Accts. receivable, net	254.7		189.9		180.0
		34.1%		5.5%	
Inventories	437.4		398.7		326.8
		9.7%		22.0%	

The figures between the columns are percentage increases from period to period.

Table 8.1 indicates that between the first quarters ended September 30, 1982 and September 30, 1983, the company's sales advanced by 102.6 percent, while accounts receivable rose by only 5.5 percent, an indication of a surge in demand. But look what happened next. Between September 30, 1983 and September 30, 1984, sales increased by only 16.7 percent and accounts receivable by 34.1 percent, just the opposite situation. Indeed, in the first fiscal quarter ended September 30, 1984, CBU's accounts receivable rose twice as fast as the company's sales. This is a clear sign that CBU's retailers were moving out its products at a slower than usual pace, while the company was shoveling out its old products in what looked like an attempt to dump them on the market in advance of new introductions. In this regard, note that while inventories rose at a slower rate, they were worthy of a more detailed analysis.

Table 8.2 indicates what is known as a "negative inventory divergence," meaning that while the raw materials and work-in-progress components of inventories declined, finished goods increased substantially.

TABLE 8.2
Commodore International's Inventory Components, 1983 and 1984

(figures in millions of dollars)

| | September 30, | |
	1984	1983
Inventories:		
Raw materials & work-in-progress	243.2	$270.3
Finished goods	194.2	128.4

It didn't take too much imagination to figure out what was happening at CBU. Raw materials, in this case electronic components, were being assembled into microcomputers and related gear, which despite an intense sales campaign were piling up as inventories of finished goods. Given the relationship between these two sets of figures, it isn't difficult to see that the dollar figures for the finished goods component of inventories on September 30, 1984 were too high.

There is one other sign that this must have been the case. In its first quarterly report in fiscal year 1983, the company had included the following:

> As the September 30, 1983 balance sheet indicates, finished goods inventory remained virtually unchanged from the June 30, 1983 level, while our raw material and work-in-progress inventory, in anticipation of very strong sales growth projected for the December 31, 1983 quarter, increased substantially during the first quarter.

CBU's 1984 first fiscal quarter shareholders' report does not contain a similar reference regarding inventory positions. So in December of 1984, I informed my readers that for the fiscal year ending June 30, 1985, CBU would report considerably lower share earnings than Wall Street was currently anticipating.[2]

Three months later, on March 20, 1985, I issued a follow-up

on CBU. The six months ended December 31 figures had been released by then, showing earnings of $1.00 per share against $2.41 for the same period the previous fiscal year, just about fulfilling my expectations. By then the stock was at the single digit level, and the situation remained bleak.

Table 8.3 shows what the inventory picture looked like.

TABLE 8.3
Commodore International's Sales and Inventories, 1982–1984

(figures in millions of dollars)

	12/31/84		12/31/83		12/31/82
Net sales: six months	$ 582.9		$640.7		$ 279.6
		(9.0%)		129.1%	
Inventories	449.3*		287.7		124.9
		56.2%		130.3%	
Components of inventory:					
Raw materials & work-in-progress	204.7		153.2		68.5
		33.6%		123.6%	
Finished goods	244.6		134.5		56.4
		81.8%		138.4%	
Total inventories	$ 449.3 56.2%		$ 287.7 130.3%		$ 124.9

*After a fiscal second quarter ended December 31, 1984, inventory write-down totaled $30 million.

What we see here is a huge buildup in inventories, probably older micros the market simply couldn't or wouldn't absorb. For the six months ended December 31, 1984, the company's sales declined by 9 percent while inventories rose by 56.2 percent. By way of contrast, CBU's sales increased by 129.1 percent with inventories advancing commensurately by 130.3 percent from the 1982 to the 1983 reporting periods.

Note too that finished goods inventory increased by 82 percent, while raw materials and work-in-progress rose by only 34 percent, indicating that CBU was still experiencing a backup of finished goods inventory. In the fiscal second quarter ended December 31,

1984, CBU had taken an inventory write-down, and I suspected more to come.[3]

This arrived in the form of a tidal wave of inventory write-downs. The September 25, 1985 edition of *Wall Street Journal* related the sad tale:

> New York–Commodore International Ltd. posted a fiscal fourth-quarter loss of $124 million, significantly wider than it projected last month, and said auditors will qualify its annual report.
>
> The loss reflected a worsening of the company's inventory position. After denying last April that any inventory write-downs were contemplated, Commodore in August projected a fourth-quarter loss of $80 million and an inventory write-down of $50 million. And yesterday, in announcing the $124 million loss, Commodore said such write-downs were larger than expected and totaled $63 million. The company also cited one-time charges of $14 million, the effect of promotional allowances and a 56% drop in sales.

Reference has been made to the fact that Commodore purchased Amiga in order to get a product to go against Apple's Macintosh. At the same time, Apple (AAPL) was mounting a major drive to crack into the office market with Macintosh, which was adjudged a product success. So was the Apple IIc, which industry experts pronounced a better and more flexible machine than the IBM PC jr. with which it was often compared. But the company continued to have management problems and, as we have seen earlier, was about to undergo a period of distress.

Part of the reason for this was a slowdown in sales of the Apple IIe, a variant of which had first appeared in 1977 and was quite long in the tooth by the mid-1980s. In the spring of 1985, it had become apparent that Apple was in trouble, and this was borne out by the earnings statement for the March, 1985 quarter which came to $0.16 against $0.15 for the same period in 1984. Since the previous quarter's comparisons were $0.75 versus $0.10, it was quite clear Apple was slowing down. Management confirmed this in May by announcing it expected both revenues and earnings for the quarter ending June 30, 1985, to drop below the levels of the 1984 quarter.

Because of this, the consensus of opinion on Wall Street was that Apple's earnings for all of fiscal 1985 ending September 30, 1985, would come to $1.10 a share. This is to say that the analysts thought that Apple would earn around $0.20 a share for the second half—quite a comedown.

Given the bloated inventory situation at the end of the March quarter, even this seemed quite high. Take a look at it in Table 8.4 and you will see what I mean.

The table illustrates that for the six months ended March 29, 1985, AAPL's sales increased by 83.9 percent while inventories rose by 113.9 percent. These figures contrast with AAPL's sales and inventories advances of 39.3 percent and 39 percent respectively for the previous year's six months.

From what we have seen in Commodore's case, you can pretty well imagine what happened in the 1985 period. Apple shoveled merchandise into the market, but not fast enough to prevent that large increase in inventories from accumulating. Of particular interest was the fact that while AAPL's raw materials and parts inventories increased by 89 percent, those of finished goods soared by 294 percent.

There were two explanations for this huge increase: either the Macintosh and IIc weren't selling well, or the Apple IIe's marathon run was just about over. Either way, this was a company in trouble. And if the latter were the situation, I would expect large-scale write-downs in the future, along with drastic price reductions on the Apple IIe to get them out of the warehouses.

TABLE 8.4
Apple Computer's Sales and Inventories, 1982–1985

(figures in millions of dollars)

	3/29/85		3/30/84		4/1/83		3/26/82
Net sales (6 months)	$1133.6		$616.3		$442.2		$264.5
		83.9%		39.3%		67.1%	
Inventories							
Raw materials and purchased parts	85.9		45.4		36.6		42.9
Work-in-progress	26.3		38.7		24.0		20.1
Finished goods	148.4		37.7		27.0		34.8
Total inventories	$ 260.6		$121.8		$ 87.6		$ 97.8
		113.9%		39%		(10.4%)	

All of this could happen pretty soon, and on May 28 I wrote that "AAPL could report a loss in either or both of the fiscal third and fourth quarters ending June 30 and September 30."[4]

Needless to say, Apple was a stock to avoid as far as I was concerned, even though the stock had already declined considerably and was trading at around 20. For the third fiscal quarter ended June 30, 1985, AAPL incurred a net loss—the first quarterly loss in Apple's history. From normal operations, AAPL recorded $3.5 million in pre-tax profit. However, due to $40.3 million of extraordinary expenses attributable to a major reorganization and consolidation of operations, AAPL's net after-tax loss totaled $17.2 million, or $0.28 a share. Apple's stock drifted downward to a low of 14 before rallying.

It turned out that AAPL's reorganization proved successful. For the first fiscal quarter ended December 27, 1985, Apple reported its highest-ever quarterly earnings, totaling $56.9 million, or $0.91 a share, compared with $0.75 a share in the first fiscal quarter ended December 28, 1984. It is noteworthy that CEO John Sculley said that one of the key reasons for the firm's improved results was "higher inventory turns." Between the first fiscal quarter ended December 28, 1984 and the first fiscal period ended December 27, 1985, AAPL reduced its inventories by an amazing 58 percent to approximately $109 million from $261 million. In early 1986, AAPL common had rallied to the mid-20s.

Varian Associates (VAR) is a well-regarded manufacturer of power tubes and solid-state devices. For the fiscal year ended September 27, 1984, VAR earned a record $3.16 per share on revenues of $928 million. For the first fiscal quarter ended December 28, 1984, the company earned $0.57 per share versus $0.53 for the same quarter the previous year. Not bad, some thought, considering the industry's bleak outlook at the time. Seeing even a small rise gave one hope in this period, and the price of VAR common firmed, the feeling being results for the second quarter would be even better.

Such optimists might have thought otherwise had they bothered to take a careful look at the accounts receivable and inventory situations shown in Table 8.5.

Table 8.5 indicates that in the December 1984 quarter, VAR's sales increased by 16 percent, while accounts receivable soared by twice that amount and inventories increased at a more rapid clip: 43 percent. By way of contrast, in the first fiscal quarter ended

TABLE 8.5
Varian Associates' Sales, Accounts Receivable and Inventories for Selected Quarters, 1981–1984

(figures in millions of dollars)

Quarter ended	12/28/84	12/30/83	12/31/82	1/1/82	1/2/81
Sales	$229.2	$196.7	$166.4	$161.5	$144.0
		16.5%	18.2%	3.1%	12.2%
Accounts receivable	194.7	146.9	131.2	137.4	142.2
		32.5%	11.9%	(4.5%)	(3.4%)
Inventories	217.7	152.2	139.5	156.0	218.1
		43.0%	9.1%	(10.6%)	(28.5%)

December 30, 1983, VAR's sales had risen by 18 percent, whereas accounts receivable and inventories advanced by only 12 percent and 9 percent, respectively. On a comparative basis, it is evident that as of December 28, 1984, VAR's accounts receivable and inventories were quite high in relation to sales, and it seemed to me this would show up in future quarters.[5]

At the time of my advisory in late March, VAR was selling for around 32. It subsequently declined to the mid-20s. Earnings for the March quarter came to $0.56 per share versus $0.71 for the previous year, and the figures for the June quarter were only $0.11 versus $0.82, with the numbers for the fiscal September quarter $0.51 versus $1.04. For the fiscal year ended September 27, 1985, VAR earned $1.81 per share from continuing operations compared with $3.16 for fiscal 1984.

By now you, the reader, may have begun to agree with me that time after time accounts receivable and inventories analysis can be a terrific barometer for forecasting negative earnings surprises, usually well before Wall Street analysts come to the party. And for a simple reason: many of them either do not utilize this superb tool or if they do, fail to credit it with as much forecasting power as it possesses.

Because I regard this chapter as the most important one in the book, I am going to provide several additional examples to illustrate this point.

Consider the situation of TIE/Communications in the spring of 1984, when the stock was selling in the high teens, having levelled off after a precipitous decline from a fraction over 40 the previous year. Yet the worst seemed behind it, as Wall Street was once again turning bullish on the issue. In the *Quality of Earnings Report* dated April 27, 1984, I observed that in 1983 the firm's inventories had advanced at a considerably more rapid rate than its sales. The actual figures were a 157 percent increase in inventories versus an 88.9 percent advance in sales. This was a red flag, a sign the stock should be avoided. The situation continued into 1984, as Table 8.6 indicates.

TABLE 8.6
TIE/Communications' Sales and Inventories, 1981–1984

(figures in thousands of dollars)

For the year ended:	12/31/84		12/31/83		12/31/82		12/31/81
Net sales	$501,066		$324,078		$171,523		$130,898
		54.6%		88.9%		31.0%	
Inventories	240,000		125,090		48,634		42,940
		91.9%		157.2%		13.3%	

As can be seen, this table indicates that in 1984 TIE's sales increased by 54.6 percent and inventories by 91.9 percent. That March I wrote that "it is our opinion that TIE's inventories imbalance will continue to compromise the Company's profitability in the year 1985."[6]

Let us now turn to DSC Communications, smaller and less well-known than TIE, but with a well-regarded line of digital telephone switches. In 1984, DSC had gone from a low of 17 to a high of 34 and closed the year at 22 1/2. In 1984, the company's earnings advanced to $1.40 a share from $1.02 in 1983. For the three months ended March 31, 1985, the company reported $0.42 per share compared with $0.30 for the same period the previous year. DSC's management acknowledged that:

> In obtaining a significant share of the independent long distance switching/systems market, the Company has met extended payment terms offered by competitors. These extended payment terms have contributed to the higher receivables balances. Other portions of the Company's business have considerably shorter payment terms. Management believes that total inventory and receivables levels relative to revenues will improve by the beginning of 1986.

At the time, DSC's receivables totaled $187.7 million versus $87 million at the end of March, 1984.

Working from the reports, I constructed Table 8.7, which by now you should be able to do on your own. Just enter the revenues, figure out the increases, and do the same for inventories.

TABLE 8.7
DSC Communications' Revenues and Inventories, 1983–1985

(figures in thousands of dollars)

	3/31/85		3/31/84		3/31/83
Revenues (3 months)	$100,514		$44,124		$22,010
		127.7%		100.4%	
Inventories	126,620		36,967		21,897
		242.5%		68.8%	

Here is how I interpreted these figures in June of 1985:

> The above table indicates that for the three months ended March 31, 1985, DSC's revenues increased by approximately 128%, whereas inventories rose by about 242%. These figures compare with revenues advancing by 100 percent and inventories by about 69% for the three months ended March 31, 1984. It is our opinion that DSC's inventories are much too high in relation to the Company's sales. This factor will probably compromise DSC's earnings in the remaining quarters of calendar year 1985.

DSC reported a loss that year, and in late December its stock was selling in the single-digit range.

Take a more familiar example, that of Texas Instruments (TXN), which for the year ending December 31, 1984, came in with earnings of $13.05 a share compared with a loss of $6.09 in 1983. To the casual onlooker it might have appeared that TXN had turned an important corner, while some might have observed that there had been large write-offs in 1983 which resulted in favorable earnings comparisons the following year. Still, on the basis of these figures, TXN seemed on track for future gains.

An analysis of the inventories situation would have resulted in a different conclusion. Let's go through the by now familiar drill in Table 8.8 which appeared in a *Quality of Earnings Report* dated February 20, 1985.

TABLE 8.8
Texas Instruments' Sales and Inventories, 1980–1984

(figures in millions of dollars)

Year ended:	12/31/84	12/31/83	12/31/82	12/31/81	12/31/80
Net sales billed	$5,741.6	$4,579.8	$4,326.6	$4,206.0	$4,074.7
	25.37%	5.85%	2.87%	3.22%	
Inventories (net of progress billings)	489.2	335.6	360.0	372.0	442.7
	45.77%	(6.78%)	(3.23%)	(15.97%)	

Note that inventories declined sharply from 1980 to 1981 and continued on for 1982 and 1983; this is a sign that TXN was cleaning shop. But for 1984, TXN's sales increased by 25 percent while inventories rose by approximately 46 percent, a sign that the old malaise had returned, and bad news from headquarters might be anticipated.

In scrutinizing TXN's 1984 Annual Report, I noted that a lower percentage allowance for doubtful accounts at year end December 31, 1984 accounted for 12 percent of TXN's earnings which came in at $13.05 in the year 1984. In the *Quality of Earnings Report* for February 20, 1985, I observed that "This item, coupled with TXN's inventories imbalance, leads us to believe that TXN will report lower share earnings in the year 1985 than Wall Street is currently forecasting."[7] In 1984, TXN common had reached a high of 149 1/2, and toward the end of the year had slipped to just above 120. By February of 1985 it was down by more than a half dozen points, but still considered a recovery candidate. Then TXN reported a deficit of $0.16 a share for the second quarter and one of $3.30 for the third quarter. Meanwhile the stock slipped badly, going to the mid-80s.

The message had been signaled in the annual report, and investors who monitored the inventory situation would have been among the first to know.

Wang Laboratories (WAN) offers a dramatic example of how inventories can get out of control due to a waning popularity of product lines. This highly regarded purveyor of "offices of the future" gear showed signs of trouble in its annual report for the fiscal year 1984, ended June 30, in which it reported earnings of $1.52 a share versus $1.16 for 1983, at which time the stock was selling in the high 20s.

Now consider the inventories situation, which should be one of the first exercises you perform when completing your initial study of the report. This is shown in Table 8.9.

TABLE 8.9
Wang Laboratories' Sales and Inventories, 1982–1984

(figures in millions of dollars)

Year ended:	6/30/84		6/30/83		6/30/82
Net product sales	$1,699.2		$1,203.0		$927.6
		41.2%		29.7%	
Inventories	562.8		316.2		254.2
		78.0%		24.4%	

We can see that WAN's inventories increased almost twice as much as net sales. The company conceded its inventories were too high, commenting that "management expects to increase funds provided from operations in 1985 with particular emphasis on inventory turnover."[8] And for the first two quarters things seemed to be working out well. Then the proverbial roof caved in as shown in Table 8.10.

TABLE 8.10
Wang Laboratories, Fiscal 1984 and 1985

(earnings per share)

	Fiscal 1985	Fiscal 1984
Sept.	$0.36	$0.28
Dec.	0.40	0.35
Mar.	0.12	0.36
Jun.	(0.77)	0.52
	$0.11	$1.51

Sometimes a phenomenon exists which I call "positive inventory component divergence," meaning simply the reverse of some of the illustrations described thus far, which were of negative inventory divergences. The positive version transpires when the raw materials component of inventories is advancing much more rapidly than the work-in-process and finished goods components. Imagine what this might mean. The company receives many new orders, and management realizes that an inventories buildup is required. So it simultaneously ships products from its finished goods inventory (which declines) while ordering raw materials in larger amounts (so this component of inventories is enlarged). This, of course, is good news, and should trigger the bullish impulses in your psyche.

Such was the situation at Raychem (RYC), a high quality material science firm that manufactures high performance products for the aerospace, construction, electronics, electrical power, process, and telecommunications industries. For the fiscal year ended June 30, 1985, we learned that RYC's earnings had declined to $2.84 a share from $3.84 in fiscal 1984. One might have been justified in concluding that the stock should be avoided, and indeed a sell-off was in progress. After having risen to a high of 93 in the summer of 1983, RYC declined to under 60 in early 1984, where it stood that summer.

An analysis of RYC's inventory position convinced me that the company would perform better in fiscal 1986 than the Street believed. The main reason for this conclusion was RYC's highly positive inventory component divergence revealed in the 1985 report. Table 8.11 gives the situation as shown there, for anyone to see.

TABLE 8.11
Raychem's Inventory Components, 1982–1985

(figures in thousands of dollars)

Inventories	1985	1984	1983	1982
Raw materials	$56,347	$36,219	$29,986	$30,659
Work-in-process	41,156	33,694	34,168	34,600
Finished goods	61,625	51,428	50,689	45,773

Note that between 1984 and 1985, Raychem's raw materials advanced at a much more rapid rate than the work-in-process and finished goods components of inventories, symptomatic of a substantial increase in production. It has been my experience that many companies that exhibit positive inventory divergences report higher earnings in the year ahead than most analysts anticipate.

It turned out that such indeed happened. For the second fiscal quarter ended December 31, 1985, Raychem earned $1.55 a share compared with $1.00 in the second fiscal quarter ended December 31, 1984. For the six months ended December 31, 1985, Raychem's earnings were $2.46 versus $1.62 for the same period the previous year.

Perhaps this is the place to observe that shareholders would have gleaned little of this from the company's quarterlies. Typically, most of these reports contain little but the barebones statistics and a brief comment from management; indeed, some don't even contain balance sheets. For example, in its shareholder quarterlies IBM lumps together receivables, inventories, and prepaid expenses. Therefore, in order to conduct a thorough examination of a company's quarterly statement, it may be necessary to secure the Form 10-Q report it files with the SEC. These contain balance sheets and make the proper segregation of data. Note that the 10-Q need not be filed until 45 days after the quarterly reporting period, and that most companies do not file their quarterlies until within five days of the reporting period deadline.

Occasionally getting information can be like pulling teeth. But it is there, and investors who have respect for their many thousands of invested dollars should understand that nothing comes without effort.

By now I'm certain you get the idea, but let's have one more case to wrap up this most important concept. Equatorial Communications (EQUA), an important player in the glamorous business of satellite telecommunications, came in with earnings of $0.49 a share for the year ended December 31, 1984, compared with $0.15 the previous year (both figures before extraordinary items, credits of $0.01 and $0.15 for 1984 and 1983 respectively). At the time the stock was in the high teens, on the way up to 20 by February. This was uncalled for, given the inventory situation revealed in the annual report, there for anyone to see, though few apparently did. (See Table 8.12.)

TABLE 8.12
Equatorial Communications' Revenues, Accounts Receivable and Inventories, 1982–1984

(figures in thousands of dollars)

For the year ended:	12/31/84	12/31/83	12/31/82
Total revenues	$38,297	$17,860	$9,634
	114.4%	85.4%	
Accounts receivable	10,204	2,763	1,320
	269.3%	109.3%	
Inventories	8,474	1,909	912
	343.9%	109.3%	

Study these figures and see if your conclusion squares with mine, which appeared in the *Quality of Earnings Report* of March 20, 1985:

> Readers should note the sizable buildup in EQUA's accounts receivable and inventories at year end December 31, 1984. In 1984, EQUA's TOTAL revenues increased by 114%, whereas accounts receivable rose by 269% and inventories advanced by 344%.
>
> As a result of EQUA's high accounts receivable and inventories position, the Company has drawn down heavily on its cash and tem-

porary cash investments. At year end December 31, 1984, EQUA's cash investments declined to $4.7 million from $17.1 million at year end December 31, 1983. During the same time span, long-term debt due within one year and long-term debt due after one year totaled approximately $12 million at year end 1984 compared with zero at year end 1983.

EQUA's accounts receivable and inventories should be closely monitored by investors. It is our opinion that EQUA has an accounts receivable and inventories imbalance that will compromise the Company's share earnings for the year ending December 31, 1985. Hence, we believe that EQUA will report lower share earnings than *Wall Street* is *currently* anticipating.

By the end of the year EQUA was selling for only 8 1/2 a share. It turned out that for the year ended December 31, 1985, EQUA incurred a loss of $0.11 a share, before extraordinary items.

In all of these examples, with the exception of the positive Raychem illustration, the companies subsequently reported earnings substantially below forecasts at the time the original *Quality of Earnings Report* commentaries were offered. The message is quite clear. Investors who ignore accounts receivables and inventories— especially in high tech and consumer-sensitive industries—run unnecessary risks without the chance of commensurate rewards. Next time you hear some wild story about a glamour stock and are tempted to buy without investigating, think about Ben Smith and that factory with the smokeless smokestacks.

CHAPTER 9

Debt and Cash Flow Analysis

DURING THE FIRST HALF OF THE 1980s two different kinds of investors explored the intricate highways and byways of corporate debt. Lured by high real interest rates, those who traditionally had been involved with equities rushed to the government and corporate markets, while a far more spectacular crew of characters devised methods of utilizing debt to acquire some of America's largest and most prestigious corporations.

We are all familiar with the first group—you may be one of that number. And readers of the financial press know full well of the other—corporate raiders and risk arbitrageurs such as T. Boone Pickens, Ivan Boesky, Carl Icahn, and the like. In these exercises investors, usually insiders, utilized debt to retire equity, transforming publicly owned companies with manageable debt to equity ratios into privately owned firms with enormous debt.

How far did this go? In 1984 nonfinancial corporations replaced $77 billion of equity with $60.8 billion in bonds and $98.9 billion in short-term debt, and the pace quickened thereafter. It is estimated that, in 1985, the gross reduction in the supply of equity capital approximated $110 billion. It became a kind of game at the large investment houses where Drexel Burnham Lambert, previously considered a second tier house, emerged as the chief purveyor of "junk bonds," a term barely known in the Street at that time, and certainly not to individual investors. Kohlberg Kravis Roberts

& Co., a relatively obscure concern, emerged as a specialist in leveraged buyouts and skyrocketed to fame and fortune.

In their hands these low rated debts became the coin used to lure stockholders into accepting their deals and cooperating in the leveraged buyouts. In time the new owners would sell off assets and use the funds to retire a portion of that debt, but this need not concern us here. Rather, consider that in the 1980s investors became more aware that debt was an important aspect of a corporate balance sheet, and that no shrewd player could afford to ignore it. Also, note that the rules of the game were changing, that a debt structure once deemed dangerous was coming to be accepted, not only by the Street, but by investors as well. The mania for junk bond mutual funds in 1985–1986 bore striking witness to this phenomenon.

Benjamin Graham, in many respects the godfather of us all, devoted much of his time to debt analysis. The prudent Graham, so popular an analyst during the Great Depression when most investors sought to maximize safety, was wary of firms that required substantial amounts to service debt. In his classic text, *Security Analysis*, Graham concluded that a corporation with a total debt equal to 35 percent of capital would be approaching the upper limit of conservative borrowing for a typical industrial concern.[1]

The Graham approach was challenged in the late 1950s by Franco Modigliani who, with an associate, Merton Miller, published several articles pooh-poohing the idea that debt structure should be a major consideration in making investment decisions. Indeed, under some circumstances, said this future Nobel laureate in Economic Science, a corporation might be justified in going to 100 percent debt. Not that Modigliani was in sympathy with the takeover tycoons of the 1980s. Rather, he suggested that any attempt to substitute a rigid ideology for careful scrutiny of the individual case was bound to result in poor investment decisions.[2]

I am of several minds regarding debt, though the Modigliani approach seems sensible enough. But this does not extend to debt analysis, which is an important aspect of the analytical process. This is particularly true for troubled companies and those in the process of being taken over, or even more importantly, fighting a takeover by issuing debt of their own.

It is important to note that the playing field has changed in recent years, and that participants have to keep this in mind when making decisions. This isn't to say that investors have to check their analytical talents and chuck Graham into the waste bin when considering where to place their funds. Rather, they have to be prepared to seek the most plausible research and carefully arrive at conclusions, while at the same time being on guard when confounded by the machinations of a takeover king.

Recall that in Chapter 5 (*Nonoperating and/or Nonrecurring Income*) I related that in acquiring Norton Simon and Esmark, Beatrice Companies was transformed into a top-heavy conglomerate whose total debt had advanced from $1 billion to $5 billion. Subsequently the company reduced its debt load by selling off $1.4 billion in assets which were divested from Beatrice.

Because of this situation, and what I regarded as the low quality of Beatrice's earnings, when the stock was in the low 30s in the summer of 1985 I suggested it be avoided. Based upon conventional analysis, this made sense. But there was nothing conventional about the investment scene at that time. Kohlberg Kravis put together a deal to take Beatrice private at $45 a share.

Where had I gone wrong? By failing to fully consider what Kohlberg Kravis would see in Beatrice—an array of well-known and established brand name items that would bring in a stream of earnings for years, perhaps decades to come, and more to the point, a substantial cash flow per share which, in recent years, had been running at twice earnings. Kohlberg Kravis obviously intended to sell off some of those branded items and use the proceeds to retire a large portion of the debt incurred in the purchase. Then, after further restructuring, and when market conditions were ripe, the new management would take portions of the slimmed-down Beatrice public in new equity offerings, reaping a huge financial reward for their efforts.

What this means is that debt and cash flow analysis are useful tools in assessing the ability of a company not only to service debt, but also to grow and flourish. However, this assumes the company will continue to exist in its present form, and not become the object of a takeover bid. It also suggests that not all "undervalued" situations will attract the takeover artists, but rather those in industries deemed attractive from a business point of view or firms that possess large unrealized assets. In recent years broadcasting and foods fell into the former group, the large oils into the latter.

If these words were read in 1984 or 1985, and even early 1986, you might be tempted to skip to the next chapter, for at that time takeovers were all the rage. But a rising stock market diminishes the urge to go private, since the higher priced equities would require much higher bid prices than previously were the case. Moreover, there are signs the leveraged buyouts have gone too far. Modigliani, who at one time seemed to smile benevolently at them, went out of his way to indicate that they fell out of the purview of his analysis. "I am not in accord" (with leveraged buyouts), he said in the autumn of 1985. "They are not to improve corporations' capital structure, but are the result of the desire to acquire corporations by those who lack the capital."[3] So continue on, but be aware that I am talking here of analysis of ongoing concerns, and not the object of some takeover artist's lust.

Start out by assembling a toolbox of ratios having to do with the capital structure of a corporation:

Long-Term Debt to Equity Ratio:

$$\frac{\text{Long-Term Debt}}{\text{Shareholders' Equity}}$$

Total Debt to Equity Ratio:

$$\frac{\text{Current Liabilities} + \text{Long-Term Debt}}{\text{Shareholders' Equity}}$$

Times Interest Earned Ratio

$$\frac{\text{Operating Income}}{\text{Annual Interest Payments}}$$

The above ratios are useful in determining (1) the extent to which nonequity capital is used in a firm; and (2) the long-term ability of a firm to meet payments to nonequity suppliers of capital.[4] This is another way of saying how much the firm must throw off in cash flow to satisfy creditors before having earnings for the common shares.

Most Wall Street analysts rely heavily upon the long-term debt to equity ratio, and this is often provided in research reports sent out to clients. While this ratio can be useful, it should be noted that in recent years, given the uncertain interest rate environment, many corporations have taken to financing a good deal of their business with short-term debt. Indeed, an imaginative treasurer with a keen insight into money market activities can earn as much for a company as a plant manager, simply by switching debt from long-term to short and vice versa at the right time. And an investment banker with some imagination can arrange debt for equity swaps and the reverse to increase earnings, decrease interest or dividend payouts, and perform all sorts of miraculous things for clients.

This is to suggest that the long-term debt to equity ratio, though still worth considering, should be viewed alongside the *total debt* to equity ratio, that takes in short-term debt as well. This can be calculated without much trouble. Simply add the short-term debt to the long and refigure the ratio according to the formula. And if you see a long-term debt to equity ratio of 20 percent, next to a total debt ratio of, say, 50 percent, reflect on the altered perception of the balance sheet thus presented.

In analyzing the debt picture of a corporation, the investor should first turn to the Income Statement and glance at the interest expense, if any. Then interest expenses should be added back to the pre-tax income of the corporation. Next, interest expense should be computed as a percentage of adjusted pre-tax income. Why? Because if you do this, you will obtain a clearer view of the financial strength of the company. Simply stated, the higher the percentage, the more leveraged the firm is, and the greater the impact of higher earnings to the upside, and lower earnings to the downside.

Now for a striking example of this situation. Recall the analysis of International Harvester, now reborn as Navistar under a management fully aware of the sour taste the old name left in the mouths of customers and investors. Table 9.1 illustrates the then International Harvester's interest expense for the fiscal years ended October 31, 1976 through October 31, 1980.

Table 9.1 indicates that a large portion of International Har-

TABLE 9.1
International Harvester's Interest Expense, 1976–1980

(all figures in millions of dollars for fiscal years ended October 31)

	1980	1979	1978	1977	1976
Pre-tax income	$(891.6)	$379.2	$193.7	$249.7	$219.4
Interest expense	288.9	148.4	125.9	117.7	121.3
Pre-tax income adjusted for interest expense (or loss)	(602.7)	527.6	319.6	367.4	340.7
Interest expense as a percentage of adjusted pre-tax income	—	28%	39%	32%	36%

vester's pre-tax income (loss) from 1976 through 1980 was being consumed by interest charges. In particular, note that between 1979 and 1980 interest expense comes to almost $289 million from $148 million.

When investors see this kind of situation develop they should hear alarms go off in their heads. Rapidly growing interest charges as a percent of income can be caused by several factors: increasing borrowings with stable income, or declining income in relation to debt. If it is the former, consider whether the borrowings were made out of distress or to capitalize upon prospects for growth, and act accordingly. But should the percentage rise substantially due to poor earnings, be on guard for future problems.

In this case turn to Statements of Changes in Financial Position in the company's annual report and scrutinize the statement. Reproduced on pp. 132–33 is what was found in the International Harvester 1980 report.

This statement reveals that in 1980 International Harvester added around $379 million to long-term debt (additions of approximately $443 million to longer-term debt minus $64 million in reduction of debt). Also, the company issued $150 million of preferred stock and notes payable increased by $397 million.

While I criticized Harvester early and often on its management commentaries and operations, I do concede that it did well in providing investors with a ratios table relating to its capitalization, which is reproduced on page 134.

Note the deterioration in the ratio of total borrowings and redeemable preferred stock to common stockholders' equity and convertible preferred stock, that of total borrowings to common stockholders' equity and preferred stocks, and long-term debt as a percent of common stockholders' equity, preferred stocks, and long-term debt. In the February 16, 1981 issue of the *Quality of Earnings Report* I wrote:

> Alas, the combination of the lengthy UAW strike, soaring interest rates, and a recessionary economic environment, have raised havoc with HR's financial ratios. Readers should take note of the fact that after a steady four years of improvement in the ratios since 1975, the year 1980 saw the ratios deteriorating below those in year 1975.

Once again, the pigeons came home to roost. For the fiscal year ended October 1, 1980, HR wound up losing $12 a share. In

Statements of Changes in Financial Position

(Thousands of dollars)
For the Years Ended October 31

	1980	1979
Working Capital (Used) Provided by Operations		
Income (loss) from continuing operations	$ (369,628)	$ 369,562
Items not affecting working capital:		
Depreciation and amortization	129,646	126,798
Undistributed earnings of nonconsolidated companies	(119,849)	(102,728)
Deferred income taxes	(59,956)	159,021
Other	961	2,033
Working capital (used) provided by continuing operations	(418,826)	554,686
Wisconsin Steel, net (loss)	(27,700)	—
Item not affecting working capital—deferred income taxes	(27,200)	—
Working capital (used) by Wisconsin Steel	(54,900)	—
Total working capital (used) provided by operations	(473,726)	554,686
Other Sources of Working Capital		
Additions to long-term debt	442,858	117,690
Issuance of preferred stock—Series C	150,000	—
Issuance of common stock	32,914	30,726
Property disposals	16,025	8,685
Total other sources of working capital	641,797	157,101

Other Uses of Working Capital		
Capital expenditures	383,763	284,907
Cash dividends	83,141	76,389
Reduction of long-term debt	63,960	102,061
Increase in investments and long-term receivables	67,136	52,060
Other	15,280	13,792
Total other uses of working capital	613,280	529,209
Increase (Decrease) in Working Capital	(445,209)	182,578
Working Capital		
At beginning of the year	1,392,398	1,209,820
At end of the year	$ 947,189	$1,392,398
Changes in Working Capital		
Current assets—increase (decrease):		
Cash	$ 111,901	$ (2,051)
Receivables	(169,548)	113,974
Refundable income taxes	132,762	8,927
Inventories	(11,265)	450,011
Other current assets	97,800	46,197
Current liabilities—decrease (increase):		
Notes payable	(397,550)	(105,932)
Accounts payable	(41,150)	(333,657)
Accrued liabilities	(147,229)	(38,517)
Current maturities of long-term debt	(20,930)	43,626
Increase (Decrease) in Working Capital	$ (445,209)	$ 182,578

See Notes to Financial Statements.

Ratios

	1980	1979	1978	1977	1976	1975	1974	1973	1972	1971
Current assets to current liabilities	1.4-1	1.7-1	1.8-1	2.2-1	2.2-1	2.1-1	1.7-1	1.8-1	2.0-1	2.2-1
Total borrowings and redeemable preferred stock to common stockholders' equity and convertible preferred stock	1.21-1	.67-1	.75-1	.77-1	.84-1	1.08-1	.99-1	.81-1	.76-1	.65-1
Total borrowings to common stockholders' equity and preferred stocks	1.15-1	.63-1	.70-1	.72-1	.78-1	1.01-1	.99-1	.81-1	.76-1	.65-1
Long-term debt as a percent of common stockholders' equity, preferred stocks and long-term debt	41%	30%	33%	36%	37%	40%	32%	28%	28%	27%

early 1981 its stock sold for as much as 26—and then plummeted to 6, as the firm was buried under an avalanche of debt and rumors of an impending Chapter XI bankruptcy echoed through the Street. This was avoided when the company arranged a capital restructuring, but the outlook was hardly cheerful. In 1982 Harvester common finally bottomed out at 2 3/4. Could this have been anticipated? Perhaps not, but anyone who noted those financial ratios in early 1981 would certainly have been forewarned that trouble lay ahead.

Now let's look at another example of a company with a highly leveraged balance sheet, namely Thousand Trails. The firm's rationale was intriguing. With the national parks crowded, Thousand Trails intended to develop large private parks, with all kinds of recreational services, in which individuals yearning for that kind of vacation could purchase time shares. The company sells memberships for cash or, more often, on an installment basis. For book reporting purposes, it records membership sales in full upon execution of contracts. Installment sales require a down payment of at least 10 percent of the sales price. All marketing costs and an allowance for estimated contract collection losses are recorded currently.

Table 9.2 indicates Thousand Trails' interest expense as a percentage of pre-tax income for the calendar years 1982–1984. Note that interest expense has been added back to pre-tax income with the adjusted pre-tax income then being divided by interest expense. The computation of interest costs is done prior to the capitalization of interest.

TABLE 9.2
Thousand Trails, Inc.

(figures in millions of dollars)

	1984	1983	1982
Earnings before deferred income taxes	$35.40	$22.63	$15.10
Total interest costs	11.01	6.41	6.76
Earnings before deferred income taxes adjusted for total interest costs	46.41	29.04	21.86
Total interest costs as a percent of adjusted earnings before deferred income taxes	24%	22%	31%

What we see here is that in 1982 Thousand Trails had a rather large ratio of interest to adjusted earnings before deferred income taxes, due to the important investments necessary in the early stages of the company's history. This declined sharply in 1983 and appeared steady the following year. A quick glance at these numbers might have led one to conclude that Thousand Trails was in good shape. But look further.

A turn to the company's Statements of Changes in Financial Position for 1982–1984 (reproduced here) reveals that Thousand Trails had indeed been expending considerable sums for resort acquisition and development and that borrowings collateralized by contracts receivable had risen significantly. Between 1983 and 1984 cash expended for these purposes increased to $59.3 million from $20.6 million and the proceeds of borrowings collateralized by contracts receivable totaled $63.3 million in 1984 against only $851,000 in 1983. Now that's a sizable jump, one that fairly demands further investigation.

In order to uncover interest expenses the reader would have to turn to the footnotes which, as has been indicated, are one of the most important parts of the annual reports too often overlooked by investors. There, in Footnote H, is an item labeled "Costs and Expenses," where one can see that interest expenses in 1984 leaped to $11 million from 1983's $6.4 million. Here is that footnote:

> The Company capitalizes interest as a component of the cost of significant improvements to resorts. Total interest costs were $6,756,000 in 1982, $6,411,000 in 1983 and $11,007,000 in 1984, of which $2,553,000, $2,454,000 and $5,883,000, respectively, were capitalized.

This leads inevitably to a look at the liability side of the balance sheet. See page 137.

Utilizing the figures from the table, we can calculate the company's total debt to equity ratio. The current portion of long-term debt is added to long-term debt for a total of $122.2 million for 1984 and $53.2 million for 1983, a 130 percent advance. We then add back the current and long-term portions of deferred income taxes which totaled $45 million in 1984 and $29 million in 1983 back to shareholders' equity of $80.9 million in 1984 and $60.3 million in 1983. (The reason we do this is because deferred income taxes are a "paper" accounting entry, which may never be paid by

Thousand Trails, Inc. and Subsidiaries Consolidated Balance Sheets

Liabilities and Shareholders' Equity December 31,	1983	1984
Current Liabilities:		
Accounts payable	$ 2,415,000	$ 5,980,000
Accrued salaries	3,714,000	6,110,000
Prepaid membership dues	1,887,000	2,706,000
Other liabilities	1,180,000	3,322,000
Current portion of long-term debt	5,896,000	9,359,000
Deferred income taxes	7,026,000	9,197,000
Total Current Liabilities	22,118,000	36,674,000
Long-Term Debt	47,343,000	112,895,000
Deferred Income Taxes	22,007,000	35,856,000
Deferred Rental Revenue		3,428,000
Commitments and Contingencies (Note G)		
Shareholders' Equity:		
Common Stock, no par value—		
Authorized, 15,000,000 shares;		
Issued and outstanding,		
10,197,145 and 10,658,476	29,358,000	30,934,000
Retained Earnings	30,941,000	49,983,000
	60,299,000	80,917,000
	$151,767,000	$269,770,000

a corporation. Also, if the corporation is liquidated, the shareholders' equity is likely to be increased by the accumulated provisions for deferred taxes.)

This type of calculation results in a total debt to equity ratio of 47 percent in 1984 compared to 37 percent in 1983, a 10 percent increase.

Now ask yourself if Thousand Trails is too highly leveraged, which is to say, has too high a level of debt. On the one hand, this is a business in which large debt is required, but on the other, the industry itself is new and untested. In my view, Thousand Trails was a high risk security, in part because of the leverage in an industry where there is no true means of knowing what constitutes a prudent balance sheet.

In 1985 Thousand Trails' share earnings plummeted to $0.16. The reason: a slowdown in sales which, on top of those high interest

Thousand Trails, Inc. and Subsidiaries Consolidated Statements of Changes in Financial Position

Year Ended December 31,	1982	1983	1984
Operations:			
Cash Received—			
Membership sales	$ 22,582,000	$ 27,738,000	$ 30,549,000
Collections on contracts receivable, including interest	19,278,000	28,619,000	44,060,000
Dues and resort revenues	7,336,000	10,507,000	15,586,000
Other	133,000	211,000	1,288,000
	49,329,000	67,075,000	91,483,000
Cash Expended—			
Marketing expenses	23,211,000	32,832,000	48,653,000
General and administrative expenses	7,739,000	11,325,000	12,510,000
Resort maintenance and operations	6,127,000	8,625,000	13,743,000
	37,077,000	52,782,000	74,906,000
Cash provided by operations before debt service and resort acquisition and development	12,252,000	14,293,000	16,577,000
Cash expended for resort acquisition and development	(12,631,000)	(20,609,000)	(59,316,000)
Interest expense	(4,203,000)	(3,957,000)	(4,984,000)
Principal payments on debt related to resort properties	(2,388,000)	(4,337,000)	(4,688,000)
Cash used in operations	(6,970,000)	(14,610,000)	(52,411,000)

Other Sources (Uses) of Cash:

Issuance of common stock	4,161,000	17,756,000	989,000
Proceeds of borrowings collateralized by contracts receivable	8,646,000	851,000	63,284,000
Purchase of resort operating equipment, net of related borrowings of $1,008,000, $1,302,000, and $3,165,000	(313,000)	(1,711,000)	(5,953,000)
Purchase of construction and other equipment, net of related borrowings of $64,000, $86,000, and $96,000	(1,177,000)	(1,232,000)	(4,266,000)
Principal payments on notes payable and credit line arrangements	(735,000)	(1,109,000)	(306,000)
Investment in preferred stock	(3,000,000)		
Other, net	(81,000)	122,000	(463,000)
	7,501,000	14,677,000	53,285,000
Increase in Cash	531,000	67,000	874,000
Cash:			
Beginning of year	172,000	703,000	770,000
End of year	$ 703,000	$ 770,000	$ 1,644,000

charges, placed the company in peril. Here is the way the situation was analyzed in the December 13, 1985 edition of *Value Line*:

> What a difference a year makes. When we reported on Thousand Trails 12 months ago, the stock was flying high at $28 a share. Since then, it has plunged to 6 7/8, driven down, we think, by the failure of a rumored merger and lower than expected earnings. Abnormally high selling expenses in the September period sent share earnings plummeting to 10 cents, only one-seventh of those tallied in the '85 interim.

Value Line was cautiously optimistic regarding the future. "But Thousand Trails is shifting gears. The company plans to spend the next several years digesting the new resorts that were added in 1984 and '85. The slowdown in expansion will lessen the need for additional debt, which should shore-up what is now a highly leveraged balance sheet." Perhaps. We shall see. But anyone performing the kind of analysis sketched here would have been able to perceive that Thousand Trails was a risky situation. As every investor knows, the greater the opportunity for profit, the greater usually is the risk. I'm not suggesting you should shy away from such risks, but only that you should know what you are getting into when you make a commitment.

A knowledge of just how much cash a company takes in from its operating activities during any given time period is the kind of information that forms the bedrock of analysis. This is known as the *Cash Flow from Operations* (CFFO), to be distinguished from the term, "Cash Flow," which refers to the sum of profits plus depreciation allowances. There are major problems in measuring CFFO because of the many and confusing methods of presentation of the data. Investors instinctively know this is an important matter. After wading through annual reports, they wonder if the company emerged from the year in better shape than it was when it began. Leopold Bernstein, one of the pioneers in the field, wrote:

> The best defense that can be used by credit and equity analysts against the misleading presentations of CFFO is to approach the analysis of financial statements armed with a clean understanding of what CFFO is and how it is computed. At present, an analyst who accepts a published figure designated as CFFO or by similar terminology runs the risk of working with inaccurate and misleading measures. A working knowledge of how CFFO is computed will enable the

analyst to assess the validity of the figure disclosed and, if need be, to adjust it to the correct amount.[5]

Professor Bernstein has developed a worksheet that will facilitate the conversion of Statements of Changes in Financial Position presented in a great variety of formats into a statement that will explain the inflows and outflows of cash including the cash generated by operations.[6] This worksheet utilizes, as an example, data from the 1984 Kellogg Company Annual Report for the years ended December 31, 1983 and 1984. Also included are the Kellogg Statement of Changes in Consolidated Financial Position from which data in the worksheet are drawn. What I have done is translate the Kellogg figures into what I deem to be a clearer and more useful set of statistics. Look them over and see if you agree.

A review of the worksheet which converts Kellogg's 1984 and 1983 Statement of Changes in Financial Position into a cash format will reveal the following:

1. Every single item in Kellogg's Statement of Changes in Financial Position must be fitted into its appropriate category in the conversion worksheet. In this example, letter keys are used in order to facilitate the reader's understanding of the conversion process.
2. Once every item in the Statement of Changes in Financial Position has been transferred to the cash flow worksheet and the major subtotals and totals have been computed, the increase or decrease of cash for the period will have been fully explained. That explanation reinforces the validity and the accuracy of the conversion process and also validates that important subtotal entitled, "Cash from Operations."

Kellogg Company and Subsidiaries

Changes in Consolidated Financial Position

Year ended December 31.

(millions)		1984	1983	1982
Financial resources were provided by:				
Net earnings	A	$ 250.5	$ 242.7	$ 227.8
Depreciation	B	63.9	62.8	55.9
Deferred income taxes and other	C	62.6	12.0	27.1
Working capital provided by operations	D	377.0	317.5	310.8
Issuance of long-term debt	J	348.1	1.5	
Issuance of common stock	K	6.7	1.1	.4
Property disposals	L	12.0	38.0	5.3
Recognition of tax lease benefits	M	3.1	6.2	12.0
Other	M	.9	.5	3.1
Total resources provided		747.8	364.8	331.6

Financial resources were applied to:

Additions to properties	N	228.9	N	156.7	121.1
Cash dividends	P	123.6	P	124.0	116.6
Purchase of treasury stock	Q	577.9			
Investment in tax leases			S	11.6	14.2
Reduction in long-term debt	O	2.7	O	3.6	75.7
Other	T	14.6	T	10.5	13.9
Total resources applied		947.7		306.4	341.5
Less effect of exchange rate changes on working capital	R	15.1	R	12.5	14.9
Increase (decrease) in working capital		$ (215.0)		$ 45.9	$ (24.8)

Changes in components of working capital:

Cash	U	$ 71.8	U	$ 35.6	$ 36.0
Marketable securities	V	(11.7)	V	53.4	(39.9)
Accounts receivable	E	25.4	E	16.4	(18.2)
Inventories	F	4.3	F	(10.9)	(3.5)
Prepaid expenses	G	(1.4)	G	4.5	7.5
Current maturities of debt	J	(320.6)	J	(13.5)	10.0
Accounts payable	H	(10.6)	H	(17.7)	5.4
Accrued liabilities	I	27.8	I	(21.9)	(22.1)
Increase (decrease) in working capital		$ (215.0)		$ 45.9	$ (24.8)

See notes to financial statements.

TABLE 9.3
Cash Statement for Kellogg Co.

(in millions $)*

Sources of Cash:		1984	1983	19__	19__	19__
From operations:						
Income before extraordinary items	A	$ 250.5	$ 242.7	$	$	$
+Expense (−Revenue) not affecting w/c:						
Depreciation & Amortization	B	63.9	62.8			
Noncurrent deferred income taxes	C	62.6	12.0			
=w/c from operations	D	377.0	317.5			

+ (−) changes in current assets and current liabilities related to operations:				
(I) D in receivables	E	(25.4)	(16.4)	
(I) D in inventories	F	(4.3)	10.9	
(I) D in prepaid expenses	G	1.4	(4.5)	
I (D) in accounts payable	H	10.6	17.7	
I (D) accruals	I	(27.8)	21.9	
I or D in other current operating accounts				
=Cash from operations		331.5	347.1	
Unusual gains (losses), net of tax (describe)				
Less noncash items				
Long-term borrowing (348.1 + 320.6)	J	668.7	15.0	
Short-term borrowing (net of repayments)				
Sale of common or preferred stock	K	6.7	1.1	
Sale of plant & equipment	L	12.0	38.0	
Other (3.1 + .9)	M	4.0	6.7	
Other				
Total Sources		1022.9	407.9	

(continued)

TABLE 9.3 (continued)

Uses of Cash:		1984	1983	19__	19__	19__	19__
Additions to plant & equipment	N	$ 228.9	$ 156.7	$	$	$	$
Additions to other noncurrent assets							
Reductions in long-term debt $xx and (I) D in current portion of lt debt $xx	O	2.7	3.6				
Dividends $xx and (I) D in dividend payments $xx	P	123.6	124.0				
Purchase common or preferred stock	Q	577.9					
Other—Exchange Rates Change	R	15.1	12.5				
Other—Investment in Tax Leases	S		11.6				
Other	T	14.6	10.5				
Total Uses		962.8	318.9				
INCREASE (DECREASE) IN CASH & MARKETABLE SECURITIES		60.1**	89.0**				

Cash (U)	71.8	35.6
Marketable Securities (V)	(11.7)	53.4
	+60.1**	+89.0**

*Derive all figures from company's Statement of Changes in Financial Position *including* net change in each working capital component. Then, calculate for yourself the sub-totals titled w/c from operations, cash from operations, total sources, and total uses.

CHAPTER 10

Dividends: The Tender Trap

CONSULT ANY COLLEGE TEXT on investments and you will find that creditors (bondholders) are rewarded for their loans by the payment of interest, while the owners of the company (the stockholders) receive dividends. In reality, however, the situation is somewhat different and certainly more complex. Both bond and stock investors are in for the relatively short haul. Many institutions may own both bonds and equities for decades, but this is no longer the case for the majority of individual investors. Few purchasers of long-term bonds intend to hold them to maturity. Rather, they buy them in the expectation that interest rates will decline and the bonds appreciate in price, and while they are waiting, they will collect satisfactory payments in the form of interest. As for stockholders, they feel no ties of ownership, but rather purchase stocks hoping the price will rise for a variety of reasons, and while they wait for this to happen, dividend payments might provide a nice cushion.

Bondholders must be paid their due, since loans have to be honored if the company is to remain in business. Dividends on stocks are another matter. Solid, substantial companies can thrive without such payouts, and indeed many do. In fact, managements might consider that such payments are unnecessary, even harmful to the operations of the company. Pay your creditors, by all means. But fork over perfectly good cash to stockholders as dividends? "Why give money to those strangers?" is the way one CEO put it in a moment of candor brought on by indulgence in strong spirits.

For that is what stockholders are. They care little about the firm's long-term welfare, but rather hope for profits from the purchase of paper. Indeed, the well-managed, healthy concern has its eye upon growth, knowing that it is made possible by a strong and intelligent labor force. Far better to reward them than the stockholders, since employees have a much stronger stake in the company than do those transient "owners," who would sell their share in an instant if they felt its prospects were poor.

Are there any good reasons for managements to pay dividends? Of course. If the company knows it will have to sell additional shares and wants to maintain the price of the common so as to make the financings less expensive than otherwise might be the case, dividends do make sense. Such is the situation with utilities, for example. Industrial concerns that are badly managed and, as a result, have stocks with low price/earnings multiples will increase dividends in the hope that the stocks will rise, and so discourage would-be raiders. Indeed, dividends often establish a price "floor" in the form of a yield that will attract investors interested in obtaining their rewards in that form.

I have a certain distrust of firms with generous dividend policies, and so should you. Consider a firm with $5 million in "excess" cash. If a healthy operation, it might use the money to fund research and development; or to lower the price of its product so as to increase market share; or for many other operations to enhance the value of the enterprise. Suppose, however, that it can't find anything in the company worth the investment. That firm might be thought of as having reached a dead end. And in such a case, it might increase the dividend to placate shareholders and stave off takeover artists.

The message is clear, and stated most forcefully by management guru Peter Drucker, who wrote that all revenues of a healthy company are used to pay for past, present, and future expenses—past (interest charges), present (wages, rents, and raw materials), and future (research and development and expansion). Indeed, said Drucker, vibrant firms are constantly trying to raise additional funds so as to capitalize on the juicy prospects they find on all sides. Ailing corporations in stagnant industries, with little in the way of new opportunities, use surplus funds to increase payouts.

These funds are also used to repurchase shares, though as will be seen there are also sensible reasons for the practice. There are two ways to increase earnings per share—earn more money, or shrink the number of shares. Generally speaking, the former is the preferred method, the latter is resorted to only when all else fails. Which would you look for in the stocks you are thinking of buying? For the answer, consider two companies. Both have doubled earnings per share, the first through growth, the second by means of shrinking the amount of equity. Which is the dynamic entity? The answer should be obvious.

Consider an actual case, that of Detroit's Big Three automakers. In January, 1984, Chrysler announced it would repurchase up to 25 percent of its outstanding shares, and the following year Ford said it would buy back 30 million of its 185 million shares. Then, in March, 1986, General Motors got into the act by stating it would expend close to $2 billion to retire chunks of its common and Class E and H shares. How might this help the firm? It will boost earnings per share and perhaps, in this way, cause their prices to rise. In the case of the Class H common this could be important, since GM has guaranteed it will be selling for at least $60 a share by the end of 1989, and at the time of the announcement the stock was going for 38 1/4. But that was more than three-and-a-half years away, and GM had plenty of time to maneuver.

Perhaps stockholders will benefit from this move, but there might have been another way to boost earnings per share: put that $2 billion into profitable operations at the firm and reap rewards from performance. Detroit's Big Three apparently have less confidence in their ability to make money from such operations and so have opted to take the buyback route. Indeed, there remained an even more intriguing option: the companies might have lowered the prices of their products, in this way aggressively challenging foreign corporations for market share. This path too was avoided.

Rapidly expanding companies cannot afford to pay dividends or repurchase shares. Companies with excess cash should use it to buy back equity, not increase the dividend sharply. And finally, corporations with dividend payouts high in relation to earnings are to be carefully studied to uncover management's reasons for such a policy.

Those who are uncomfortable with this approach might take heart by considering the words of Benjamin Graham and other fun-

damentalists to whom high and increasing payouts were hallmarks
of a powerful company whose stock should be purchased. This attitude was nurtured by the Great Depression, when businessmen
were understandably timid about growth and expansion and investors insisted upon generous dividends. The Graham view is quite
clear on this point:

> Success of the typical concern has been measured by its ability to pay
> liberal and steadily increasing dividends on its capital. In the ma-
> jority of cases, the price of common stock has been influenced more
> markedly by the dividend rate than by the reported earnings. In other
> words, distributed earnings have had a greater weight in determin-
> ing market prices than have retained and reinvested earnings. The
> "outside," or non-controlling, stockholders of any company can reap
> benefits from their investment in only two ways: through dividends
> and through an increase in the market value of their shares. Since
> the market value in most cases has depended primarily upon the div-
> idend rate, the latter can be held responsible for nearly all the gains
> ultimately realized by investors. This predominant role of dividends
> has found full reflection in a generally accepted theory of investment
> value which states that a common stock is worth the sum of all the
> dividends expected to be paid on it in the future, each discounted to
> its present worth.[1]

Reflect, however, that any investor who took those words to
heart would be effectively barred from purchasing shares in aggressive young companies in exciting new industries, and would remain away from many established growth companies. Indeed,
Graham recognized that the idea was losing currency during the
bull market of the 1950s and 1960s, so different from the depression
conditions during which his maxims had such great force. In a footnote to the above paragraph, he related that "We use the term 'generally accepted' because in recent years this view has been questioned." And in the appendix, Graham adds: "We may suggest an
extension of the 'dividend stream theory' to read: a common stock
is worth the discounted value of future expectable dividends over
any assumed period of time, plus the discounted value of its expected market price at the end of the period."[2]

It remains to be said that dividend policy is the most important
aspect of management's demeanor toward stockholders, and re-

quires careful attention from prudent investors, no matter what their own convictions regarding the matter happen to be. Note from the outset that an analysis of the policy in any given situation can enable the investor to ascertain the backbone and acumen of corporate managements better than most other aspects of their activity.

My own view, based upon empirical evidence, clearly is that, all things being equal, a corporation is better off in the long run paying minimal or no dividends. In addition to the reasons sketched above, consider that under our laws, corporate dividends are subject to a double tax. The corporation is taxed on profits, and when a portion is sent to individual stockholders, they are taxed again. By contrast, interest on bonds is seen by the IRS as a cost of doing business, and so merits a deduction from gross earnings. The government fairly invites companies to finance operations through debt rather than through equity.

Why then pay dividends, or if it is difficult or unpleasant to cut or end them, at least forego increases? One reason might be the role of institutional and professional investors, who account for some 80 percent of activity on the nation's financial markets. Some corporate boards feel that a relatively liberal dividend policy will pacify the money managers. However, this is not necessarily the case, since an army of portfolio managers is scurrying around trying to achieve above-average investment returns and, in the background, many predators are hovering over corporations with the idea that they can exact from assets and a dividend stream a higher return than can existing management. Yet most managements associated with mature corporations regard dividends as akin to motherhood, apple pie, and the American flag.

The reduction and/or elimination of a dividend is generally considered a sign of failure and trouble. When this occurs the corporation will be blitzed with letters from irate stockholders and cursed by securities analysts who have recommended the shares. The stock will usually decline, and possibilities of a reassessment of the bonds by S&P and Moody's will be pondered. In other words, it can be a most unpleasant experience, one most managements can hardly relish contemplating. Little wonder that CEOs would figuratively kill rather than pass a dividend. Within this context, Hicks

Waldron, Avon's CEO, related to the *New York Times Magazine* as follows:

"A matter of some urgency facing the Corporate Management Committee is that business is not living up to projections. Consequently, the company is in danger of suffering rather poor earnings in the second quarter. Poor earnings would put pressure on the company's $2.00-per-share annual dividend." Thus, Waldron has implored everyone to pare expenses, in hopes of lopping off $15 million. Any C.E.O. will go to imaginative lengths to ring out the right numbers before he will report a bum quarter. (Once, when I asked Waldron if it is fair to say that he does everything he can to avoid releasing numbers that are below plan, he replied, "Do everything is an understatement. Kill is the word. You have to have the killer instinct for the bottom line.")[3]

It might be considered the better part of valor for a corporation to pursue a modest dividend policy, paying out only a small fraction of earnings to shareholders. Yet so strong is the urge to win plaudits some boards go ahead and make a fetish of annual boosts.

Rand Araskog of ITT argued that it was his way of rewarding the stockholders. "They haven't had too much action out of the common shares over the past ten years," he noted, adding that the annual boost of a few pennies a share was the firm's way of making peace with them. Yet at the same time his company was borrowing funds in order to make the payout.

To be fair, it really wasn't Araskog's baby; the dividend policy had been initiated by Harold Geneen, as one of the ways to celebrate his supposed successes at the firm. When Geneen came on board as CEO in 1958, ITT had revenues of less than $800 million a year; when he stepped down in 1979, revenues had reached $18 billion and he had molded an international conglomerate that owned upward of 250 companies comprising over 100 businesses.[4] More to the point, he had stamped his personality on ITT, and little that his successors, Lyman Hamilton and then Araskog, could do changed this. In November, 1982, Araskog proclaimed that in "exemplifying their continuing confidence in the future of our Company," the Board had approved the nineteenth consecutive annual increase in the dividend. And he continued the policy as long as he could.

Here, in cold, stark figures, is the sad tale of ITT's attempts to cut its financial arteries so as to present a pleasing picture to those investors:

Selected Statistics for ITT, 1971–1985

Year	Earnings per Share	Dividends per Share	Common Share Dividend Payout Ratio	Long-Term Debt (millions)	Common Shares
1971	$3.37	$1.16	34%	N/L*	75.0
1972	3.72	1.20	32	N/L	95.6
1973	4.08	1.32	32	N/L	94.5
1974	3.57	1.46	41	N/L	94.4
1975	3.12	1.54	49	N/L	94.3
1976	3.81	1.64	43	$2,295	94.2
1977	3.99	1.82	46	2,351	104.5
1978	4.49	2.05	46	2,872	112.2
1979	2.59	2.25	87	2,964	115.8
1980	5.95	2.45	41	2,847	122.3
1981	4.63	2.62	57	3,336	130.2
1982	4.68	2.70	58	2,890	133.2
1983	4.50	2.76	61	2,783	137.7
1984	2.97	1.88	63	2,589	139.7
1985	2.99	1.00	36	2,700	141.0

*N/L: Not listed by *Value Line* in 2/21/86 survey.

Source: Reprinted from *The Value Line Investment Survey*, February 21, 1986. Copyright © 1986 Value Line, Inc.

Note that ITT's percentage dividend payout ratio was in the low 30s in the years 1971–1973, moved up to the mid-40s during the mid-1970s, and then trended upward to a range between 57 and 63 percent in 1981–1984. During the same time span, ITT's long-term debt averaged about $2.9 billion, but common shares outstanding increased to approximately 140 million from 112 million in 1978.

Anyone looking at the dividends in relation to earnings over the years might have been excused for recalling the Russian tale of the troika being chased by wolves. The faster the carriage went, the faster the wolves seemed to advance. And even when the carriage slowed down, the animals continued their chase. When would the dividend surpass the earnings, one might have asked? Even a casual reader could see that ITT has locked itself into an overly generous dividend policy, and that was exacerbated by the growing capital needs of many of its businesses and disappointing results in others.

Araskog finally bit the bullet in July, 1984: ITT would cut its quarterly dividend from $0.69 to $0.25. This prompted a ten point decline in the price of the common, from 31 to 21, in a single session.

The ITT example is a textbook illustration of what happens when a corporation becomes locked into the ritual of annual dividend increases. Brian Fernandez, an analyst with Nomura Securities, concluded the result was inevitable. "Nobody realizes the terrific strategic box that Geneen built for the company by not clearly thinking through the future cash requirements of all of the businesses," he said when it was all over. And Araskog plaintively remarked, "The dividend has been such history for ITT for 20 some years. . . . It had become a deeply embedded thing that was hard to move."[5] It probably was not a coincidence that Araskog didn't cut the dividend until after Geneen left the ITT board.

In the aftermath of the dividend debacle, when ITT was selling in the low 20s, the Salomon Bros. brokerage house published a report on ITT, labeling the stock a buy based on an asset play. Portfolio strategist Michael Metz of Oppenheimer purchased ITT stock shortly after the dividend cut on the judgment that ITT shareholders would be better off if the corporation were dismembered, the pieces sold, and the proceeds distributed. He contended, "There is no reason for this company to exist—period." In mid-year 1986, ITT was selling at about $45 a share, based upon a rebound in share earnings with a potential asset play kicker.[6]

Look at Western Union, which for many years had an astonishing policy of paying out more than half its earnings in dividends, even though the firm's capital spending perennially exceeded cash flow. Finally, after losing $3.24 per share in 1984, Western Union eliminated the dividend, and the stock collapsed.

One might argue that several of ITT's companies were in growth areas, while Western Union was a perennial candidate for rebirth as a high tech operation. Rosy views of future earnings, then, might have contributed toward the desire to raise the former payout and maintain the latter. Also, corporate management is well aware of the fact that a generous dividend policy can prove to be of valuable assistance in helping the company sell its stock at a good price. This is an oft-invoked argument for an ample dividend. But what about troubled companies in ailing industries? These have no

Selected Statistics for Western Union, 1971–1985

Year	Earnings per Share	Dividends per Share	Common Share Dividend Payout Ratio	Long-Term Debt %	Common Shares
1971	$1.12	$1.40	125%	N/L*	10.2
1972	2.63	1.40	53	N/L*	12.8
1973	0.53	1.40	264	N/L*	13.7
1974	0.25	1.40	560	N/L*	14.0
1975	2.12	1.40	66	N/L*	14.0
1976	2.10	1.40	67	47.7%	15.2
1977	2.41	1.40	58	43.8	15.2
1978	2.35	1.40	60	46.5	15.2
1979	(0.34)	1.40	—	46.5	15.7
1980	1.80	1.40	78	45.6	15.7
1981	3.06	1.40	46	44.5	17.0
1982	3.34	1.40	42	40.0	23.9
1983	1.79	1.40	78	46.5	24.1
1984	(3.24)	1.05	—	51.3	24.4
1985	(2.50)	—	—	48.5	24.4

*N/L: Not listed by *Value Line* in 2/21/86 survey.

Source: Reprinted from *The Value Line Investment Survey*, February 21, 1986. Copyright © 1986 Value Line, Inc.

such excuses for making large payouts to owners of common shares. Such was the experience of Bethlehem Steel, which often reduced dividends (but didn't eliminate them) in bad years only to boost them in better times.

This surely is an exercise in monetary sadism. None of us can peer into the future with any consistent degree of success, but after all, steel is a cyclical industry. Bethlehem didn't have to increase its dividend in 1973, or if management felt compelled to do so, there might have been a more modest increase. And what about payouts in years during which the corporation lost money? These aren't necessary either. I calculate that if the company had refrained from paying a dividend between the deficit years of 1982 and 1985, it could have saved approximately $112 million, which would have been sufficient to pay off 10 percent of the long-term debt at year end 1985.

I am certain you get the message by now, and additional examples might be considered redundant. But, before offering suggestions as to how investors should interpret dividend policies, I would like to offer three more examples—Avon, Teledyne, and Lit-

Selected Statistics for Bethlehem Steel 1971–1985

Year	Earnings per Share	Dividends per Share	Common Share Dividend Payout Ratio	Long-Term Debt (millions)	Common Shares
1971	$3.14	$1.20	38%	N/L*	44.5
1972	3.02	1.20	40	N/L*	44.5
1973	4.72	1.65	35	N/L*	43.5
1974	7.85	2.30	29	N/L*	43.7
1975	5.54	2.75	50	N/L*	43.7
1976	3.85	2.00	52	$1,023	43.7
1977	(10.27)	1.50	—	1,155	43.7
1978	5.15	1.00	19	1,000	43.7
1979	6.31	1.50	24	1,008	43.7
1980	2.77	1.60	58	1,010	43.7
1981	4.83	1.60	33	972	43.7
1982	(9.60)	1.30	—	1,271	43.7
1983	(7.31)	0.60	—	1,134	46.3
1984	(3.32)	0.60	—	1,265	46.5
1985	(2.45)	0.30	—	1,232	52.0

*N/L: Not listed by Value Line in 2/21/86 survey.

Source: Reprinted from The Value Line Investment Survey, February 21, 1986. Copyright © 1986 Value Line, Inc.

ton—each of which offers a special twist and illustrates an important point.

In recent years Avon's dividend policy had bordered on the incredulous. Consider that from 1980 to 1985, management had paid out on the average of 91 percent of its earnings in the form of dividends. Indeed, unless one knew better, one might have concluded that the top brass was retaining next to nothing for growth. The problem is compounded when one considers that Avon, the leader in sales of cosmetics door-to-door, has been hurt by the rapidly increasing feminization of the work force, in that many would-be Avon Ladies are now engaged in more remunerative full-time employment, while the number of housewives, the company's prime customers, is declining. The money Avon paid out in the form of dividends during this trying period might have bettter been utilized to pay for its diversification into more promising areas. Instead, management continued its exceptionally high dividend payouts and divested itself of one of its core holdings, Mallinckrodt, a health care and specialty chemical company.

Start out by considering the basic statistics:

Selected Statistics for Avon Products, 1976–1985

Year	Earnings per Share	Dividends per Share	Common Share Dividend Payout Ratio	Long-Term Debt (millions)	Common Shares
1976	$2.90	$1.80	62%	6.7	58.1
1977	3.30	2.20	67	5.0	58.1
1978	3.92	2.55	65	3.0	58.2
1979	4.17	2.75	66	4.1	60.2
1980	4.01	2.95	74	2.6	60.2
1981	3.66	3.00	82	4.8	60.2
1982	2.75	2.50	91	297.3	74.4
1983	2.21	2.00	93	318.4	74.5
1984	2.16	2.00	93	440.5	85.4
1985	2.05*	2.00	98	617.8	79.1

*Does not include the sale of Mallinckrodt, which was classified as a discontinued operation at year end 1985.

Source: Reprinted from The Value Line Investment Survey, January 24, 1986. Copyright © 1986 Value Line, Inc.

Because Avon paid out most of its earnings in the form of dividends, it had not been able to build up retained earnings in amounts sufficient to support long-term debt additions. The above table indicates that between year end 1981 and year end 1985 Avon's long-term debt advanced from approximately $5 million to $618 million.

As Avon's troubles grew, and the price of its common shares declined, rumors appeared that the company would soon be the object of an unfriendly takeover bid. How might this be avoided? Management decided on maintaining the dividend so as to transform this once alluring growth stock into an income producing entity, thus maintaining the price by a high yield.

Avon also planned a stock repurchase program, both to increase earnings per share and dissuade potential takeover artists. In October, 1985, Avon revealed it had signed an agreement with Merrill Lynch under which the latter would purchase up to 10 million shares of Avon's common stock, with the company having an option to repurchase these shares through February, 1986. The purpose of the agreement was to enable Avon to match its stock repurchase outlays with expected future funds inflows. How was the money for this to be generated? Through the sale of Mallinckrodt, Avon disclosed that the Board had authorized the repurchase of 20 million shares of common, or about 25 percent of the total outstanding.

Then, in late January, 1986, Avon informed shareholders it had sold Mallinckrodt for $675 million, and that this money would be used for the scheduled repurchase of those 10 million shares to acquire The Mediplex Group Inc., and to reduce debt. Thus, Avon divested itself of an entity that produced 23 percent of its total operating income 1983–1985 in order to slash its equity base. And through all of this the dividend remained intact. It recalled the familiar chase scene in silent movies, in which in order to preserve themselves, the crew of a train throws everything flammable into the boiler to keep it going, and in the end has nothing but the engine left.

In October, 1985, when Avon revealed its stock repurchase plan, the shares were selling for about $24 on the NYSE. I thought it would be interesting to develop two hypothetical models, one of which would utilize the $675 million dollars from the sale of Mallinckrodt to repurchase a total of 20 million shares. After reducing the common shares outstanding by 20 million using the Mallinckrodt proceeds, my model would also assume that Avon completely eliminated its $2.00 per share annual dividend and utilized the dividend savings to repurchase common shares for the next five years at a price between $30 and $35 per share. This model is presented below:

MODEL I

Effect on Earnings per Share After Utilizing the Proceeds from the Mallinckrodt Sale to Repurchase 20 Million Common Shares—Then Dividend Is Eliminated and Funds Therein Are Utilized to Repurchase Common Shares of Stock between the Years 1986 and 1990

(in $ millions)

Year Ending:	1985	1986	1987	1988	1989	1990
Net Income		$135[1]	$135	$135	$135	$135
Common shares—						
beginning of year	60[2]	60	56	52.3	49.1	46.3
Less—Repurchase of shares		4[3]	3.7[4]	3.2[5]	2.8[6]	2.6[7]
Common shares—year end		56	52.3	49.1	46.3	43.7
EPS		$2.41	$2.58	$2.75	$2.92	$3.09

[1] Assumed level of earnings excluding Mallinckrodt.
[2] Assumed number of shares after repurchase of shares from Mallinckrodt sale.
[3] Dividend saving 60 mil shares × $2 = $120 mil ÷ $30 price per share = 4 mil shares.
[4] '' '' '' 56 '' '' × $2 = $112 '' ÷ $30 '' '' '' = 3.7 '' '' ''
[5] '' '' '' 52.3 '' '' × $2 = $104.6 '' ÷ $32.5 '' '' '' = 3.2 '' '' ''
[6] '' '' '' 49.1 '' '' × $2 = $ 98.2 '' ÷ $35 '' '' '' = 2.8 '' '' ''
[7] '' '' '' 46.3 '' '' × $2 = $ 92.6 '' ÷ $35 '' '' '' = 2.6 '' '' '' .

This model assumes that Avon's net income would remain flat at $135 million per year from 1986 through 1990, and indicates the amount of common shares that can be acquired each year by utilizing the former stream of earnings for the purpose of repurchasing shares. The result of this exercise is that by the year 1990, Avon's share earnings would have increased to $3.09 per share from the 1986 base of $2.41, even though net income during the same time span would not have risen at all. In other words, while repurchasing shares rather than using the money to expand operations and increase earnings is of dubious merit, it does make sense for a firm to repurchase shares rather than pay large dividends. The higher per-share earnings would be transformed into a higher price for the common, and the stockholders would be rewarded by the market mechanism through capital gains rather than by the company in the form of earnings.

However, it should be noted that under the 1986 proposed tax reform bill most of the difference, if not all of the difference, in tax treatment between dividends and capital gains will disappear.

I then engaged in another hypothetical exercise labeled Model II. Here I assumed that Avon would not sell Mallinckrodt, but would completely eliminate its common dividend and utilize the savings to repurchase shares at a price between $30 and $35 in 1986–1990.

MODEL II
Impact upon Earnings per Share Assuming There Was No Sale of Mallinckrodt— The Dividend of Avon Is Eliminated and the Dividend Savings Are Utilized to Repurchase Common Shares of Avon between the Years 1986 and 1990

(in $ millions)

Year Ending:	1986	1987	1988	1989	1990
Net Income	$180[1]	$180	$180	$180	$180
Common shares—					
beginning of year	80[2]	74.70	69.72	65.43	61.69
Less—Repurchase of shares	5.3[3]	3.98[4]	4.29[5]	3.74[6]	3.53[7]
Common shares—year end	74.7	69.72	65.43	61.69	58.16
EPS	$2.41	$2.58	$2.75	$2.92	$3.09

[1]Assumed level of earnings—no sale of Mallinckrodt.
[2]Assumed number of shares (rounded from 79.9).
[3]Dividend saving 80 mil shares × $2 = $160 mil ÷ $30 price per share = 5.3 mil shares.
[4]'' '' 74.7 '' '' × $2 = $149.4 '' ÷ $30 '' '' '' = 4.98 '' '' .
[5]'' '' 69.72 '' '' × $2 = $139.4 '' ÷ $32.5 '' '' '' = 4.29 '' '' '' .
[6]'' '' 65.43 '' '' × $2 = $130.9 '' ÷ $35 '' '' '' = 3.74 '' '' '' .
[7]'' '' 61.69 '' '' × $2 = $123.4 '' ÷ $35 '' '' '' = 3.53 '' '' '' .

In this instance I used a net income figure of $180 million per year between 1986 and 1990. The difference between the $135 million figure used in Model I and the $180 million in Model II is the additional $45 million of net income derived from the retention of Mallinckrodt by Avon.

Note the interplay that results when a former stream of dividends goes toward the repurchase of common shares. In this model, we find that between 1986 and 1990, Avon's earnings have advanced to $3.09 from the base of $2.41 per share. Hence Avon, without selling Mallinckrodt, could arrive at almost the same share earnings as in Model I—while still having this core division!

Dr. Henry E. Singleton is one of the more imaginative American businessmen, and his company, Teledyne, is an intriguing concern, as a result of Singleton's dividend and stock repurchase policies as well as operations. Singleton has made it crystal clear that there will be no dividends so long as he has anything to say about it, and he has passed this view along to the next generation of managers. So Ben Graham's stricture that the stock price should reflect anticipated future dividends might mean Teledyne should be selling at zero. Yet more often than not, Teledyne common is the highest priced equity on the NYSE list. The reason is Singleton's stock repurchase policy, which might be called "Operation Shrink," in reference to the vastly reduced equity base made possible through the utilization of cash flow. Singleton initiated the policy in 1972, when he retired 22 million shares of common, reducing the outstanding amount from 82 million to 60 million.

By year end 1984, as a result of further repurchases, Teledyne's equity base was down to 11.7 million shares. During this span, earnings per share rose from $0.64 to $46.66. The price of Teledyne common soared from a low of $6 in 1972 to a high of $338 in 1985. Were the stockholders rewarded? Of course. The rewards came from the market in the form of capital gains, this being the least expensive way for any management to earn shareholders' gratitude. Doubly so, because the gains in reference to individual shareholders aren't taxed till the shares are sold, and then at the long-term capital gains rate. Again, readers should note that impending tax law changes will erase either all or most of the distinction in tax treatment between earned and unearned income and capital gains.

Teledyne is a textbook example of what a determined management can do when it devotes itself to setting a long-term course of creating additional value in the marketplace via a substantial reduction of common shares outstanding rather than by paying generous dividends.

Finally, Litton Industries offers the case of a glamour stock that started out by not paying a dividend, switched to a cash payout policy, and then abandoned it in favor of a program of stock repurchases.

The company paid only small stock dividends until 1979, when the cash payouts began. These were modest at first ($0.23 that year) but they rose steadily, so that in 1984 the dividend came to $1.90 per share. As of July, 1985, Litton had approximately 42 million shares outstanding, and decided to shrink the amount substantially. In the fourth quarter of the fiscal year ended July 31, 1985, Litton issued subordinated debt securities in the sum of $1.3 billion in exchange for 15 million common shares. This reduced the equity base to around 27 million shares and was the first step in the process.

Let's look at some of the mathematics involved in this shrinkage. In the spring of 1986 Litton was paying around $140 million of interest expenses a year to service its $1.3 billion of debt incurred in the exchange. On an after-tax basis, the net cost to Litton is approximately $77 million per annum. At the time of the exchange the company had gone to a $2 per share annual dividend, which was equal to a cash outlay of approximately $84 million a year. However, when Litton had completed its debt for common share exchange, it discontinued paying any common share cash dividends. Therefore, it turns out that the dividend savings totaling $84 million a year (42 million original shares times $2 per share) more than covered the $77 million net interest cost.

By now some observers might want to know the reaction of Litton's shareholders to the elimination of the dividend. Those who were counting on it to meet expenses must have regretted the change and were best served by selling their shares and purchasing debt or equity that returned a steady stream of interest or dividends. Another option would be to sell off some shares to raise cash. But as a result of these moves Litton's earnings per share now were higher than they had been earlier, and this was one of the reasons for the advance in the price of the common shares, which went from 65 to the low 80s by March, 1986. True, this was a bull period on the

Street, but Litton common outperformed both the Dow and S&P. Moreover, the company was in better financial shape than it had been in a long time. By then Litton had accumulated a cash hoard totaling $1.6 billion, equal to $60 a share. Hence, after incurring a sizable sum of debt to retire around 35 percent of its outstanding common, Litton was in a position of possessing assets to enable it to further shrink that equity base. Indeed, in October, 1985, the board announced it would repurchase another 2 1/2 million shares from time to time.

The impact of the move on Litton's per share earnings was dramatic. For the six months ended January 21, 1986, Litton's net income totaled $90.7 million compared with almost $142 million for the previous year, a decline of 36 percent. But due to the decline in equity from 42.5 million shares to 27.8 million, earnings per share fell by only 3 percent.

I do not necessarily believe dividends are an evil unto themselves; certainly they have a role to play in rewarding shareholders. But managements should reflect that their first goal is to develop the enterprises for which they work, and paying dividends when the business is short of capital is foolish. So is increasing payouts when the money might be used to repurchase shares.

The bottom line here is that investors must keep an eye on dividend policy, and consider that for most industrial concerns, regular boosts in the face of irregular earnings can be a warning signal. So can the refusal of managements to lower dividends when earnings fall and/or capital requirements rise. Companies with high dividends and rising debt may be borrowing money to pay shareholders, a practice often resorted to by managements in fear of being ousted by some corporate raider. True, the stock of companies such as these may be attractive because the Street may anticipate a hostile bid, but for most investors who are seeking stocks that will advance on their performance and earnings per share, low dividends can mean high profits.

CHAPTER 11

The Importance of Understanding Accounting Changes

THERE IS an old tale, told with great relish by veteran accounting professors to neophytes, regarding a firm in search of an accountant. The field narrowed to three, each of whom was interviewed, and then asked to look at the books and calculate the firm's taxable income for the year. The first candidate replied, "$2.3 million," and the second, after obtaining additional information, thought it would come to $2.4 million. The third glanced around, pulled down the blinds, and asked the board, "How much do you want to show?" Naturally, he got the job.

The joke illustrates something accountants know quite well and the general public, including investors, hardly at all, namely that according to the methods used, a company can report a very wide range of earnings. It may not seem right or fair, but it is, due to the way one totes up assets and liabilities, expenditures and income.

Consider for example that generally accepted accounting principles permit a firm to write off a factory over 20 years, using straight line depreciation. Suppose the property cost $20 million originally. Would you say it was worth only $5 million after fifteen years? That is what the company's books would indicate, but given the nature of the real estate market, that building might fetch $30 million or more. Yet every year the firm deducted an item of $1 million for factory depreciation, when perhaps it would have been more realistic to add a million for appreciation.

Or think about what constitutes an asset. Do the firm's reputation and patents count for anything? Of course they do, but many companies carry goodwill at zero and understate the value of patents. What about the value of undeveloped land acquired many years ago, carried at cost, which might be a few dollars an acre for property worth millions?

A good accountant can make a company's books sit up and sing or lie down and die. Harold Geneen, the redoubtable CEO of ITT, was for many years an accountant, one of the most imaginative of the breed, and he was often accused of doing just that. Geneen was guilty of no crime, or even a mild violation of professional ethics. All he was doing was applying what accountants call "Generally Accepted Accounting Principles," which cover the spectrum from liberal to conservative, under whose tent many camels may gather. Indeed, so loose is GAAP that a few years ago, in disgust, accountant Abraham Briloff suggested the term be changed to "Commonly Reported Accounting Principles," or CRAP.

Many years ago, the accounting firm of Arthur Andersen & Co. published a chart entitled "Accounting Magic," that graphically illustrates the tremendous difference that can be shown by two identical companies, one utilizing liberal accounting practices (i.e., research cost, pensions, and capital gains), the other conservative ones. Some of the illustrations are outdated, but the basic idea remains. The chart is on pp. 166–67, with Andersen's explanations therein.

Accounting Magic—Illustrating Different Results from Alternative Accounting Principles

The chart which follows was prepared to show you how the use of alternative generally accepted accounting principles might affect the earnings reported in a given case. Column 1 shows the profit results of an assumed Company A that faces economic conditions realistically and so reports them in its earnings statement. Columns 2 to 7 show the effect of alternative accounting principles that are also generally acceptable. Column 8 shows Company B's earnings, with no change in operations except the application of alternative methods of accounting followed, yet Company B reports net profits of over twice as much as Company A.

It is wholly possible to have the stock of these two comparable companies selling at prices as much as 100% apart, merely because of the differences in accounting practices.

You can judge for yourself whether, if you were a stockholder, you would rather have the accounting of Company A or that of Company B followed by your company, if it meant the stock would bring you twice as much cash value upon sale. The answer is too obvious to dwell upon.[1]

Company A, whose figures are in Column 1, utilized very conservative accounting practices, while Company B, in Column 8, took advantage of every possibility to show higher earnings offered under GAAP. The difference, as you can see, is that between $0.80 per share for Company A and $1.79 for Company B.

Company A used LIFO (last in, first out) inventory practices, while Company B opted for FIFO (first in, first out). In a period of rising prices, this means that Company A, which acquired inventory a few years ago at, say, $1 a unit, which now costs $2, deducted $2 from the inventory value when the unit was shipped and sold. Company B made a $1 deduction, since that is what it cost. So under these procedures, the cost of the inventory was twice as much for A than it was for B, thus increasing the Costs and Expenses segment. In the Andersen model, this added $400,000, or $0.32 a share, to B's profits.

Column 3 indicates that Company A used accelerated depreciation, writing off its assets rapidly, while Company B did it more slowly, thus lowering its costs of doing business in any given year. The difference: $100,000, or $0.08 a share.

Company A charged research and development as the expenses were paid, while Company B did so over a five-year period. This added another $80,000 to its bottom line, or $0.06 a share.

How about pensions? Company A put this item down to current expenses, while Company B counted only the present value of the pensions vested, for another $150,000, or $0.12 a share, as seen in Column 5.

Both companies utilized incentives, but while Company A paid cash ($200,000), Company B utilized stock options, which cost nothing in the current year, saving it $200,000, or $0.16 a share.

The two companies realized capital gains, perhaps on the sale of property. Company A deemed this not to be ordinary income, and accounted for it as a special item. Not so Company B, which added $150,000 to its bottom line, this another $0.25 a share. (Readers should note that due to subsequent changes in accounting rules, the "special item" terminology is obsolete.)

Note that Company A's profits before income taxes came to

Accounting Magic

All "in Conformity with Generally Accepted Accounting Principles"

	Company A Col. 1	Use of Fifo in Pricing Inventory Col. 2	Use of Straight-Line Depreciation Col. 3	Deferring Research Costs Over 5 Years Col. 4	Funding Only the Pensions Vested Col. 5	Use of Stock Options for Incentive Col. 6	Including Capital Gain in Income Col. 7	Company B Col. 8
				Company B's Profits are Higher Because of				
Sales in units	100,000 units $100 each							100,000 units $100 each
Sales in dollars	$10,000,000							$10,000,000
Costs and expenses—								
Cost of goods sold	$ 6,000,000							$ 6,000,000
Selling, general and administrative	1,500,000							1,500,000
LIFO inventory reserve	400,000	$ (400,000)						—
Depreciation	400,000		$ (100,000)					300,000
Research costs	100,000			$ (80,000)				20,000
Pension costs	200,000				$ (150,000)			50,000
Officers' compensation—								
Base salaries	200,000							200,000
Bonuses	200,000					$ (200,000)		—
Total costs and expenses	$ 9,000,000	$ (400,000)	$ (100,000)	$ (80,000)	$ (150,000)	$ (200,000)		$ 8,070,000
Profit before income taxes	$ 1,000,000	$ 400,000	$ 100,000	$ 80,000	$ 150,000	$ 200,000		$ 1,930,000
Income taxes	520,000	208,000	52,000	42,000	78,000	104,000		1,004,000
	$ 480,000	$ 192,000	$ 48,000	$ 38,000	$ 72,000	$ 96,000	$ —	$ 926,000
Gain on sale of property (net of income tax)	—						150,000	150,000
Net profit reported	$ 480,000	$ 192,000	$ 48,000	$ 38,000	$ 72,000	$ 96,000	150,000	$ 1,076,000
Per share on 800,000 shares	$ .80	$ .32	$ .08	$ .06	$ .12	$ .16	$ .25	$ 1.79

Market value at—

						Company A	Company B	
10 times earnings	$ 8.00	$3.20	$ .80	$ .63	$1.20	$1.60	$2.50	$17.93
12 times earnings	$ 9.60	$3.84	$ .96	$ .76	$1.44	$1.92	$3.00	$21.52
15 times earnings	$12.00	$4.80	$1.20	$ .95	$1.80	$2.40	$3.75	$26.90

( ) Denotes deduction.

Explanation of Columns 2 to 7, Inclusive

Column	Company A	Company B
2.	Uses Lifo (last in, first out) for pricing inventory	Uses Fifo (first in, first out)
3.	Uses accelerated depreciation for book and tax purposes	Uses straight-line
4.	Charges research and development costs to expense currently	Capitalizes and amortizes over five-year period

(If R & D costs remain at same level, the difference disappears after five years. The difference of $80,000 in the chart is in the first year, where A expenses $100,000 and B capitalizes the $100,000 but amortizes 1/5.)

Column	Company A	Company B
5.	Funds the current pension costs—i.e., current service plus amortization of past service	Funds only the present value of pensions vested

(Difference in pension charges might also arise where, as in in the case of U. S. Steel in 1958, management decides that current contributions can be reduced or omitted because of excess funding in prior years and/or increased earnings of the fund or the rise in market value of the investments.)

Column	Company A	Company B
6.	Pays incentive bonuses to officers in cash	Grants stock options instead of paying cash bonuses
7.	Credits gains (net of tax thereon) directly to earned surplus (or treats them as special credits below net income)	Includes such gains (net of income tax thereon) in income

$1,000,000 and its taxes, $520,000. Company B's profits were $1,930,000, and its taxes, $1,004,000; so A's net income was $480,000 and B's $1,076,000.

Few on Wall Street take such different accounting methods into account. All the analyst and investor know is that for the year, Company A had $0.80 per share earnings and Company B, $1.79. If both firms' stocks were selling for 15 times earnings, A common would be at $12, and B at $26.90.

Now ask yourself which stock you would prefer to own. Since Company B's shares are so much higher, the answer is self-evident.

All of this should seem fairly obvious. Yet academicians and others are divided on the issue and its implications. There is a widespread school of thought, based upon the Efficient Market Hypothesis (EMH) that holds the prices of stocks are based upon economic reality rather than such accounting differences. It states that if two companies are identical in every way they would have the same stock price, even though they utilize different accounting methods, the sole *caveat* being that the accounting does not affect cash flows.[2] Professor George Benston of the University of Rochester's Graduate School of Management claims that his research indicates that, on the average, earnings changes produced by accounting are not associated with changes in stock prices except when the new methods result in lower taxes. In short, the market appears to be able to see through accounting gimmickry.[3] Another respected researcher, Professor Alfred Rappaport of the Kellogg Graduate School of Management at Northwestern University, claims the market is not fooled by changes in accounting methods—for instance, a switch from accelerated to straight-line depreciation that boosts reported earnings per share, but does not affect cash flows.[4] This is a matter of heated contention within the academic community, with the Street looking on with great interest.

Some believe that most individual investors simply ignore such matters, while the professionals—the individuals who manage large pools of money—are quite conversant with them. And since in our increasingly institutionalized market the pros dominate, it would appear the academics have a point. But I have my doubts on this score, having too often witnessed the contrary. And so have managers of corporations. They know that a switch from conservative to liberal accounting can pay off. This is because changes in accounting that serve to elevate reported share earnings have a permanent uplifting effect that becomes embedded in the stock price of an individual security.

This point of view is supported by Arthur R. Wyatt, a former Arthur Andersen partner and currently a member of the Financial Accounting Standards Board, who posed the question: "If EMH is valid, why do profit-motivated businessmen frequently enter into forms of transactions that are not very profitable (when compared with alternatives) solely or primarily because those forms will produce financial statement results that they believe will make their companies look better?" Wyatt goes on to say that "while EMH research to date appears to provide substantial support for the hypothesis, it seems equally clear that the real world of accounting either ignores or disputes the validity of the hypothesis and those of the research."[5]

A form of Gresham's law exists in accounting, where poor practices tend to drive out good. This is because a corporation that takes a conservative approach knows that, all things being equal, a rival with liberal accounting will show higher earnings, and therefore sell at a higher stock market price.

I don't mean to suggest that a corporation can lower the quality of its reported share earnings with impunity through the adoption of liberal accounting techniques. If a corporation's stock is selling at a fairly high price-earnings ratio, a lowering of earnings quality could indeed result in an erosion of the multiple. But a corporation utilizing conservative accounting practices, and selling for either a stock market or below market price-earnings ratio, knows it can boost earnings, and with this the price of its stock. The temptation to do so is understandably irresistible. Imagine the CEO at his desk, looking over his firm's figures during a disappointing year, knowing that with a few perfectly legal accounting changes, all in accord with Generally Accepted Accounting Principles, the level of his share earnings can be raised, sometimes substantially. How many of them would hold back?

In October, 1983, I published the results of a survey indicating that out of 704 NYSE-listed corporations only 16 percent utilized accelerated or partially accelerated depreciation methods for shareholder reporting purposes. Only 7 percent conservatively deferred and amortized their investment tax credits for shareholder reporting in contrast to employing the more liberal flow-through method.[6]

One reason managements make the change is to enhance the

image of their performances, and another is to obtain personal financial rewards. More than 90 percent of the nation's top managers hold stock options, and so have a strong stake in seeing the price of their companies' stocks rise. Also, many of them receive bonuses based upon the level of earnings per share. To them, the price of the firm's stock is more than a simple ego trip—it can be the difference of hundreds of thousands, even millions, of dollars.[7] And of course, a higher stock price may keep potential corporate raiders from the door. Let us turn now to some examples of how this works.

Gelco Corp. (GEL) is in the business of providing fleet management services, mostly in the form of leased trucks. On December 31, 1979, Gelco acquired CTI International, a container leasing company, for $250 million. It turned out that Gelco paid a very high price for CTI because CTI's net income peaked at $26.6 million in 1979. A CTI International prospectus dated September 10, 1980, relating to the issuance of $50 million of 15 percent notes, commented that:

> Since 1978, principally as a result of competitive conditions in the container leasing industry, CTI has not significantly increased its overall lease charges despite inflation-caused increases in the cost of services required under most leases.

In a *Quality of Earnings Report* dated December 15, 1981, I commented that Saul Steinberg, Chairman of Reliance Group, is to be congratulated for the sale of CTI to Gelco Corp. for $250 million. In essence, Steinberg unloaded a capital-intensive business with sizable borrowing tied to the prime and/or LIBOR (Eurodollar) rates, but whose revenues since 1978 have not been able to reflect adequate rate relief regarding inflation-caused increases in costs of services.

Effective January 1, 1980, Gelco lengthened the depreciation periods for container equipment manufactured by CTI, changing the useful lives from 10 years to 12 1/2–15 years, and the salvage value was upped to 15 percent from 10 percent. Because CTI International is a subsidiary of Gelco and its operations are consolidated with those of Gelco for shareholder reporting purposes, this move provided Gelco with substantially higher earnings per share.

Table 11.1, derived from information found in Gelco and CTI filings with the SEC, demonstrates the impact upon Gelco's per share earnings of the liberalized accounting methods. The year 1980 is missing because I was unable to secure information for this period

TABLE 11.1
Gelco Corp.—CTI Container Subsidiary

(figures in millions)

	Year Ended 12/31		Year Ended 7/31		
	1979	1981	1982	1984	1985
Container rental equipment	$348.1	$492.8	$548.6	$482.4	$433.6
Depreciation on rental equipment	$34.4	$29.7	$34.7	$37.9	$36.5
Depreciation on rental equipment as a percentage of container rental equipment	9.88%	6.03%	6.33%	7.86%	8.41%
Difference between Co.'s 9.88% 1979 depreciation rate and reported rate		3.85%	3.55%	2.02%	1.47%
Gelco tax rate		15.7%	19.4%	26.9%	40.7%
Shares		10.2	11.8	13.8	13.7
Earnings per share		$4.67	$2.51	$0.82	$1.63

and the year 1983 is omitted because Gelco reported a deficit of $0.87 that year.

Now to discover the exact impact the changes in accounting procedure had upon the reported earnings, the statistics for which are outlined below.

First of all, note the difference between CTI's 1979 depreciation rate of 9.88 percent while the reported depreciation rate of 6.03 percent in 1981 is 3.85 percent. Multiply this depreciation rate differential of 3.85 percent by the $492,800,000 reported for container rental equipment and the result is $18,973,000. (See the first line of Table 11.2 on page 172.) Now, to follow the computations of the table, multiply the $18,973,000 by the 15.7 percent Gelco tax rate and you get the tax effect of $2,979,000. Subtract this from the $18,973,000 and the result is $15,994,000, the amount that can be attributed to accounting changes. Divide that by the number of shares outstanding (10.2 million) and you get $1.57 per share, which is 34 percent of Gelco's reported earnings. Without these changes, then, Gelco would have reported $3.10 instead of $4.67. I then did the same for the other years; the results are shown in Table 11.2.

Compare the adjusted EPS with the reported figures and you will have a striking example of how accounting changes can affect this vital statistic.

TABLE 11.2
Adjustments for Accounting Changes for Gelco, 1981, 1982, 1984, and 1985

(figures in thousands of dollars) Refer to text for explanation of compulations

1981	1982	1984	1985
$18,973	$19,475	$9,744	$6,374
× 15.7%	× 19.4%	× 26.9%	× 40.7%
$2,979	$3,778	$2,621	$2,594
18,973	19,475	9,744	6,374
−2,979	−3,778	−2,621	−2,594
15,994	15,697	7,123	3,780
10.2	11.8	13.8	13.7
$1.57	$1.33	$0.52	$0.28
34%	53%	63%	17%
Adjusted EPS $3.10	$1.18	$0.30	$1.35

There appears little doubt Gelco had bought the wrong company at the wrong time and would have been far better off without CTI. Devotees of the Efficient Market Hypothesis should consider what those earnings would have appeared to be had not the liberalization of earnings taken place. Table 11.2 illustrates that in 1981, 1982, 1984, and 1985, the impact of reporting changes accounted for 34, 53, 63, and 17 percent, respectively, of Gelco's reported share earnings.

Everyone knows of Union Carbide's (UK) difficulties resulting from the Bhopal explosion in November of 1984. The stock plummeted; there was talk of bankruptcy. Then came the unwelcome takeover attempt from GAF in late 1985 and the sale of some of the most attractive parts of the firm's business in 1986 as management strived to remain independent. UK common behaved in a most erratic manner, not unusual for the paper of a firm in such bewildering and uncertain circumstances.

UK had reported earnings of $7.15 per share in 1976, when the stock topped out at 76 3/4. This was followed by declines in both figures—to $6.05 a share in 1977 and $6.09 the following year, when the stock dipped to 33 5/8. Earnings rose to $8.47 in 1979, but the stock responded by rising only to a high of 44 1/2. Stronger medicine was needed, and in 1980 management decided to elevate earnings through accounting changes.

UK started out by extending the expected useful life of machinery and equipment, instead of utilizing the Internal Revenue Service's "guideline lives." Concurrently management adopted the flow-through method of accounting for investment tax credits instead of the deferred method. In announcing these changes, UK management said that it was a rather innocuous alteration, merely an attempt to bring the company's practice in line with what most of its competitors were doing.

Table 11.3 (p. 174) is a graphic illustration of the impact of these changes on UK's reported share earnings.

Consider that the change affected earnings not only for 1980, but subsequent years as well. Note that the accounting changes increased UK's 1980 earnings by $1.63 in 1980 and sizable amounts in subsequent years.

How did all of this affect UK's stock price? Table 11.4 (p. 175) shows that from 1977 to 1979 UK common sold for a lower P/E ratio than any of its competitors. Then came the boost in 1980, which caused the P/E to fall even lower, and this attracted bargain seekers. The company reported earnings of $9.56 per share in 1981, but as can be seen, $1.40 of this came from accounting changes. No matter; Wall Street responded by bidding the price of UK common to a high of 62 1/8. In 1983, when reported earnings came to $3.02, $1.40 of which was due to the accounting changes, the stock advanced to a high of 73 7/8, only a shade below its all-time high.

In summary, from 1977 through 1981 Union Carbide had the lowest P/E multiple in the chemical group, with the exception of Monsanto Chemical in the year 1978. However, in 1984 the ratio had risen to the level of or surpassed all of the rest except Dow. And this in spite of the fact that in late 1984 the stock price of Union Carbide plunged as a result of the Bhopal incident.

What a difference a shrewd accountant can make. And mind you, all of this was perfectly legal.

If we were to believe those who hold to the Efficient Market Hypothesis, we might have expected Union Carbide's P/E to decline, not rise. But in the real world, the accounting changes paid off in higher stock prices. What is the cure for an ailing P/E? An accountant with a sharp pencil and a sharper mind.

TABLE 11.3
Impact of Accounting Changes Upon Union Carbide's Earnings

	1977	1978	1979	1980*	1981	1982	1983	1984
Depreciation Expense ($ mill)	$359	$417	$470	$326	$386	$426	$477	$507
Depreciation Exp. As a % of Avg. Plant Equip.	5.0%	5.35%	5.60%	3.55%	3.92%	4.10%	4.43%	4.64%
Investment Tax Credits ($ mill)	$15.4	$19.6	$26	$53	$61	$58	$20	$43
Tax Rate	30%	32.5%	30.2%	33.3%	27.0%	14.4%	—	36.0%
Reported Earnings Per Share			$8.47	$10.08	$9.56	$4.47	$3.02	$5.16
Dividend			$2.90	$3.10	$3.30	$3.40	$3.40	$3.40
Depreciation Acct. Change				$1.37	$1.11[1]	$1.00[1]	$1.40[1]	$1.27[1]
ITC Acct. Change				$0.26	$0.29[1]	$0.26[1]	—	$0.15[1]
Total Accounting Changes				$1.63	$1.40[1]	$1.26[1]	$1.40[1]	$1.42[1]
Reported Earnings Per Share			$8.47	$10.08	$9.56	$4.47	$3.02	$5.16
Adjusted EPS Excluding Depreciation & ITC Accounting Changes				$8.45	$8.16[1]	$3.21[1]	$1.62[1]	$3.74[1]
Accounting Changes As a % of EPS				16%	15%[1]	28%[1]	46%[1]	28%[1]

*Year of depreciation & ITC accounting changes.
[1]Estimates calculated by The Quality of Earnings Report.

TABLE 11.4
Average Annual P/E Ratio—Chemical Basic Industry

Company		1977	1978	1979	1980*	1981	1982	1983	1984
Dow Chemical	EPS	$3.01	$3.16	$4.33	$4.42	$3.00	$1.14	$1.50	$2.50
	Avg. Ann'l. P/E Ratio	11.1	8.2	6.5	7.6	10.3	20.5	21.6	11.8
DuPont		$3.69	$5.39	$6.42	$4.83	$5.81	$3.89	$4.47	$5.89
		10.9	7.3	6.7	8.5	7.6	9.0	10.6	8.1
Hercules		$1.36	$2.36	$3.89	$2.60	$3.09	$1.97	$2.76	$3.61
		14.5	6.6	5.0	7.7	7.3	10.7	13.0	9.0
Monsanto		$3.73	$4.15	$4.56	$2.05	$5.75	$4.24	$4.72	$5.42
		9.2	6.2	5.8	13.2	6.2	8.3	10.1	8.4
Rohm & Haas		$1.69	$2.15	$3.70	$3.63	$3.61	$2.92	$5.33	$6.73
		11.6	7.8	5.5	6.0	8.4	10.0	11.3	8.8
Union Carbide		$6.05	$6.09	$8.47	$10.08	$9.56	$4.47	$3.02	$5.16
		8.3	6.4	4.6	4.4	5.7	10.6	21.3	10.2

*Year of depreciation & ITC accounting changes.

Source: Reprinted from *The Value Line Investment Survey.* Copyright © 1986 Value Line, Inc.

If IBM appears more often than any other corporation in these pages, it is because it is and has been the most admired American business enterprise for the past half century, and is far and away the market's bellwether issue. It also had some interesting recent changes in accounting. IBM was once one of the few corporations that utilized the same depreciation rate for shareholder and tax purposes, both accelerated, which is a conservative method of computing depreciation.

In 1984 IBM switched to straight-line depreciation of rental machines, plant, and other property acquired after 1983 for financial reporting purposes, which meant these charges would drop significantly, as a percentage of depreciable assets, causing earnings to rise. Partly as a result of this liberalized policy, the company's 1984 depreciation expense fell to $2.987 billion from $3.362 billion the previous year. These figures were equal to 10.15 percent and 11.52 percent of rental machines and plant and other property for 1984 and 1983 respectively. The lower percentage depreciation expense was equal to $0.37 a share after tax.

As indicated, such changes will continue to impact earnings favorably for years to come. In 1985 IBM's depreciation expense again declined, this time to $2.894 billion from 1984's $2.987 billion. These figures were equal to 8.39 percent and 10.15 percent of properties for 1985 and 1984, respectively. The effect of the lower depreciation rate this time came to $0.55 per share, after tax.

Nor was this all. In 1984 IBM lowered the cost of its retirement plan expenses by raising its assumed actuarial rate of return on plan assets. There was nothing unusual in this; many companies were taking the same action so their plans would more accurately reflect the realities of the marketplace. Prior to 1984, IBM had assumed a 5.5 percent rate of return on assets; in 1984 the rate was raised to 7.5 percent on plan assets through 1993. This meant that IBM's contributions to pension costs would be reduced, since less money would be required given the higher anticipated yield. The total costs of IBM retirement plans in 1983 had come to $1.180 billion; for 1984, the figure was $1.096. The reduced pension plan expenses came to $0.08 per share.

IBM lowered the costs of retirement plans the same way in 1985, when the rate went to 8 percent, this to continue through 1995. In addition, IBM lengthened the amortization of prior service costs to 15 years from 10 years. As a result of these changes in actuarial assumptions, coupled with favorable actual results on investments made by the plans, IBM's retirement plan expenses declined to $868 million in 1985 versus the $1.096 million the previous year. The reduced pension expenditures were equal to $0.21 per share after tax.

In 1984 IBM reported earnings of $10.77 a share. The combination of reduced percentage depreciation expense and lower retirement plan expenses accounted for $0.45 per share ($0.37 plus $0.08). IBM's earnings that year were $1.73 more than in 1984. Thus, 26 percent of the company's increase in earnings was accounted for by changes in accounting.

The same happened in 1985, when IBM reported earnings of $10.67. The combination of lower percentage depreciation costs and reduced retirement plan expenditures totaled $0.76. IBM's earnings that year declined to $10.67, $0.10 less than in 1984. However, were it not for the beneficial impact of these two items, IBM's earnings would have declined a total of $0.86.

Think of it this way: as far as most people are concerned, IBM's 1984 and 1985 earnings were $10.77 and $10.67. Without the accounting changes, they would have been $10.32 and $9.91. How do you think Wall Street would have reacted to that kind of comparison when the figures for 1985 were released in early 1986? What would that have done to the price of IBM common?

Few Wall Street analysts take note in their research reports of items such as this. In other words, they fail to inform clients that fully 7 percent of IBM's 1985 earnings were derived from accounting changes that first took place in 1984. What about the Efficient Market Hypothesis, which holds that the stock's price would take this into consideration?

Of course, there are many factors going to make the P/E ratio at any given time, and I'm not about to suggest that accounting changes can work all kinds of magic with the stock's price. Consider, however, the way IBM common jumps every time a major analyst boosts or cuts an earnings estimate, and that in 1985, with the benefit of that extra $0.76 from accounting changes, IBM sold for an average P/E ratio of 12.4, compared with 10.8 for 1984.

It remains to be said that IBM is not selling for an outlandish P/E ratio, and that the company's liberalized changes in accounting have not negatively impacted the stock's multiple. So if you own IBM, give a silent prayer for those Armonk accountants who came up with the changes.

CHAPTER 12

Coming Clean
After the Big Bath
and/or Restructuring

THE SCENARIO IS PLAYED out regularly in executive suites and reported fully on financial pages. Management had faltered, due to incompetence, errors, poor forecasting, the emergence of aggressive and imaginative rivals, the obsolescence of plant and product, or simple bad luck. Sales and earnings are down, and the company's reputation is in tatters. Or it may be that they are forced from office by raiders or internal critics. With as much dignity and grace as can be mustered the worn-out leaders retire, making way for a set of new faces and new ideas.

After a series of conferences the rejuvenated or fresh executives appear before the press and securities analysts and grimly note that things were worse than they had thought. A turnabout will be possible, they say, given hard work, sacrifice, and dedication. But not before a thorough housecleaning takes place.

Veteran business observers know well what will take place. Management is setting the stage for a "big bath."

As might have been guessed, the big bath refers to the practice of writing off every dubious asset in sight, and some that are not so questionable. Marginal operations are sold for whatever can be obtained, while existing plant, equipment, and inventory are written down to as low a level as management can defend to its outside auditors.

All the while management continues to warn of tough times ahead, the rhetoric heating up as the time arrives to renegotiate labor contracts. The stock market responds as the price of the company's common declines. There are some additional quivers as the moment arrives to release the next quarter's results. Often revenues are constant, or even rise, but there are all sorts of special items in the report, and the end result is always the same: tremendous losses accompanied by management claims that the worst is over, and better times seem just over the horizon.

Of course they are. The situation may have been bad, but not as horrendous as pictured, or might have been guessed from the write-offs. Management has done all in its power to present the bleakest picture possible, knowing that what remained of the company was all flesh, muscle, and bones, and no fat, that the accounting maneuvers that had overstated the negatives of the company would enable management to present a sunny picture next time around, for which they will obtain credit. "Look at what we inherited," they will crow, "and look how we resuscitated the company in just a few short months!"

This isn't to suggest all that had happened was accounting changes and maneuvers. In such instances real reforms *do* take place, and there are many cases in which management, especially new management, under such circumstances does call for revived interest on the part of investors. Several such examples will be presented, and at this point I should add that I peruse the newspapers and magazines for just such situations. But all the while I know the big bath has been drawn.

Big bath accounting is given a tremendous boost under the previously discussed GAAP. Corporate management and accountants realize that all of the costs of restructuring are crowded into one quarter or year, while the benefits will be realized later on, but let it go at that. This point was brought out clearly by Professor Robert J. Swieringa of Cornell University, who related:

> Generally accepted accounting principles require that estimated (current and future) costs associated with restructuring be charged against income in the year in which the decisions to restructure are made. A liability reserve is established and the actual expenditures (which are incurred in subsequent years) are charged against this reserve. The effect of this procedure is to match restructuring costs with the decision and not with the periods during which the restructuring occurs or when the benefits are realized.[1]

The reasons managements take the big bath are obvious: it enables them not only to cast aside past mistakes, but to make themselves look good once the turnabout takes place. Count on them to congratulate themselves (and the stockholders) at the next annual meeting. But investors usually profit too. After all, many managements are often reluctant to abandon enterprises about which they had been so optimistic, for to do so would be to admit horrendous errors. Also, it is not considered good form to write down assets dramatically, for this suggests a glaring deficiency in management and a lack of meaningful internal corporate financial controls.

Wall Street analysts generally favor the big bath over a series of write-downs, because it suggests the company is finally "coming clean" (no pun intended) on its current situation, while a series of write-downs can erode a corporation's reputation and its price-earnings multiple. There is nothing the Street abhors more than surprises, and little it favors more than the aura of complete revelation. At least there will be no more major shocks, say the analysts, as they prepare to judge the company on its future prospects rather than past blunders.[2]

Indeed, big baths have become quite common for this very reason. In the fourth quarter of 1985 accounting write-offs reached a crescendo, *Forbes* financial columnist Ben Weberman labeling them "Rumpelstilzchen Accounting." He wrote that "Rumpelstilzchen spun straw into gold. Last quarter, dozens of leading businessmen spun past sins into current virtues."[3]

If anything, big bath accounting is increasing in popularity. By the end of the fourth quarter of 1985 each of 28 sizable corporations had written off $100 million or more of assets, and the total write-downs came to $9.5 billion. In writing of this development, *Business Week* commented that the overriding tactic was "Take your licks now. Then, after the economy strengthens, you look great to your shareholders and on Wall Street. On the other hand, if recession hits, the worst of the hard choices may be behind you."[4]

Large and small corporations alike are increasingly admitting the reasons for the write-offs, with shrewd executives making the moves appear a sign of present and future strength and not past blunders. For example, when CSX announced a major restructuring involving a pre-tax charge of $954 million, CEO Hays T. Watkins related, "The actions will have a very positive effect on future cash flow, earnings, and rates of return."[5] Likewise, Allied-Signal wrote off $725 million in the 1985 fourth quarter, with Chairman Edward L. Hennessy, Jr. telling reporters that "the bulk of the write-down was related to a very aggressive streamlining of this company," going on to state that "we've cut corporate overhead by $250 million a year, eliminated 3,000 jobs, reorganized into three areas of focus—aerospace/electronics, automotive, and engineered materials—and arranged to spin off our non-core businesses into a new company. We are well-poised for the future, looking forward to 1986 with a focused, efficient, and profitable group of businesses."[6] In announcing a $1.2 billion charge against earnings to cover substantial increases in insurance claims in the fourth quarter of 1985, Cigna CEO Robert D. Kilpatrick said that while "we probably made a mistake of underestimating reserves every year for at least a decade," the charge will serve as "a kind of clearing the decks of the old liabilities," and the move "improves our earnings outlook for 1986 and beyond."[7] The stock market took this as a sign of strength. Cigna common had dropped by 10 percent shortly prior to and immediately after the announcement, but within a few days rebounded vigorously, and a month later posted a new high for the year.

This is not at all unusual. Several years ago Victor S. Pastena, a professor of accounting at the Columbia Graduate School of Business, discovered that while prices of the common stocks of companies announcing big baths usually fell a month or so before the actual announcement of the write-downs, their prices tended to rise thereafter. Pastena concluded that investors are "unduly pessimistic at the time of a write-off but subsequently make an upward judgment about the company and its future prospects."[8]

The above three cases involve corporations in which present managements admit past mistakes, claim to have rectified the errors, and appear determined to steer a better course in the future. Then there are situations in which an orderly transition in top management takes place, but it turns out the new leader has a management style much different from that of his predecessor. A striking case was the way Ralston Purina (RAL) underwent a major overhaul starting in 1982.

Here is what happened. In his letter to shareholders dated De-

cember 4, 1981, CEO R. Hal Dean announced he would be stepping down the following January to be succeeded by William Stiritz, who had been elevated to the presidency less than a year before.
It seemed a smooth enough transition for a company whose revenues, earnings, and stock price had remained static in recent years.
There appeared little likelihood anything would change at what
had become a hidebound enterprise. Or at least, this was the general sentiment.

In a quiet, unassuming manner, Stiritz began a program that
included asset write-downs and redeployment and the disposal of
marginal operations. Almost simultaneously he initiated a program
of repurchasing shares on the open market. It was the beginning of
one of the most outstanding corporate turnabouts in recent history.
While much of the business press was concentrating on more dramatic stories, such as Lee Iacocca's admittedly masterful performance at Chrysler, Stiritz, who to this day is barely known outside
of the industry, was reshaping Ralston Purina in an equally intelligent fashion. It shouldn't have come as any surprise. Stiritz told
all in the shareholders' letter appearing in the 1982 Annual Report.

In this letter Stiritz outlined his strategy and tactics, which
were at the same time sensible and plausible. These included di-
vestment of tuna vessels, the mushroom business, and European
consumer products pet food businesses, all moribund, which resulted in after-tax charges of $122 million, or $1.16 per share. Four
core businesses were identified as one of the company's three
strengths, the others being a strong balance sheet and a "wealth of
talented and experienced employees." The weaknesses were that
Ralston was operating in mature markets with little growth potential and additional underperforming operations. So as to capitalize
on strengths and minimize or eliminate weaknesses, Stiritz intended
to expand the core business wherever possible, continue the divest-
ment program, and make acquisitions in related fields.[9]

This should have alerted shareholders and analysts alike to possible changes at the company. Of course, this kind of thing happens
scores of times each year, and in most cases little happens. But when
the changes do begin to take place, additional monitoring should
begin.

The changes began almost at once, spearheaded by divestiture
and repurchase of stock. In addition, Stiritz managed to squeeze

fat out of ongoing operations and increase profit margins. These changes were reflected in his shareholders' letter the following year. According to plan, the divestments continued, restaurant operations were revamped and turned in record earnings, and then 72 of them were sold. Stiritz used surplus capital to repurchase 10.2 million shares of common. He also stated his primary objective in a way calculated to please shareholders:

> One of management's primary objectives is to increase shareholder value. In order to accomplish this goal, we seek to maintain our rate of return on shareholder equity in the top quarter of the food industry. In addition, we must outperform competition and gain market share. We are making important progress toward these objectives as we strive to become the best managed food company.

Hyperbole? Perhaps. But Stiritz was delivering on promises, and that is what counted. Net earnings for fiscal 1983 were $256 million compared to 1982 earnings of $69.1 million, which were reduced by $128.1 million as a result of divestment provisions and operating losses. Exclusive of these items, 1983 earnings were up by 30 percent.[10]

The campaign continued in 1984—more divestitures and restructuring. But now Stiritz moved into new areas, making an important acquisition. At the time Continental Baking was a decent enough corporation, but one underperforming insofar as its market was concerned. Stiritz meant to change this, and so he did. In the 1984 letter, he reiterated his objectives, noted the closure of a West Coast cannery that had been performing below par, and noted continued improvement in the restaurant business, an industry which observers had concluded was being readied for sale.[11]

Finally, in the 1985 letter, Stiritz recapitulated his program and again shared his thoughts regarding the future with shareholders, who had reason to be pleased with results. Consider Stiritz's record from 1982 through 1985, and compare it with that of the company in the preceding four years (see Table 12.1, p. 184).

From 1978 to 1981, RAL's earnings per share rose by less than 12 percent; from 1982 to 1985, they advanced by 81 percent. The price of RAL common went from under 11 in 1982 to 49 in 1985, as the price-earnings ratio increased from an average of 7.2 to 12.4,

TABLE 12.1
Ralston Purina, Selected Statistics, 1978–1985

(revenues in billions of dollars)

Year	Revenues	Earnings per Share	Dividends per Share	Shares Outstanding
1978	$4058	$1.44	$0.50	107.8
1979	4601	1.19	0.58	107.9
1980	4886	1.51	0.64	108.0
1981	5225	1.61	0.72	108.0
1982	4802	1.74	0.78	101.5
1983	4872	2.58	0.84	95.1
1984	4980	2.90	0.92	86.3
1985	5864	3.15	1.00	80.2

Source: Ralston Purina, Annual Reports, 1978–1985. Fiscal years ending September 30.

this being the market's way of recognizing the superb job Stiritz had done. "Don't expect the final chapter in Ralston's restructuring 'story' to be written for several years," related Value Line in its August, 1985 number. "Since fiscal 1982, when the company wrote off several operations and began buying back its stock, these shares have outperformed the market by a wide margin."[12]

A similar if more dramatic restructuring took place at Gulf + Western (GW) after CEO Charles Bluhdorn died suddenly in early 1983. One of the great wheeler-dealers of his day, Bluhdorn had taken GW from a regional auto parts company to one of the more dazzling conglomerates of the 1960s and 1970s. At the time of Bluhdorn's death, GW owned Paramount, Madison Square Garden, Financial Services Associates, several publishing companies, New Jersey Zinc, Kayser-Roth, Consolidated Cigar, South Puerto Rico Sugar, and a grab-bag of machine tool companies, as well as a sizable portfolio of shares in other companies.

Bluhdorn had realized that the sum was less than the parts. GW common was going on a plateau, and in an attempt to provide it with some glamour he had started selling off some operations and restructuring others. But it was too little and too late. Besides, Bluhdorn was reluctant to bring down so much that he had erected. Clearly this task would have to be undertaken by someone else, an individual willing to take the big bath. As it turned out, his successor, Martin S. Davis, filled the bill quite well.

It would be unfair to say that Davis started fresh, since he did continue some of the changes Bluhdorn had initiated. But Davis went much further, selling off operations, partially liquidating a large investment portfolio, repurchasing shares, and in general accomplishing for GW what Stiritz was doing at Ralston Purina.

The numbers here weren't as impressive as those of Ralston Purina, at least at first glance. But look at them carefully.

It would appear from these figures that GW had become the incredible shrinking corporation, and such indeed was the case. Davis was busily selling off divisions that provided revenues but performed badly when it came to earnings, using the funds to repurchase common shares. The flat earnings under his leadership were taken as a sign of strength, an indication the new management was able to maintain profits in the face of a massive reorganization program. As a result, GW's P/E ratio expanded from 6.1 in 1983 to 9.2 in 1985. In future years, as profits grow, I would expect a further increase in this ratio, which I consider one of the most important assets a corporation possesses.

As with Ralston Purina, the GW plan was sketched in the first letter to shareholders put out by the new administration. It was there to be seen by anyone who took the trouble, but since the Street still felt that anything Charlie Bluhdorn put together had to have more than a few booby-traps attached, one of Davis' priorities was to establish credibility. This he did, by bold actions which were discussed in future letters. The letter opened with the usual fluff: "Fiscal 1983 was an unparalleled period in the 25-year history of Gulf + Western." Toward the end, however, Davis sketched the strategy for the future, by which he has to be judged. These included a restructuring into three operating groups geared toward the consumer markets: Davis said he planned to divest approximately 20 percent of operations and liquidate the company's sizable stock portfolio, the proceeds to be used to pare debt. Considerable progress had already been made. GW had sold its building products business and Arlington Racetrack, and had plans for disposing of a long list of others, all of which was stated in the letter.[13]

The plan was carried out in 1984 and into 1985, by which time Davis had initiated a major stock repurchase plan as well. Clearly this amorphous, flabby giant Charles Bluhdorn had cobbled together in a different era was being reshaped to meet the realities of the mid-1980s, as shown in Table 12.2.

TABLE 12.2
Gulf + Western Selected Statistics, 1982–1985

(revenues in billions of dollars)

Year	Revenues	Earnings per Share	Dividends per Share	Shares Outstanding
1982	$5332	$2.05	$0.75	74.01
1983	3993	3.38	0.75	77.25
1984	4182	3.62	0.90	70.04
1985	1759	3.51	0.90	62.27

Source: Gulf + Western, *Annual Reports, 1982–1985. Fiscal years ending July 31.*

To conclude, the big bath and/or restructuring is usually a sign that an improvement will soon transpire and a signal to investors that a careful monitoring of the stock is in order.

Epilogue

I HAVE DELIBERATELY SOUGHT to end this book on a positive note, since so much of the rest might appear at first blush to be otherwise. It is in the nature of American business to always try to put its best foot forward, to make what often is a tarnished reality appear quite rosy. Three decades of going over the materials turned out by corporations may have given me a jaundiced view of things, but far too often suspicions have turned into a conviction that all is not what it seems on the surface. Investors have to be aware that Wall Street is not a casino and their funds are not chips in a game.

Any investment decision calls for the assumption of risk, for without risk there can be no reward. I have no quarrel with this. Some investors are only at home with T-bills, others feel comfortable with blue chips, while there are those who love to gamble on penny stocks. You may fall into one of these categories or some other. No matter: when making your decision, accumulate and sift through as much information as you can, and do so with a practiced eye.

The aim of this book is to provide you with the tools and techniques useful in such operations. While in many cases the mathematics have been worked out, there really is no compelling reason for you to do the same, especially to the last decimal place. Rather, if you have learned to read the prose and understand the meaning of the numbers—and what is behind both—you will be well served.

One final point merits mention. As everyone involved with the markets knows, trading today is dominated by the large institutions. Often small investors wonder how they can compete with the high-powered, well-remunerated hotshots who devote almost all of their waking hours to the market. This is understandable, and the reason so many of them find refuge in mutual funds, where for a small management fee their own hotshots call the tune for them. Yet I am convinced that the individual investor who is willing to devote a relatively small amount of time to effective research can do better than the institutions much of the time. In fact, did I not think so, this book would never have been written.

There are several reasons for this. The institutions can't move in and out of large positions rapidly without disturbing the markets. Because managers are under pressure to outperform the averages they often take unwise chances. Others, fearful of second guessing, find comfort with the big blue chips—led of course by Big Blue (IBM) itself. I continually go back to that episode at Bank of America discussed in the *Introduction*, where the portfolio managers lived in fear of moving against the crowd. Individuals can do this much better than can institutions. Analysts spend a great deal of time looking at the stocks, visiting managements and becoming friendly with individuals there, are wined and dined, and under such circumstances it is difficult to put out a sell. Small investors have no such problems. Those who utilize the techniques discussed here need only put in a call to their broker to buy or sell, and get in and out of positions with an ease that many portfolio managers envy.

If I have been successful, by now you will be trained to go through those reports that come in the mail every few months and know what they are all about. I sometimes have been asked how long it takes me to analyze annual reports and quarterlies. There is no clear answer, since some require more work than others. But in the course of a year I look through the documents of approximately 500 companies, and so clearly don't spend weeks, even days, on any of them. I suspect that readers who have understood what I have been getting at in these chapters would need no more than half an hour or so on an annual report and 15 minutes on a quarterly to understand the points I have been trying to make. This information at hand, the decision to buy or sell will be yours.

No one can tell you how to get rich or succeed in investments. All someone can do is provide the tools for intelligent decisions. Such is the purpose of this book.

NOTES

CHAPTER 1. Don't Trust Your Analyst (pp. 1–12)

1. Susan Lee, "Selling Short—Why It Works and Why You Probably Shouldn't Do It," *Forbes*, April 22, 1985, p. 100.
2. Anne B. Fisher, "How Good are Wall Street's Security Analysts?" *Fortune*, October 1, 1984, p. 130.
3. *Wall Street Letter*, June 3, 1985, p. 1.
4. Claire Makin, "Has the Compensation Bubble Burst?" *Institutional Investor*, December, 1984, p. 109.
5. *Wall Street Journal*, January 20, 1984; Lee, "Selling Short," p. 99.
6. "Richard Hoffman: Who's Afraid to Say 'Sell'?" *Institutional Investor*, March, 1985, p. 13.
7. Mary Rowland, "The Perils of Saying 'Sell.'" *Institutional Investor*, January, 1984, p. 219.
8. Vartan G. Vartan, "When a Stock Falls Abruptly," *New York Times*, January 13, 1984.
9. "Wall Street vs. Washington," *Barron's*, June 17, 1985, p. 20.
10. David Dreman, "Portrait of Dorian Guru," *Forbes*, May 20, 1985, p. 268.
11. Rowland, "The Perils of Saying 'Sell,'" p. 219.
12. *Portfolio Letter*, February 11, 1985.
13. Fisher, "How Good are Wall Street's Analysts?" p. 133.
13a. Examiner's Statement of Investigation—Baldwin United Corp.—

United States Bankruptcy Court, Southern District of Ohio, January 15, 1985.

14. Damon Darlin, "Picking a Loser: Young Analyst Defied 'Experts' and Foresaw Baldwin-United's Ills," *Wall Street Journal*, September 30, 1983.

14a. Ibid.

15. Rowland, "The Perils of Saying 'Sell,'" p. 219.

16. Fisher, "How Good are Wall Street's Security Analysts?" pp. 132–33.

17. Randall W. Forsythe and Kathleen Kerwin, "Day of Reckoning: Adding Up the Score on Continental Illinois," *Barron's*, May 21, 1984, p. 15.

18. Richard Gibson and Wendy Wall, "Bank Analysts Try to Balance their Ratings," *Wall Street Journal*, May 29, 1984.

19. Kenneth Labich, "Guess Who's Bought Whoops Bonds?" *Fortune*, April 19, 1985, p. 54.

CHAPTER 2.   And Don't Trust Your Auditor *(pp. 13–20)*

1. "A Look At Annual Reports," (New York: Drexel Burnham Lambert, March 12, 1985), p. 3; Robin Schatz, "Critical Opinion: Why Investors Should Take Heed of the Auditor's Report," *Barron's*, March 18, 1985, p. 24.

2. Lee Berton, "Number of Qualified Opinions is Increasing," *Wall Street Journal*, June 5, 1985.

3. "Red Flags in the Footnotes," *Personal Investor*, July, 1985, pp. 55–56.

4. "A Look At Annual Reports," p. 3.

5. Berton, "Number of Qualified Opinions Is Increasing."

6. "SEC Role, Accounting Profession Scrutinized," *The SEC Today*, February 22, 1985.

7. Jim Montgomery, "FDIC Says Over 90% of Tennessee Bank's Dubious Loans Weren't on Books Year Ago," *Wall Street Journal*, February 22, 1983.

8. Gary Klott, "Auditors Feel the Heat of a New Scrutiny," *New York Times*, May 13, 1984.

9. Barbara Kallen, "Truth in Packaging," *Forbes*, March 12, 1984, p. 96.

10. Remarks of the Hon. John D. Dingell before the SEC Accounting Forum in Washington, DC on May 20, 1985.

11. Lee Berton, "Audit Fees Fall As CPA Firms Jockey for Bids," *Wall Street Journal*, January 28, 1985.

12. Mark Stevens, *The Big Eight: An Inside View of America's Eight Most Powerful and Influential Accounting Firms* (New York: Macmillan, 1981), p. 68.

13. Ibid., p. 34.

14. Ibid., p. 34.

15. Gary Klott, "Auditors Face U.S. Scrutiny," *New York Times*, February 18, 1985.

16. Mark Stevens, "Is Your Accounting Firm Still an Accounting Firm?" *Financial Executive*, July, 1985, p. 29; Gary Klott, "Auditing Role Seen in Jeopardy," February 21, 1985.

17. "Penn Square Bank Fired Auditing Firm That Questioned Reserve for Tax Loss," *Wall Street Journal*, July 29, 1982.

18. Klott, "Auditors Feel The Heat of a New Scrutiny."

19. Testimony before the Oversight and Investigations Subcommittee, Committee on Energy and Commerce, United States House of Representatives, February 20, 1985.

CHAPTER 3.   Person to Person: A Shareholder Letter *(pp. 21–43)*

1. Todd S. Purdum, "What's New In Annual Reports," *New York Times*, April 21, 1985.

2. Hill and Knowlton, *The Annual Report: A Question of Credibility* (New York: Hill & Knowlton, October, 1984).

3. Kevin Maney, "Read Between Lines of Report," *USA Today*, April 22, 1985.

4. Ibid.; Purdum, "What's New in Annual Reports."

5. Ibid.

6. *Quality of Earnings Report*, February 16, 1981, pp. 13–19.

7. Andrew Corp., *1985 First Quarter Report*.

8. Andrew Corp., *1985 Second Quarter Report*.

9. Apple Computer, *1985 First Quarter Report*.

10. Apple Computer, *1985 Second Quarter Report*.

11. *Electronic News*, June 17, 1985.

12. Coleco, *1973 Annual Report*, pp. 2–4; *1974 Annual Report*, pp. 2–5; *1975 Annual Report*, pp. 2–5.

13. Coleco, *1976 Annual Report*, pp. 2–5; *1977 Annual Report*, pp. 2–4.

14. Coleco, *1977 Annual Report*, pp. 2–5.

15. Coleco, *1980 Annual Report*, pp. 2–5.

16. *Chicago Tribune*, December 1, 1983.

17. Dan Dorfman, "The History of Hype at Coleco," *Chicago Tribune*, December 1, 1983.

18. Coleco, *1984 Annual Report*, p. 5.

19. Koppers Co., *1984 Annual Report*, pp. 2–3.

20. AMP Corp., *1984 Annual Report*, p. 2.

CHAPTER 4. Differential Disclosure *(pp. 44–54)*

1. Procter & Gamble, *1984 Annual Report*, pp. 2–5; 36; *Quality of Earnings Report*, September 25, 1984, p. 116.

2. John Koten, "For P&G's Rivals, the New Game Is to Beat the Leader, Not Copy It," *Wall Street Journal*, May 1, 1985.

3. Convergent Technologies, *1983 Annual Report*, pp. 2–3.

4. Ibid., p. 19.

5. Ibid., p. 3.

6. Convergent Technologies, *1983 10-K Report to the Securities & Exchange Commission.*

7. Ibid., Convergent Technologies, *1983 Annual Report*, p. 4.

8. Ibid., p. 18.

9. Academy Insurance, *1983 Annual Report*, pp. 2–3.

10. *Quality of Earnings Report*, April 27, 1984, p. 81; June 11, 1984, p. 98.

11. *Portfolio Letter*, June 18, 1984, pp. 1, 11–12.

12. Ibid.

13. Academy Insurance, *1984 Annual Report*, p. 23.

14. Academy Insurance, *First Quarter 1985 Report.*

15. Matt Moffett and Bryan Burrough, "Texas Banks Are Battered Again On Their Oil, Real Estate Loans," *Wall Street Journal*, March 25, 1985.

16. Texas Commerce Bancshares, *1984 Annual Report*, p. 53.

17. Texas Commerce Bancshares, 1985 Proxy Statement.

18. Bryan Burrough, "Texas Commerce Says It Was Cleared by Comptroller over Loans to Directors," *Wall Street Journal*, August 22, 1985.

CHAPTER 5.   Nonoperating and/or Nonrecurring Income
            (pp. 55–70)

1. John Heins, "Let Us Make One Thing Perfectly Clear . . . " *Forbes*, May 21, 1984, p. 186.

2. Robert J. Schoenberg, *Geneen* (New York: Norton, 1985), p. 242.

3. Leopold A. Bernstein, *Financial Statement Analysis Theory: Application and Interpretation* (Homewood, Ill.: Dow Jones Irwin, 1983), p. 692.

4. Stuart Weiss, "A Hunt for Artificial Sweeteners In Earnings Statements," *Business Week*, February 25, 1985, p. 86.

5. Lauren R. Rublin, "No Piece of Cake: Beatrice Bought Both Esmark and Trouble," *Barron's*, May 27, 1985, p. 16; Arthur M. Louis, "The Controversial Boss of Beatrice," *Fortune*, July 22, 1985, pp. 110–16.

6. *Quality of Earnings Report*, May 28, 1985, p. 63.

7. *Value Line*, May 3, 1985, p. 991; June 1, 1985, p. 1459.

8. Heins, "Let Us Make One Thing Perfectly Clear . . . " p. 186.

9. Stuart Gannes, "IBM Dials A Wrong Number," *Fortune*, June 9, 1986, p. 34.

10. TIE/Communications, *1983 Annual Report*, p. 15.

11. *Quality of Earnings Report*, November 29, 1982, pp. 299–300.

12. Anne B. Fisher, "Where Have Baldwin-United's Millions Gone?" *Fortune*, April 18, 1983, p. 99.

CHAPTER 6.   Declining and Increasing Expenses *(pp. 71–84)*

1. IBM, *1984 Annual Report*, p. 40.

2. *Quality of Earnings Report*, April 2, 1985, pp. 42–45.

3. *Quality of Earnings Report*, November 26, 1984, p. 149.

4. *Quality of Earnings Report*, July 18, 1983, p. 149.

5. *Quality of Earnings Report*, November 25, 1983, pp. 228–29.

6. *Quality of Earnings Report*, February 20, 1985, p. 19.

CHAPTER 7.   Shareholder Reporting versus Tax Reporting
            (pp. 85–105)

1. Linda Sandler, "An Appraisal: Tax Plan May Hurt Manufacturers, Many Other Issues," *Wall Street Journal*, June 3, 1985.

2. "To Haave and Haave Not," *Barron's,* August 5, 1985, p. 14.

3. United States, 95th Congress, Second Session, *Congressional Record,* January 26, 1978, vol. 124, no. 6, p. 168.

4. *Wall Street Journal,* October 9, 1985, p. 46.

CHAPTER 8.   Two Key Ratios: Accounts Receivable and Inventories *(pp. 106–125)*

1. Kathleen Sylvester, "Silicon Valley Crashes," *Newsday,* August 25, 1985.

2. *Quality of Earnings Report,* December 6, 1984, pp. 225–26.

3. *Quality of Earnings Report,* March 20, 1985, pp. 33–34.

4. *Quality of Earnings Report,* May 28, 1985, pp. 67–68.

5. *Quality of Earnings Report,* March 20, 1985, p. 22.

6. *Quality of Earnings Report,* March 20, 1985, p. 32. So it did. TIE turned in a deficit in 1985, and at year end the stock was selling in the single-digit range.

7. *Quality of Earnings Report,* February 20, 1985, pp. 18–20.

8. *Quality of Earnings Report,* September 25, 1984, pp. 168–69.

CHAPTER 9.   Debt and Cash Flow Analysis *(pp. 126–146)*

1. Benjamin Graham, *Security Analysis: Principles and Techniques* (New York: McGraw-Hill, 1962), p. 542.

2. "Modigliani on Debt," *Barron's,* October 21, 1985, p. 73.

3. Ibid., loc. cit.

4. George Foster, *Financial Statement Analysis* (Englewood Cliffs, N.J.: Prentice-Hall, 1978), p. 31.

5. Leopold A. Bernstein and Mostafa M. Masky, "Again Now: How Do We Measure Cash Flow from Operations?" *Financial Analysts Journal,* July/August, 1985, p. 77.

6. This worksheet has been prepared by Leopold A. Bernstein, Professor of Accounting, Bernard M. Baruch College, The City University of New York.

CHAPTER 10.   Dividends: The Tender Trap *(pp. 147–162)*

1. Benjamin Graham, David L. Dodd, and Sidney Cottle, *Security Analysis: Principles and Techniques* (New York: McGraw-Hill, 1962), p. 480

2. Ibid., pp. 480, 742.

3. N. R. Kleinfeld, "The Life of a C.E.O.," *New York Times Magazine*, December 1, 1985.

4. Robert J. Schoenberg, *Geneen* (New York: Norton, 1985), p. 242.

5. Michael Brody, "Caught in the Cash Crunch at ITT," *Fortune*, February 18, 1985, p. 54.

6. Ibid.

CHAPTER 11. The Importance of Understanding Accounting Changes *(pp. 163–177)*

1. Arthur Andersen & Co., *A Search for Fairness in Financial Accounting to the Public* (Chicago: Arthur Andersen, 1969); Presentation by Leonard Spacek before the Financial Accounting Class, Graduate School of Business Administration, Harvard University, September 25, 1959.

2. James W. Deitrick and Walter T. Harrison, Jr., "Professional Notes, EMH, CMR and the Accounting Profession," *Journal of Accountancy*, February, 1984, p. 82.

3. George J. Benston, "Personal Investing—The Stock Market 'Knows' What Is in All Those Financial Statements before They Reach Investors," *Fortune*, April, 1976, p. 73.

4. Alfred Rappaport, "Don't Sell Stock Market Horizons Short," *Wall Street Journal*, June 27, 1983.

5. Arthur R. Wyatt, "Efficient Market Theory: Its Impact on Accounting—Examples Show That the Real World of Accounting Is Ignoring the Efficient Market Hypothesis," *Journal of Accounting*, February, 1983, p. 56.

6. *Quality of Earnings Report*, October, 1983.

7. Amanda Bennett, "Executives Face Change in Award of Pay, Stock Options," *Wall Street Journal*, January 28, 1986.

CHAPTER 12. Coming Clean After the Big Bath and/or Restructuring *(pp. 178–186)*

1. Robert J. Swieringa, "Increasing Profits in a Down Economy: Examples of Accounting Magic," April 21, 1983. (Privately circulated.)

2. Lee Berton and Gay Sands Miller, "Accountants Debate Tightening Rules for 'Big Bath' Write-Offs by Companies," *Wall Street Journal*, February 11, 1986.

3. Ben Weberman, "Rumpelstilzchen Accounting," *Forbes*, February 24, 1986, p. 30.

4. Robert Mims, "Write-Off Times: Why the Fourth Quarter Was So Bad," *Business Week*, March 17, 1986, p. 116.

5. Daniel Machalaba, "CSX Announces Major Restructuring, Will Take $954 Million Pre-Tax Charge," *Wall Street Journal*, December 12, 1985.

6. "Allied-Signal Loses $279 Million," *Electronic News*, February 10, 1986.

7. Alex Freedman and Francine Schwadel, "Cigna Will Take a $1.2 Billion Charge in the Fourth Quarter," *Wall Street Journal*, January 31, 1986.

8. Deborah Rankin, "The Issue of 'Big Bath' Writeoffs," *New York Times*, January 31, 1978.

9. Ralston Purina, *1982 Annual Report*.

10. Ralston Purina, *1983 Annual Report*.

11. Ralston Purina, *1984 Annual Report*.

12. *Value Line*, August 30, 1985, p. 1492.

13. Gulf + Western, *1983 Annual Report*.

INDEX

INDEX

INDEX